Media Engineering

About the Wiley-BT Series

The titles in the Wiley-BT Series are designed to provide clear, practical analysis of voice, image and data transmission technologies and systems, for telecommunications engineers working in the industry. New and forthcoming works in the series also cover software systems, solutions, engineering and design.

Other titles in the Wiley-BT Series;

Media Engineering

A guide to developing information products

Steve West and **Mark Norris**

BT, UK

JOHN WILEY & SONS

Chichester · New York · Weinheim · Brisbane · Toronto · Singapore

Copyright © 1997 John Wiley & Sons Ltd,
Baffins Lane, Chichester,
West Sussex PO19 1UD, England

National 01243 779777
International (+44) 1243 779777

e-mail (for orders and customer service enquiries): cs-books@wiley.co.uk
Visit our Home Page on http://www.wiley.co.uk
or http://www.wiley.com

Other Wiley Editorial Offices

John Wiley & Sons, Inc., 605 Third Avenue,
New York, NY 10158–0012, USA

VCH Verlagsgesellschaft mbH, Pappelallee 3,
D–69469 Weinheim, Germany

Jacaranda Wiley Ltd, 33 Park Road, Milton,
Queensland 4064, Australia

John Wiley & Sons (Canada) Ltd, 22 Worcester Road,
Rexdale, Ontario M9W 1L1, Canada

John Wiley & Sons (Asia) Pte Ltd, 2 Clementi Loop £02–01,
Jin Xing Distripark, Singapore 0512

Library of Congress Cataloging-in-Publication Data

West, S. (Steve)
  Media engineering: a guide to developing information products /
S. West and M. Norris.
    p. cm.
  Includes bibliographical references and index.
  ISBN 0-471-97287-8
  1. Multimedia systems. 2. Software engineering. I. Norris,
Mark. II. Title.
QA76.575.W45 1997
070.5'797 — dc21

                    97–1038
                      CIP

British Library Cataloguing in Publication Data

A catalogue record for this book is available from the British Library

ISBN 0 471 97287 8

Typeset in 10.5/12pt Sabon by Vision Typesetting
Printed and bound in Great Britian by Bookcraft (Bath) Ltd
This book is printed on acid-free paper responsibly manufactured from sustainable forestation, for which at least two trees are planted for each one used for paper production.

Contents

Foreword

Somewhere between 94.2 and 94.6 MHz, in the sea of electromagnetic waves that we all swim, is where the vast majority of my work ends up! And it stays there for, maybe, half-an-hour, or so. Between the allotted times, an awful lot of sub-atomic particles jiggle in unison, and my work exists, engulfing a few million cubic kilometres of space and then its gone. As a Radio Producer, who has spent most of his time putting together programmes that, I hope, a substantial number of people will enjoy, I feel the highly ephemeral nature of the medium creates an interesting paradox: having created a high quality 'information product', when it's going out, it couldn't be easier to get hold of; but when it's gone out, it couldn't be harder! But, of course, all this is about to change: as a consequence of the information revolution, all I have to do is plonk my programme on a server and anyone can get it, whenever they like. But what has any of this got to do with Media Engineering? For me, the answer is architecture.

Secretly, (well not all that secretly now), I've always fancied being an architect. That fantastic fusion of art and science, of form and function, of traditions and new technologies. Plus the fact that even prefabs tend to last longer than your average radio programme! And this relationship that buildings have with time is important. For a building to last decades or even centuries, it has to be well designed, well engineered and well built. And for that to happen, the architect has to integrate seamlessly the content – the space that the building encloses – and the structure – the way those enclosures are supported. Sometimes that integration is invisible, like the exquisite curved ceiling that floats above you as you stand beneath the Duomo in Florence. And sometimes that integration is the most visible part of the building; the exoskeleton of lifts, ducts, girders and gantries that hold together the Lloyds building in London, for example.

What Mark and Steve have done is to allow me to become a practising architect in cyberspace. For a radio programme with a life expectancy of one score minutes and ten, who cares about maintenance cost? But for a multimedia information product which might last weeks, months, maybe even years, the ability to understand the separation of the content from the structure, and its real-time integration as people use the information, is going to be vital. The evidence that this is not happening is clearly visible to anyone who regularly browses the World Wide Web. What with dead-end pages and failed links, frustration, not information, is the product. Yet, as this book explains, the techniques are available, and the tools not far behind. So, with the plumb-line of file naming conventions and the scaffolding of a well-thought-out directory structure I intend to start building. And what's even better – I don't even need planning permission.

Peter Croasdale
Senior Producer, BBC Science

Preface

Once upon a time, you could sit in your house or your office and pretty much let life pass you by. You could get along quite nicely, just by keeping your own affairs in order. That was before technology put the world in front of you, in living colour, on a computer screen. Now you are continually bombarded with words, pictures and concepts that have some impact on you. It wouldn't be so bad if it all made sense but, more often than not, you are left to pick your way through an array of data and to decipher strings of technobabble.

In this brave new world it is becoming increasingly important to capture and present reams of information in a digestible format. Encarta, which is probably the world's leading computer encyclopaedia, contains over nine million words and covers a vast range of topics, from distributed computing to dinosaurs. Likewise, the Web pages developed by the authors for BT's internal computing standards provide a vast amount of technical guidance delivered to the desktop of thousands of software engineers. Yet both are easy to use and enable you to get a grip on even the most complex of topics. This was no fluke – in both cases, a considerable amount of time and effort was taken to structure the information and link facts and figures together. Likewise, there are many examples of information systems that allow the user to discover what they need to know systematically and intuitively. And even more that don't.

In putting this book together, we have drawn on our experience of contributing to Encarta and implementing BT's on-line systems. Our aim has been to explain how you go about designing and building volumes of assorted information into a coherent resource that is fit for consumption by a variety of users. In doing this, we work from a basic thesis – that the core problems of designing multimedia information are amenable to the same concepts and disciplines that have been devised in software engineering. In both cases the key is to control the complexity of an intangible product through sound organization, technique and practice.

Our fundamental premise is that it is not the technology of multimedia (compact disk, Internet, etc.) but the systematic structuring of information that really matters. For all the flashy distractions of glossy technology, we focus on the latter and present a framework and methods for solving the problem. We have called the approach DIVA, and the book is structured around its development and practical implementation. The theory presented is not something that we invented for the media world out of thin air – it is based on our long experience of similar engineering problems which have been encountered in the realm of software engineering, but tempered with the practical lessons we have learnt whilst implementing multimedia systems for real.

The first two chapters set the scene for DIVA. Chapter 1 explains the pressures that motivate its development and Chapter 2 the basis of its construction. We start to introduce DIVA itself in Chapter 3, which explains the principles that we have found to be fundamental in creating information products. Chapters 4 and 5 give much of the practical detail – notation, procedures and guidelines – that you would need to implement the DIVA principles.

Chapter 6 illustrates this by stepping through one of our DIVA-badged information products. To close, we summarize the key messages of the book before indulging in a little prediction about the future of media engineering.

The appendices contain background and fine detail that may appeal to some, but not all, readers. Appendix 1 is a set of checklists and templates that would be useful to a practitioner. The main text assumes some knowledge of the World Wide Web and other technology: Appendix 2 provides background reference on the Internet, Markup languages and authoring tools. The technical support is extended in Appendix 3, where we show how to realize one of the DIVA concepts using Java code. Finally, we offer a fairly extensive glossary in Appendix 4 as a guard against the worst excesses of the on-line industry in overloading the English language.

Our simple aim throughout is to give you the wherewithal to navigate the treacherous but uncharted waters of Media Engineering.

Acknowledgements

We are most grateful to a select band of helpers who immediately related to the concept of media engineering, reviewed drafts of the book and contributed sound advice and little pearls of wisdom.

Our thanks go to Professor Dave Bustard of the University of Ulster, Lesley Norris of MET Design Studios, Rosemary Seagrief of Webster's Encarta, John Helleur, MBE, Peter Dadson and Gaynor Beale-Garland of BT.

Their guidance, advice and wisdom has done a lot to ensure that our ideas relate to their real world concerns.

Thanks are also due to Mark Pickford of Salford University for his sterling work on the Software Engineering Library and to Ann-Marie Halligan at John Wiley & Sons for her help and encouragement in getting our ideas into print.

Before we forget, we must mention Sarah West's cat "Molly" whose page on the Internet inspired us to invent *Media Engineering*.

Finally, we are both grateful to Chris West for his contribution of graphic design skills.

About the Authors

Steve West has 15 years experience in communications, software and Information Technology. He has worked on a wide variety of projects, including the management of BT's work with the X/Open consortium and generation of corporate IT strategy. Recently he has been responsible for the development of the on-line reference material, accessible over WWW by several thousand designers and software engineers within BT. Steve has been known to play the blues guitar, but he tends not mix this with Media Engineering.

Mark Norris has almost 20 years' experience in software and network systems, project and strategic management and has worked for periods in Japan and Australia. He has published extensively over the years, including several previous books in the Wiley-BT series, and is on the board of the BT Technology Journal. He is a Chartered Engineer and a Fellow of the IEE. If he ever gets any spare time, Mark shuns technology in his quest to become a halfway decent squash player.

1
The Information Age

What information consumes is rather obvious: it consumes the attention of its recipients. Hence a wealth of information creates a poverty of attention and a need to allocate that attention efficiently among the over-abundance of information sources that might consume it.

Herbert A. Simon

Information, they say, is power. But if you cannot assimilate the information available to you, is the power it bestows negated? Our key contention in this book is that information has to be engineered just like any other product if it is to deliver to its potential. And this is why we have invented the idea of Media Engineering.

The last few years of the 20th century have undoubtedly heralded the dawn of a new age. One in which access to information has become globally available, thanks to a powerful combination of computers and networks. And one in which the provision of information is increasingly important: it is of note that there has been more produced in the last 30 years than during the previous 5000 [PP94] and many would now share Herbert Simon's feeling that this deluge of information needs to be managed.

So what, you may well ask. What relevance does this have outside of a small group of specialists and enthusiasts? Surely most of us just carry on as usual, with a few extra facilities when it comes to exchanging ideas – surfing the net is fun, but it doesn't really get you anywhere.

Both history and recent experience suggest otherwise. A significant change is afoot with many organizations now using computer-based information as a prime source of reference. The words and pictures on the screen are no longer simply background data – they are the main object of attention, the definitive copy [MG94].

History has done little to prepare us for all of this. The traditional constraints on preparing and presenting information do not translate into a world where the computer is the focus of attention. No longer is text a sequence of statements – a linear story or argument supported by explanation, reason or illustration. More complex structures are possible – it is standard practice to have computer-based documents that allow users to jump from one place to another, as they wish. What is more, the links between sections of on-line material can change at the drop of a hat and it is very easy for the message to be corrupted for want of the right structure.

The good news is that we have the prospect of vast amounts of infinitely malleable, instantly changeable data along with an array of tools for moulding it as we please. Less welcome is the observation that the concepts and methods needed to turn a wealth of data into useful information are somewhat lacking. This is something we aim to address in this book by introducing the discipline of media engineering.

Our intent is to present a systematic approach to preparing computer-based documents. This does not extend to the content as this can only be prepared or selected according to the provider's preference. Nor do we deal with the way in which information is presented – we wouldn't dream of advising on artistic flair and good taste. But we do take you step-by-step through the mechanics of building screen media that can readily be navigated and are easily maintained.

In some ways, there is little new in all of the guidelines, techniques and advice we give throughout the book. Indeed, one of the early realizations in our work was that many of the lessons about handling complexity and controlling diversity have already been learned in the software engineering arena. There are some differences, of course, and that is where we go next—to consider the nature of the problem that we are trying to tackle.

To start with, this chapter sets the scene. To understand how best to use new media, you must first appreciate its characteristic strengths and limitations. It also helps to know your target audience and the facilities they are likely to have available. By the end of this chapter, we should have painted a clear picture of where and when media engineering is relevant, who should adopt it and why. The details of how and what come later.

1.1 MEDIA AND MESSAGES

All forms of media, including the latest electronic (multi)media, offer some advantages over direct human interaction [II36], but also suffer from significant limitations. In this section we argue that it is those limitations which ultimately define the medium and how you exploit it. Following this line, we attempt to identify the key limitations that are defining the new multimedia that are the subject of this book.

Let's begin, though, with the areas where media, in the most general case, scores over human experience. There are three real plus points. Firstly, many of them are persistent and not only outlast a fleeting human experience but may outlast many human lifetimes. For instance, Babylonian clay tablets have survived for several thousand years. Secondly they can be very large in capacity and can hold immense breadth and depth of content. Indeed, the Internet seems almost limitless. Thirdly they can have a structure imposed on them to ease their accessibility – in effect, a story line can be added to make the content more palatable.

However, no single medium (electronic or otherwise) offers the richness of actual human experience. When we communicate, person to person, with other people, we employ a huge range of media and subtlety of expression. We use speech, gestures and other body language; we can draw schematic pictures; in fact we can exploit the full range of our five senses including touch and smell.

By comparison, all other media have severe limitations. For example, communication by telephone is limited by whether the users have access to telephones; by the fact that only sound is transmitted; by the limitation of the bandwidth to about 4 kHz. The same analysis of limitations can be applied to any communication medium.

1.1.1 Who's who

To understand the effect of limitations, it is worth looking at how we might categorize media. Some key characteristics are:

- *The delivery channel.* This might be 'a printed book; broadcast television; a compact disk, etc.

- *The content type.* For example, written words; sound, pictures or moving pictures.

- *Persistence.* Whether the information only exists instantaneously or can be recovered at a later stage.

- *Content.* The actual information that is conveyed—its meaning, significance, relevance and currency.

- *Structure.* The way the information is organized. An encyclopaedia is probably organized into articles arranged alphabetically, for example. A book would, in contrast, follow a predetermined story line.

- *Access.* Random or sequential.

This last category (access) may need a few words of explanation: The distinction we are drawing separates media that provide a stream of information determined by the information source from those where the sequence of access is determined by the recipient. Broadcast TV would fall into the former category (at least in the case of countries like the UK which have only a small number of TV channels) – the viewer receives programmes in the order they are transmitted by the broadcaster. An encyclopaedia would be an example of the second category: the user can dip into it at any point and home in on the required information.

To run some familiar media through this categorisation, a World Wide Web browser requires a network link, delivers all content types, is persistent (but liable to change beyond the users control) and has all manner of content from excellent to dubious. The structure is a series of linked pages and the access is random. By way of contrast, the typical novel is simple in content but more persistent (as long as you don't lose it). Most published novels have a recognizable brand which carries with it some assurance of content. The structure is invariably built in and the normal access method is sequential.

In the case of the multimedia that are the subject of this book, it is the first of the above examples that applies. Great flexibility exists, with a considerable amount of opportunity for inappropriate use. The absence of established comfort factors offered by books – their colour, where they sit on the shelf, and other orientation/context aids – means that the onus for ordering facts and figures is all too easily placed on the reader. Information providers can, to a large extent, excuse themselves the responsibility of designing the logical flow of their data.

So we need to think a little more about how we exploit available media. In doing this, we look again at the various media characteristics. They may appear to be distinct, but are in practice interlinked in a complicated way. Our expectation as information consumers is that particular media channels will deliver particular types of information. We would, for example, be surprised if we went to the cinema and what appeared on the screen was nothing more than a sequence of scrolling text which told a story. Likewise a book with moving pictures would be something of a novelty.

Putting this another way, our established media have evolved a set of conventions regarding the information content, structure, access type etc. Moreover, these conventions are most strongly attached (in our minds) to the delivery mechanism rather than any of the other characteristics: we know broadly what to expect when we turn on a TV, open a book, or play a record. Some of these conventions are inherent in the limitations of the technology – a textbook does not usually replay sound; broadcast television doesn't let the user home in on particular information; a record cannot print text.

Other conventions are simply built around user expectations – particularly the expectation that the delivery medium will be exploited to best advantage. These conventions grow up over a period of time, out of experience. We need only look at early examples of any medium to see this – for example many of the cinematic epics of the 1920s were more like filmed records of stage plays than movies as we now understand them.

The development of so-called multimedia has offered us a number of new delivery options (the floppy disk, the CD and the Internet). As mass communications media, these are still in their infancy, although their penetration of world markets is growing at an astonishing rate. The full set of conventions and customer expectations that will be attached to these new delivery mechanisms has not yet developed but it is probable that once again people will expect the content to be constrained only by the limitations of the medium [Gor91].

At the time of writing, the observed characteristics of multimedia products are:

- They are very strong on textual content and linking of text (hypertext).

- They are strong on embedded pictures but often the quality (resolution and colour range) is selected to be adequate for on-screen display but is disappointing when printed. This is an interesting example of the publisher's assumptions about media limitations which may not match the user's expectations.

- Sound and video are included but not particularly well integrated with other media and the quality is often limited by current PC technology.

- Structure is variable. Some multimedia products are very poorly structured when viewed at anything but the most superficial level. The Internet has almost no discernible structure.

- Size is usually very large. This is not so much a limitation, more a challenge. Most people can relate the story of a book or a television programme to you: few can recite the contents of a CD ROM.

- Their searching capability is strong, as befits the enormous information space that has grown up in the past few years.

- They change rapidly. There is a tendancy for a stream of publications, each an increment of its predecessor, to appear. Information currency and persistence is reduced.

What is missing is a clear picture of where these characteristics place information-based, multimedia products. This is not an unexpected situation, given the maturity of the area. Furthermore, it is an opportunity to explore the options that might lie ahead.

1.1.2 So what?

If the above analysis is correct, the ultimate expectations of the consumers will be that media are exploited to the bounds of their limitations. And for computer-based media this means:

- *Very large capacity.* This is already the case – large encyclopaedias (such as Microsoft's Encarta) with millions of words and thousands of images fit on to a single CD-ROM. Within a few years, optical media which can hold the equivalent content of thousands of books will be available. Even within existing optical technology, compression techniques can pack huge amounts of information into small spaces.

- *Integrated sound and video.* Technologies for this are improving all the time (e.g. MPEG cards in PCs). Furthermore, the increase in capacity of media reduces the current trade-off between using the capacity for relatively small amounts of video or large amounts of text.

- *Full searchability.* The Internet offers good search engines, such as Lycos, which build their indexes in background and hence permit rapid searching of millions of pages. Currently Lycos will do the equivalent of searching about eighteen million pages in a few seconds. We say it is 'equivalent' to searching the pages because, in practice, it is only searching the index to the pages.

- *Good structure and navigability.* The presentation of cogent information has long been a challenge, one that draws praise when done well and spreads confusion when done poorly. As you read an article on a computer screen, it should be no more difficult to understand or follow than its textbook or magazine counterpart.

It is the last of these characteristics which is the least amenable to simple technological improvement. As noted already, the development of higher-density optical (and magnetic) storage media continues unabated; digital sound and video technologies are maturing and search engines are being refined for searching the whole Internet.

However, structure and navigability are not simple technological issues: there is no available technology which imposes a structure on random information. Despite the considerable advances that have taken place in 'search engines', 'web crawlers' and other systems which infer the content or structure from the finished system, none of these is a substitute for designing-in a structure that guides the user through the relationships between items of information. Furthermore, other developments in technology militate against the imposition of simple structure. For instance, the increasing capacity of optical media exacerbates the structure limitation rather than improving it.

As an analogy, major international libraries such as the Bodleian in Oxford contain so much information that it is impossible simply to browse through them looking for one particular item. The only way to access what you want is through indexes and catalogues. If an item is lost from the catalogue it is effectively lost completely. Already the Internet is similarly too large to search for individual items without the aid of search engines or indexes. In the case of compact disks, the current generation of the technology is still just about browsable, but this situation will doubtless change over the next few years with increased capacity of optical media and with improved data compression techniques. The authors both expect to be around when all human knowledge can be stored on a single disk.

All of the factors discussed here leave us in a position where the organization and presentation of information needs to be reviewed if we are to take advantage of the information age. We have called the collection of techniques for doing this 'Media Engineering'. And that is what we now move on to introduce.

1.2   MEDIA ENGINEERING

First of all, a definition (albeit a fairly loose one). When we say Media Engineering, we are talking about the organization of large amounts of computer-based information. This information may be held locally or remotely, it may be private or public, it may be general or specific. Whatever its nature, there is invariably a lot of it and it is rarely in any sort of order. So, some sort of control and technique is required in rendering it useful.

In short, media engineering is the application of a systematic and disciplined approach to the development, operation and maintenance of information products.

This is more than design. It extends the job of the media engineer into

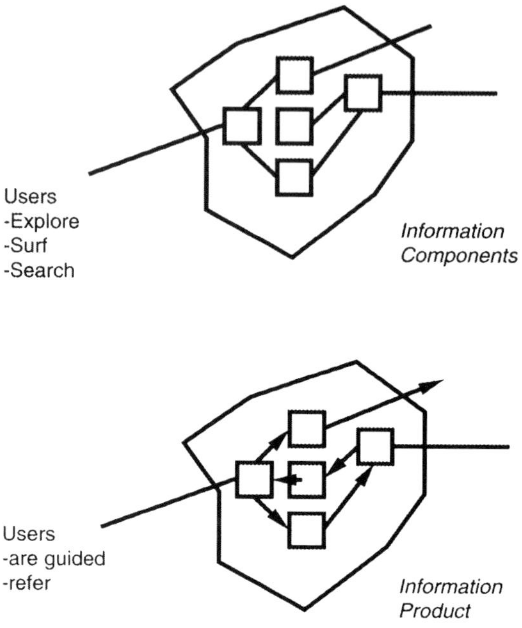

Figure 1.1
The move from surfing to guided tours

keeping the product live and flexible post release. And this means that a capacity to evolve has to be built in at the start, as an integral part of the development process.

This is what the remainder of this book is about. We aim to provide a set of concepts for controlling complexity along with the process steps for their practical application. And, in recognition of the vagaries of the real world, we also include guidelines and specific details of the technology that is available for realizing well-structured on-line documents.

The essential drive for Media Engineering comes from the use of dynamic, rather than sequential, presentation. The use of hypertext on computers means that the non-sequitur and logical schism that every book author worries about can readily be removed by inserting a corrective link. Conversely, poorly placed links can leave the reader unable to infer any logical relationship between pieces of information: fine if you are playing Dungeons and Dragons but, as a rule, not a happy result.

So, with such a basic change in capability, the implication is that the way in which information is designed also changes. There are new rules in the writing game.

Figure 1.1 illustrates the general thrust of all this. It illustrates a move from the user having to search an increasingly large information space under their own steam (aka surfing) to a situation where information is presented as a cogent resource.

The concepts of searching and surfing (known and loved throughout the Internet community) are not going to disappear. But with burgeoning demands on the information consumer, they will be complemented with information excursions, the viewer being guided through a subject. In the current model, it is up to the user to create their on-line map. In the media engineering model, the map starts to become part of the information product.

There is precious little guidance available on how to provide this level of support as yet. Some associated elements are well documented. For instance, there are more than adequate guides on page design, production languages and delivery technology. We don't talk about these in any great depth as there are plenty of good books on Networks, the Internet, World Wide Web page design, setting up servers etc for the implementer to refer to [Abo92, AN95, PLM95, FN97]. The *products* for building and distributing information are well documented. It is the *process* for structuring the information that we are more concerned with.

The second defining statement on media engineering relates to its intended audience – who it is for. The answer involves the following, fairly short, piece of reasoning.

Consider this. Many of the barriers to providing information to a mass market disappear with computer-based information systems. You no longer have to be a press baron to get your views across to a huge number of people.

This allows a new equation to become reality: author = publisher. The producer of a book, a guide or some publicity does not have to rely on a third party to make their work available. It is almost as easy for them to distribute it as it was to produce it in the first place. So an old order (rather like the privilege of reading and writing, the preserve of the clergy in the middle ages) is broken and there are many more (potential) players in a previously bounded marketplace.

The publishing revolution gave authors access to professional technicians who would undertake information presentation, replication and distribution on their behalf. The media revolution has placed the tools of presentation, replication and distribution directly in the hands of the authors.

So, with increased speed of production (it's on the streets, before review, still hot) and greater variety of source (minimal cost of entry to the market), a new need arises. If many more people are publishing at potentially great speed, some level of control will have to be adopted to

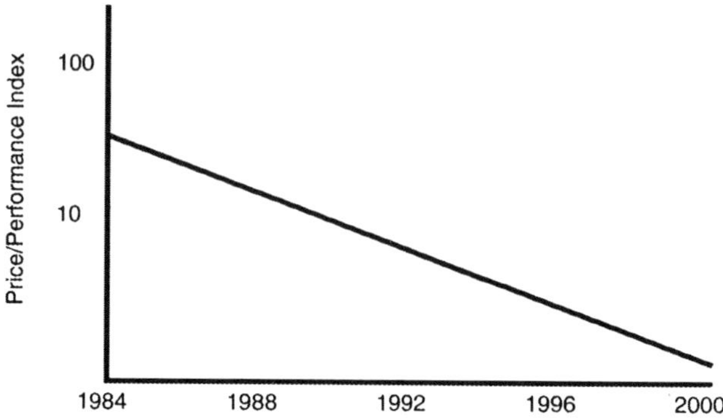

Figure 1.2
The inexorable growth of computer power

ensure the cogency of what results. The new press barons – the Media Engineers – need some technique in order to ply their trade to good effect.

Having sketched out what Media Engineering is and who needs it, let's consider the environment in which it is applied.

1.3   THE MESH

It is the dramatic increases in computing power and memory that have made richer information forms possible. The basic text and editing facilities of the 1970s now seem a dim relic of history when compared with the linked multimedia of the 1990s. And the advances go well beyond just more attractive documents. We have seen ·the genuine realization of the computer's latent capacity to provide easy to use documents.

There is little evidence that the price/performance ratio of computers will do anything other than continue to fall – all of the historical evidence points this way (as is illustrated in Figure 1.2), as do all expectations.

It is accepted wisdom that Moore's law, which states that computing power and capacity double every eighteen months, will hold true well into the next millennium. So, with prices falling and processors becoming redundant (and recycled) so quickly, the number of people who can participate in the media revolution has the potential to grow, and continue growing, at a staggering rate.

As well as more power to hand, the average computer user has an ever increasing community of peers, as is illustrated in Figure 1.3.

Here we show the growth of the best-known network of computer networks – the Internet.

The significance of this is encapsulated in Metcalfe's law, which says that the value of a network (defined as the usefulness of the service it

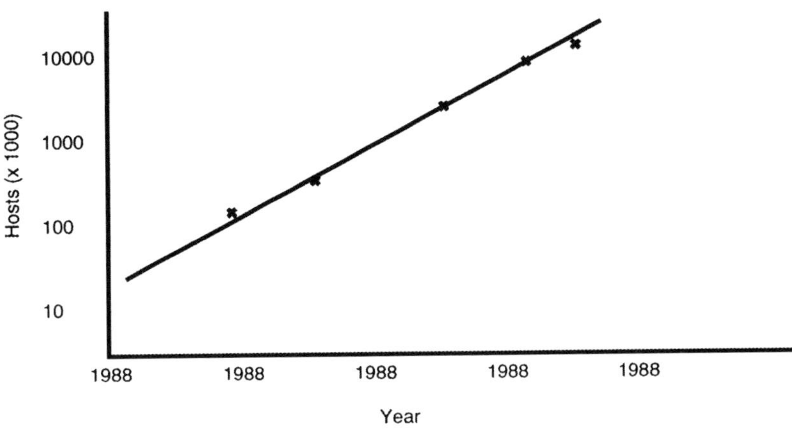

Figure 1.3
The rise and rise of computer networks

renders to its users) is roughly proportional to the square of the number of users. This point is readily illustrated with the telephone network. Alexander Graham Bell's first phone was fairly useless as he only got to speak to Mr Watson. But when phones popped up in every corner of the globe, the network reached its full potential – and changed society forever.

So it is for computers and the information they share. If we add both of these factors, it is clear that Infosurge is no imagined phenomena. It is here to stay and is something that an increasing number of us should aim to exploit or, at least, to learn to make the best of.

If we turn our attention from boxes and links to look at information, the picture is much the same – more and more of it being provided, shared and consumed. The illustration below shows the Internet Society's predictions for World Wide Web traffic. At first glance it appears that network-borne information is on the verge of saturation. There is another way to interpret things. It could be that the amount of Web traffic that is predicted over the next few years represents as much as the users can possibly take, at least in terms of volume. And given that there is likely to be a high level of consumption, the difference between good quality information and the rest will surely become more of an issue.

It has to be said that Figure 1.4 is speculative (albeit based on the best guess from a most authoritative source). One is reminded of 'jokes' about mathematicians and engineers – the mathematician says that the sequence of prime numbers 1, 2, 3, 5, 7, 11, 13 has no pattern but the engineer claims that all odd numbers are prime (the 2 was an experimental error). Semantics, aside, one thing that is clear is that manufacturers expect on-line and multimedia products to grow in importance – we have already

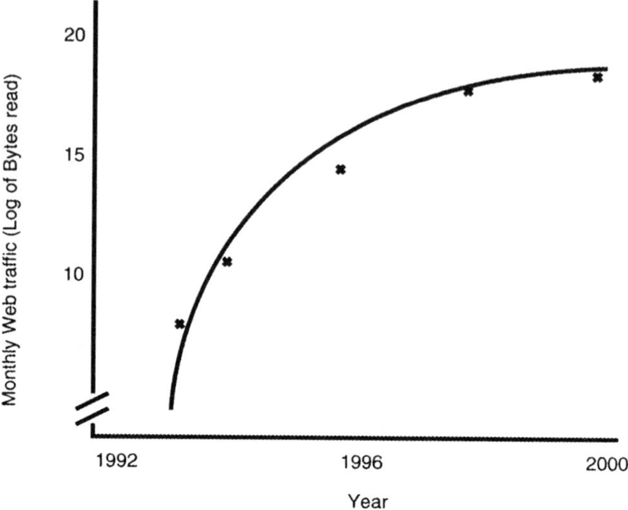

Figure 1.4
The growth of internet browsing

seen many applications designed to exploit distributed and networked computers [NW96].

Despite the plethora of available technology, there is not that much accumulated wisdom on how you use it. It seems to be a tradition in the computing, as well as other, industries that tools and utilities are in place before the methods for using them are established. An example familiar to many would be the concrete tower blocks of the 1960s, a triumph of technology over good practice. Closer to the case in question, we only have to point at all the Web pages that are created simply because someone had the wherewithal to do so.

As software engineers, it comes as no surprise to the authors that you can do more with a computer than you really should. Discipline is needed for the safe wielding of power tools and this is best borne of experience!

We now move on to look at some of the experience to date with computer-based information. What is the nature of the beast and what is it that we are really trying to do.

1.4 MELTDOWN

One thing that we should be very clear on before going any further is why it is important to design information. After all, many people will have quite happily used the search engines available on the World Wide Web to locate items of interest. No-one is mandating rules for the presentation in this arena, so why not stick to open formats and let the user seek out what they want?

Most people who have tried to find more than a very specific piece of information will feel that something better is needed when it comes to on-line structure. With the world so diverse and interlinked, few have the time or energy to build a complete picture for themselves from the ground up.

Going back to Herbert Simon's words at the beginning of the chapter, we do need to treat information with some deference. It is a valuable asset and some care and attention should be devoted to its packaging. It should be possible to capitalize on the speed and ubiquity of networked computers without losing the logical thread that runs through a set of data to provide the reader with new insight.

In short, there are some requirements that any systematic method of engineering information should meet. For example, the user should have a clear and consistent view of:

- where they are

- where they can go

- how to get there quickly (and how did I get here in the first place)!

And the provider should know:

- what their 'units of information currency' are;

- what options for presentation they have;

- how they can change or update their asset.

Media engineering is intended to meet these requirements. Indeed it has been assembled in direct response to them. All of the ideas, tools and techniques in the book draw on the authors' experience of providing computer-based reference, education and advisory material. This has come through a number of routes from contributing to large compact-disk-based references such as Encarta to implementing BT's on-line systems.

Our basic thesis is that the core problems of designing multimedia information products are amenable to the same concepts and disciplines that have been devised in software engineering. After all, both call for the same ability to design a useful product from an intangible resource. And both have to cope with high levels of product complexity and change.

Furthermore, it is not the technology of multimedia (the compact disk, the Internet, etc) but the systematic structuring of information that really matters. In this text we focus on the latter and present a framework and methods for solving the problem. The theory presented is based on our experience of software engineering: the practical detail on the lessons we have learnt in doing it for real.

1.5   SUMMARY

We have used this chapter to introduce the concept of Media Engineering. In doing this, we have tried to put together a picture of a world in which the explosive growth in computer power and data networks has opened up the previously restricted world of information provision. The quality of this information (or rather, its organization and distribution) is something that will increasingly concern virtually all of us. And this is precisely where Media Engineering aims to help.

In order to set the context, we have tried to deliver a number of messages about the opportunities and limitation of computer media. The main ones are:

- that it allows you to take in information not linearly, as presented in a book, but through the linking of ideas and concepts;

- that it has very strong potential in some aspects of supporting this (for instance, facilities for exploration, multimedia etc.);

- that there is a difference between capability and delivery ; it takes discipline to capitalize on the potential.

There is little doubt that the Internet, the compact disk and the networked computer are here to stay. No-one should ignore them, many should be interested in how to exploit them to create, use and distribute large amounts of information. The ideas and techniques in Media Engineering introduced here and elaborated later are focused on navigating a large and growing information space – building a map of the maze.

REFERENCES

[Abo92]   Aboba B. *The Internet Catalogue*, John Wiley & Sons (1992)

[AN95]   Atkins J. & Norris M. *Total Area Networking*, John Wiley & Sons (1995)

[Gor91]   Gore A. Infrastructure for the global village, *Scientific American*, September (1991)

[II36]   Ilyich I. *Deschooling Society*, Harper & Row (1971)

[MG94]   Lyons M. & Gell M. Companies and communications in the next century, *BT Engineering Journal*, **13**(2) (1994)

[NW96]   Norris M. & Winton N. *Energize the Network – Distributed Computing Explained*, Addison Wesley Longman (1996)

[RLM95]   Person R., Laby L. & Merkel B. *Web Publishing with Word*, Que (1995)

[PP94]   Pritchett P. *New Work Habits for a Radically Changing World*

2
Déjà Vu

Nothing holds up the progress of science so much as the right ideas at the wrong time.

Vincent de Vignaud

Let's start with the bad news: all of the problems that we are about to meet in Media Engineering are the same as those that have dogged the software industry for over 25 years. And now some good news: the software industry has solved most of them. There is even better news: the solutions translate pretty well into the media engineering world, so there is a useful historical parallel from which we can learn.

That is what this chapter is all about. We explain some of the ideas and techniques that software engineers have thought through, developed and applied to good effect. Along the way we explain how they can help with media engineering. In the next chapter we start to apply them to the job in hand. This chapter concentrates on setting out the basic concepts that have proved themselves.

First, though, a little history. Back in the mid-1960s, a new term was coined. This was the 'software crisis' and it reflected the fact that the production of software-rich systems was running into the brick wall of complexity. The real cause of this problem was that software had, within a few short years, gone from a specialist activity to a potential solution for all our technological problems. Everyone was doing it but there were no real norms or rules in place.

The initial response to the software crisis was to invent a new term – software engineering. The hope was that a systematic approach to software development would soothe the industry's ailment.

The situation was not unlike one that many of us are now familiar with – lots of people solving their marketing, sales, advertising and operational ills by transferring their information on-line.

Back then, there was within the software industry a general recognition that something had to be done to help with the management of projects. Some of the best minds in the area rounded on the questions of how the software development process should be handled and what sort of methods needed to be applied.

Within a relatively short space of time a whole raft of methods, concepts and models appeared. The fact that some of these are as valid nearly 30 years on is testament to their value. What is more, many of these ideas have found application beyond their original remit of software development.

As it turned out, the software crisis turned out to be more of a chronic illness. The work done to counter the immediate problem, like many remedies, had a limited shelf life. It was not that long before greater levels of complexity confounded some software ventures and so yet more powerful solutions had to be devised. Thus software engineering became an evolving discipline, continually struggling to devise ways of building bigger, faster and sexier systems under some sort of control.

The crisis has yet to bite the on-line and multimedia industries. But it will. With so many turning this way for a lead in business it seems inevitable that enthusiasm will outstrip management capacity. One well known saying in the software world is that quality cannot be painted on afterwards. In much the same way, the adoption of media at an early stage may well avert, or at least alleviate, a crisis later on.

2.1   THE GLOBAL COTTAGE INDUSTRY

The parallels between the software industry and the evolving information industry go beyond the professional development community. Just as many have turned their hand to building venture software, so many small players can and will continue to contribute information products. The great attraction, in both cases, is that the barriers to entry are very low – a computer, some software plus (optionally) some talent and a network connection in both cases.

Nowhere is this more evident than on the World Wide Web. In a few short years, the variety and volume of information that you can access has exploded. Some of this has to be welcome. It is now relatively easy to track down a host of facts and references that would previously have taken several weeks and much shoe leather to locate. There is, however, an element of being entertained in your home by people that you wouldn't have in your home. The quality, cogency and validity of what is on-line is by no means guaranteed.

In the case of information products delivered on compact disk there is

Craft

- Talented individuals
- Design by intuition
- Knowledge growth slow, casual
- Little concern over economy of material

Commercialisation

- Procedures are established
- Systematic training
- Rules of thumb established
- Economic production is a concern

Engineering

- Analysis as a basis for production
- Theoretical principles established
- Performance, scalability dealt with

Figure 2.1
The evolution of an engineering discipline

not the same proliferation of content. Here, the means of publication and distribution is vested, to a large extent, in professional publishing houses. However, with plummeting costs of mastering technology for compact disks, this facility to publish is rapidly being brought within the grasp of the 'ordinary PC user'. So this medium is likely to follow the trail blazed by the World Wide Web.

It is worth standing back from some of the inevitable gloss and hype of multimedia for a few seconds and taking a look where the on-line information industry is in terms of maturity. Figure 2.1 gives some of the typical stages in the development of an engineering discipline.

It should be clear from this that the on-line information business is still very much at the level of a craft industry. It may be high-tech and is certainly global – but even a global cottage industry is still a cottage industry. And the main implication of this is that it is difficult to discriminate between one trader and another. With the quality of the end product heavily reliant on individual talent, the consumer is in something of a vulnerable position. What is more, the intangible nature of the

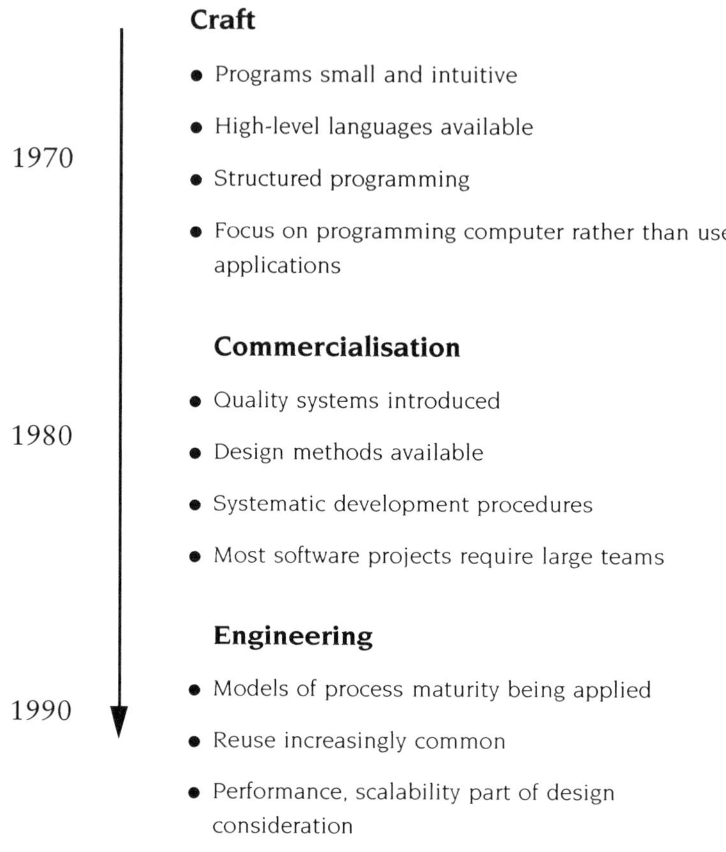

Figure 2.2
An overview of software engineering evolution

product and the fact that virtually anyone can set up as an information trader makes supplier selection a matter of intuition, good luck and chance

In truth, the current situation is probably closer to that of a rather hectic, loud and busy street market.

There is much that needs to be done before the whole situation becomes more ordered, less hit and miss. We are still a way off being able to systematically build information products of comparable size or with the same level of reproducibility as software products.

So, to see how we might get to this from here, it is worth considering the way in which software engineering has evolved. We can fill in many of the generalities of Figure 2.1 with specific developments.

It is not that long since software supply and production was in much the same state as we now find in the world of on-line information. A favoured route into the software business used to be via computer games (some

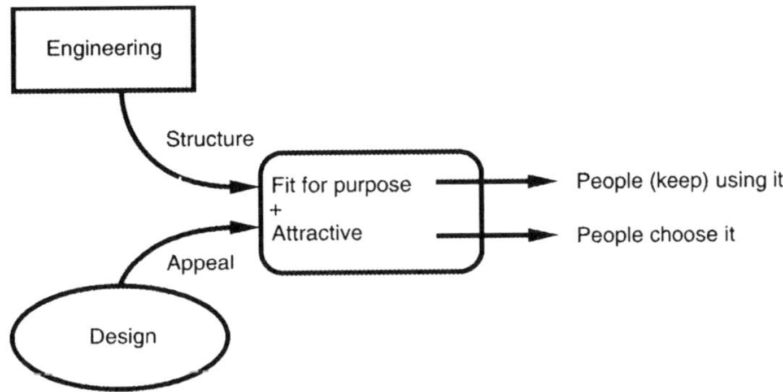

Figure 2.3
The balance of science and art

worthy feats of engineering, others little more than glossy but fragile toys).

As the software industry matured through to the commercial stage, only those who moved with it continued to contribute. Many fell by the wayside and moved down the value chain to become journeymen (literally, paid by the day). It was only those who embraced the new methods and techniques designed to cope with scale and complexity who went on to produce industrial strength systems.

And the message is that we can see what is needed to put a global cottage industry onto a firmer footing by following the lead from a strikingly similar area. That is not to say that we can learn all of the answers by looking back at the evolution of software engineering: the balance of art and science, illustrated in Figure 2.3, is not the same. Information products will have less functionality but will probably always require more attention to presentation, design and packaging.

Even so, structure and usability will inevitably be the differentiating factor between equally attractive offerings. And as the industry matures, these are likely to become key determinants of product quality.

One final point to make about the global cottage industry is that it is unlikely to disappear. With just about every author, potentially, their own publisher, there will always be room for the information smallholder. Furthermore, the high design content in on-line information products means that skilled craftsmen will always be in demand. It is for the engineering part of the above diagram that we turn to the world of software for some illumination of the way ahead.

2.2   BACK TO BASICS

Software can be deceptive. At the simplest level, it is no more than a series of statements coded into a standard format. The problem arises when such straightforward elements are used to produce artefacts of great complexity that are expected to operate reliably and efficiently and to evolve with changing requirements. Many organizations could not function without their software-rich systems.

Information products are much the same. They too are built using a few simple components. As they become increasingly vital to an organization, a similar set of management principles to those in place for software become necessary.

A simple fact from the world of software illustrates the issue very well. With hardware costs falling year on year, the cost of software in high technology business have rocketed – they now account for about 80% of the systems budget. With the balance between systems in development to systems in maintenance about 30:70, this means that over half of the system concerns lie in keeping the installed base in step with a changing world. So the fruits of good engineering lie not so much in a better product but a more durable one. The same issue will surely increasingly apply to information products.

The link between software and Media Engineering should come as no great surprise. One of the reasons that software engineers are in the vanguard of the information revolution is that they are on intimate terms with many of the new concepts. They have already spent years struggling with the problem of how best to structure and link a complex array of abstract ideas, requirements and technical capabilities. Some of the ideas that have proved useful in dealing with this are quite simple – much more structured common-sense than rocket science.

Having said that, it would be invidious to reduce the accumulated wisdom of a major industry down to a few paragraphs but here goes.

The methods and concepts that have been developed, along with some of the lessons learned, provide a useful starting point in mastering copious amounts of information. Here are a dozen or so of the most pervasive and useful ideas. These form the basis of the techniques developed in subsequent chapters.

- *Abstraction.*
  The killer of many a software project was complexity – so much that no-one could get a good understanding of what it was they were dealing with. The real lesson that emerged was that complexity can only be controlled though abstraction – the omission of unnecessary detail. The

real trick – one that has received much attention in the software world – is what to omit.

Getting the right abstraction is not easy. Visual tools gave comfort but didn't solve the problems then – and probably won't for media engineering. Even now, there is no general solution in software engineering. Design notations and structuring (both explained below) have both played their part. The general approaches that have endured are structured decomposition (breaking a large system into smaller, simpler components), stepwise refinement (the gradual addition of detail, showing each step to be a valid development), information hiding (suppressing local concerns), separation of concerns (designing the data separately from the processing) and high-level languages (which allow the engineer to work at a higher level of abstraction rather than focusing on implementation detail).

Once a suitable level of abstraction has been found, what do you do with it? The second lesson from the software world is that it is important to be systematic – you need a reliable and reproducible way of moving from the abstract through to the concrete. There is many a slip twixt specification and final product, so the steps along the way have to be measured (for example, how much coupling and cohesion is there between two components) and controlled. The need for reproducibility is embraced in many of the design notations that have been developed.

Much of this is not planned. There is a natural evolution as ideas – often quite simplistic ones – take hold and are accepted as 'the way you should do it'. For instance, one of the far-reaching ideas in the production of software code was to deem the GOTO statement harmful. This seemingly simple assertion was underpinned by a view that unconditional jumps from one part of a programme to another would obscure the logical flow of programme structure and make maintenance more difficult.

- *The Lifecycle.*
  This is the overall framework within which work takes place, rather like the scenes of a play. As well as guiding you through the process, the concept of a lifecycle can be used to insert checks and balances at key points, ring alarm bells when you are off course and give you some basis for measurement and estimation.

  Lifecycles (of which many flavours now exist in the software industry) are fundamental to the effective quality management of many development projects. They provide the route map for traceable and reproducible developments.

  The concept of the lifecycle is inherent in any engineering discipline.

It comes to the fore in software because of the intangible nature of the product. It is fairly obvious that you need to design a bridge before building it. The sequence of events is not so clear in software (or indeed media) engineering, so the adoption of a lifecycle provides a shareable view of what is going on.

- *Design Notation*.
When working with intangible and abstract ideas, you need some way of expressing your thoughts and proposals and writing them down in a way that other people will understand.

  A good notation gives you something against which you can check thinking, set out a test plan and refer to at a later date, when errors have to be fixed and modifications made. By way of example, a flowchart is a familiar notation for expressing any logical sequence of operations to be performed. It gives you a means of expressing how various entities interact and provides something to check an implementation against.

  In software, the initial focus was on structuring high-level code. As complexity took hold, so a plethora of design methods appeared. Some focused on the flow of control, some on the manipulation of data, some on the interaction of the software system with its intended environment. Whichever angle was taken, the engineer was furnished with a way of tackling a complex problem, a notation for recording their decisions and (usually) some guidelines to check the soundness of what they had done.

- *Use Cases*.
The proof of any pudding lies in the eating. And it is end users who consume information, just as they do software systems. The ultimate test of fitness for purpose lies in the user's perception, so it is worth having this as an initial target rather than a retrospective touchstone.

  Use cases provide a way of recording the expectations a user might have, the actions they might take and the most likely ways in which they will use (and abuse) a delivered product. With much of the functionality of software systems hidden from the end user, the elicitation of use cases can be a demanding task.

  The immediacy of information products makes it somewhat easier to establish what a user will or will not like – most will be able to tell you what they want to see and in what order. The function of the use case is to gather a set of such requirements into one place so that they can be built into a single product.

- *Objects*.
When dealing with any complex entity, it is important to separate various concerns and encapsulate information into manageable chunks. The natural units used in software design are called objects.

These provide the building blocks of a software system. Objects have associated with them rules and guidelines that tell you what you can (and cannot) do to them, how they work with each other and what they provide.

A few, very simple concepts, when applied consistently, can form a powerful set of building blocks for building even the most complex of systems. In the software industry, object-oriented design has been used to construct large systems for some years. And this is founded on three properties of objects – encapsulation (the hiding of internal behaviour), polymorphism (a means of getting compatibility between objects) and inheritance (building on the properties of an already established object). There is a lot more that could be (and has been) said about objects but the basics are very easy to grasp and apply.

- *Compilation.*
Another consequence of complexity is that you cannot expect to hand craft everything. Sheer volume quickly takes hold and a significant amount of automation is required to keep control. This has long been accepted by software engineers, who would not dream of translating their programs into the low-level code that actually drives the computer. Tools such as the compiler, which carry out this translation as well as performing many sanity checks, have long been accepted as basic necessities.

- *Linking and Binding.*
At some point, the various components of a system have to be assembled into a whole. And so, we move on from the basic translation of the compiler into the linking and binding of the assemblage of working bits. Again, most software engineers accept that references in one object will be automatically matched to required locations and that incomplete links will be neatly bound at an appropriate point in the process. There are various options for linking and binding that are useful in Media Engineering.

- *Configuration Management.*
When dealing with a large number of software components which only exist as (often strangely) named files on a computer disk, it is very easy to lose track of what is what and what is where. Especially after the enthusiasm of the first release is past and you are into updating the product for the third (or, more likely, 23rd) time.

Software products built of thousands of components, delivered to hundreds of sites in tens of variants manage to cope with this. An important part of the lifecycle is to identify configuration items (the source components from which a product is built) and establish release baselines (compatible sets of source components that constitute a viable product). This requirement extends across all of the versions and variants of the product that need to be deployed.

Once this is done a mechanism for change control has to be put in place, so that the products can evolve under some form of control. A change control process would, typically, consist of a queue of change requests, an evaluation/integration stage and a release queue.

- *Naming.*
When a product is built from many components, it is important to have consistent and meaningful names so that you can keep track of what is called, by whom. Naming conventions (or, rather, lack of them) have been the rock on which many software projects have foundered.

A little effort expended in this area has been known to pay dividends in the past and can be expected to do so again. It is very annoying to lose files when you forget what they are called, or lose track of which version of a document you are working on. A good naming scheme helps you to home in on a component by knowing its function in life, rather than an arbitrary name. For instance 1–ABA–00123–CD is a typical documentation code from big software project. Anyone on the project would instantly know that it was a system level (ABA) flowchart (CD) relating to module 123. More importantly, if they were searching for system level flowcharts on module 123, they would have some chance of finding them!

- *Tools.*
Machines are more accurate than people, and accomplish routine tasks more speedily, so with software systems of any size, automation is essential. Basic tools, such as compilers and editors, have been available for many years. Tools to support design are more recent additions to the software engineer's arsenal. The software industry has served itself here with a raft of computer aided software engineering (CASE) tools.

After an outbreak of initial enthusiasm (when some believed that CASE tools would commoditize software production), a wide range of useful aids have emerged to support the software engineer. The old adage that 'a fool with a tool is still a fool' is just as true as ever, though.

- *Non-functionals.*
A lot of important practical aspects are invisible in a logical, paper design but are very obvious when a product performs (even more so when it doesn't). Much of the early work on software engineering focused on programme function, consistency and accuracy. The 'non-functional' issues of usability, scalability, maintainability and the

like emerged a little later, as it became clear that cost of ownership of software systems was as (if not more) important than the cost of the initial development.

Media Engineering (and, in this, we include our own efforts from here on) will have to address the issue of non-functionals head on. Performance and usability are two issues that will differentiate good information products from the also-rans. Neither of these attributes can be retrofitted to a poorly designed system: like all of the non-functionals, they need to be designed in from the start.

- *Structure.*
  A couple of the previous points have touched on having some accepted means of decomposing a complex problem into simpler constituent parts that can subsequently be put back together to form a cogent whole. For the software engineer, object orientation and other design notations put this on a rigorous basis.

  One of the informal concepts in this area that has come to be applied in software design is the separation of the logical from the physical: the what from the how. This sort of approach is useful in that you can map one logical design onto a variety of physical realizations. In practice, this allows for flexibility in the face of change – the same logic can be re-implemented in different ways – and also allows for different levels of performance and scalability to be catered for.

  The separation of structure and content is a key part of media engineering.

- *Reuse.*
  As software engineering has matured, standard components have started to appear. At first, some standard functions (e.g. mathematical routines) were made available and, more recently, a few larger software components that carry out complex actions have been produced. At a local level, many software houses maintain a library of commonly used utilities from which a selection can be made when building a new product. This is particularly pervasive in the computer games industry where there are standard backgrounds, algorithms and characters.

  One thing that has come to the fore in the world of software development is the idea of application programmer interfaces (API). These provide the engineer with a means of including either reusable components or hand-crafted code into a product. The API is the software engineers equivalent of the standard thread on a nut that has to fit a specific bolt. Only problem is that the complexity of real APIs is considerably greater than that for the thread on the nut, so software reuse is not as successful as in other disciplines.

- *Testing.*

  About 40% of the effort that goes into a software product is devoted to testing. Sometimes this is intentional but more often goes under the name of alpha-trialling, rework or bug fixing. The real scam in the software engineering industry is that many vendors charge you for so-called software maintenance which, in truth, is you paying them to fix the bugs that they sold you in the original product!

  A good product is not just free from error (bugs), it is also fit for its intended purpose. A test regime should address both of these concerns and verify that the product meets its specification (i.e. operates as it should) and validate that the product is fit for purpose (i.e. performs as the customer and/or user expects).

  This means that testing is not something tacked onto the end of the lifecycle. It should go right through the lifecycle – requirements can be tested, as can plans and designs. The same continuous evaluation principle applies to Media Engineering.

That's as far as we go for now. All of the above concepts apply directly in media engineering and, with ever-increasing product complexity, need to be applied. We could have said more as there are a couple of notable exceptions from our list. One is measurement criteria, the second is quality assurance. Their omission is not an oversight, rather a reflection of the fact that neither has yet been satisfactorily dealt with in the software engineering community. It is not that efforts have not been made – indeed there are lots of ways of measuring the productivity of software production, the complexity of a software product, defect levels in code and the maturity of a development process. What has yet to be established is how what can be measured relates to what you really want to know – how good the product will be or how long it will take to develop. Predictive and qualitative measures have run into the problem that software development is heavily reliant on people and they are not easy to neatly categorize.

With Media Engineering at least dependent on people, it seems unlikely that it is going to adequately cover the issues.

In order to see how these ideas that we have listed relate to each other (and to the real world), it is worth delving a little deeper. This is probably best achieved by looking at the overall process of software production – the end-to-end picture into which all of the above fit. The next section outlines how some of the concepts apply, and where there are established lessons, know-how and guidelines that can be derived.

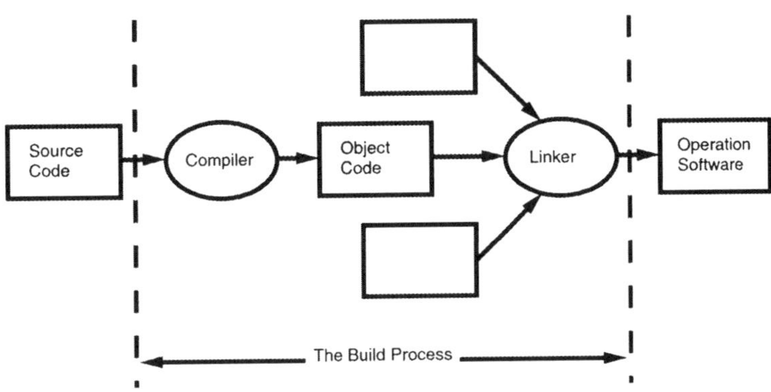

Figure 2.4
The production stages for a software product

2.3   HOW SOFTWARE IS BUILT

To a very rough approximation, the diagram below illustrates the main steps in building a software product. This part of the diagram, marked as the 'build process' is now the focus of attention.

On the left of the diagram we have the basic building blocks of the product – the objects required to construct a working system. Since these elements have been crafted by software engineers, they just happen to be lines of source code in C++, Cobol, Java etc. The build process is a set of steps that take this collection of base components and forges them into a product.

There are a number of transformations that have to be effected to the collection of components before the final product can be released, the first of these being the generation of machine-readable object code from the designers source. This is where compilation comes in. It would be unreasonable to expect a human to reliably translate a high-level programming language into machine code. It can be done but few people live that long! The compiler carries out the translation automatically. There are some assumptions and preferences in this process but the compilation of source code into object code is taken as a standard utility by the software engineer.

So our first step takes us from one source file to one object file. In practice, it is the norm to have a number of people developing a software product. This means that after each team member has compiled their contribution, there is work to be done in coalescing their efforts. This is where linking comes in. The linker resolves symbolic references into real locations, tells you if there are any conflicts between components and can indicate where components are missing. It is only after all of the compiled components are linked together that you have an operational product.

There are a couple of observations on the build process that are worth making. The first is that there is a lot of work that precedes the build phase in software production. A lot of effort has been expended in defining the methods and concepts to help the designer in producing components that fulfil stated product requirements. Indeed, the precursor to the build process often consists of a set of quality gates that determine when design stops and coding begins, when testing stops and when maintenance begins.

The second observation is that the build process is an automated one. Everything between the dotted lines in the above diagram remains (largely) untouched by human hand. The inputs and outputs from the process are managed but even moderate levels of complexity make it impossible to hand build the product.

Control over an established software build process is effected by ensuring that a known set of source code components are used and that they are put together in a known way. This is done with the 'makefile utility' (which comes bundled with many development computers). It takes a set of software components, defined in a user template, and builds them into the product.

2.4   FOUNDATIONS

As indicated above, there is a lot of preparation that needs to be done before any building work takes place. We now go a little deeper into some of the design and control issues that are employed in software development.

First, the overall design of the product. There are many different (and sometimes conflicting) factors that the software designer has to take into account before deciding how to approach the design phase of a software development. Some of the more pressing ones are explained below along with the reasons why they need to be addressed.

- *Constraints.*   There are a number of reasons why the full range of choices open to a designer would be restricted. Some of these are contractual (purchasers require certain procedures to be followed or methods to be used) others are technical (existing hardware and software limits the freedom to design from scratch). Yet others are cultural.

- *Customer expectation.*   The level of customer involvement in a software project may influence (and be influenced by) the design strategy adopted. If the design process is easy to monitor, the customer can contribute. This is not always desirable nor is it always sought. Software developments tend to range between extremes. At one, the customer states their requirements and returns later to pick up the finished article (the dead cat over the wall scenario[1]. At the other extreme, the customer is presented with a series of prototypes and there is a mutual evolution towards a solution.

The nature of hypermedia places it technically and culturally at the latter extreme. Media Engineering is considerably more immediate than many software projects, so customer, user or client guidance is that much more relevant. The received wisdom in the software world is that the user may not always be right, but the user is always . . . the user[2].

- *Type of System.* The nature of the system being developed does, to some extent, lead the choice of design methods and tools. For example, the most appropriate methods for a real time system might be state tables, for a database design, a specialized query language etc. In media engineering, the temptation is to use all of the bells and whistles all of the time. The lesson here is to select the right horse for the right course!

- *Type of Application.* The implications of designing a security or safety critical system are very different (and make different demands on the design process) from the design of an in-house prototype. It is unlikely that media systems would have the same characteristics as the most extreme software systems (e.g. those that control a nuclear power station) but there still remain a wide range of application areas for media engineering. To address these requires a broad set of technologies, including some secure socket layer (SSL), proxy and firewall deployment.

- *Whole lifecycle view.* Design choices should be taken with a view to their long-term implications. It is important to know whether the development is a one-off, time critical project or (at the other extreme) a core development likely to be maintained through many revisions. As well as designing for the anticipated durability of the product, the user-perceived boundaries have to be managed. So, when building for the World Wide Web, external links are part of your system.

- *Non-functional requirements.* Designers often concentrate on the what a system does rather than how easy it is to use, how reliable it is

---

[1] The trade story being that the developers claim that the cat may be dead now but it was alive when they flung it over the wall!

[2] A sentiment we must attribute to Charley Moore.

likely to be, how quickly it will operate etc. It is the non-functional requirements that will, increasingly, become the differentiating factor in Media Engineering, just as they have done in software engineering.

All of the above are as pertinent to Media Engineering as they are to software, and similar preparation is called for. Software developers are fortunate (perhaps) to have many established methods to choose from. Their task is to select appropriate methods, techniques and options for specific applications. We have to build our own – starting in the next Chapter – but at least we can build on the foundations of some well-tried principles.

2.5 SUMMARY

Very little in this world is truly new. What appears, at first sight, to be novel and different often has parallels with something already known and understood. The theme of this chapter has been to suggest that the production of complex information products is a case in point and that software engineering provides many useful ideas, techniques, hints and tips. In explaining the natural progression of any engineering discipline, we have tried to show that the on-line and multimedia industry is in much the same state as the software business was in the late 1960s. Our contention has been that it will develop in much the same way, too.

Given this basic premise, the main part of this chapter explains some of the basic concepts that underpin modern software engineering. Most of them are very simple and can readily be applied to other endeavours. Yet they have all shown themselves to be very powerful and capable of rising to significant challenges. The ideas introduced here as the basic precepts for media engineering are:

- *Abstraction.* The omission of detail to allow focus on the essential issues, and thus keep complexity under control.

- *The lifecycle.* The view of development as a linked set of stages, each with a defined purpose of its own.

- *Design notation.* Some means of being able to record and reason about something very abstract.

- *Use cases.* Making sure that the end user view is catered for by explicitly including it as part of the design.

- *Objects.* Having some recognizable building blocks, with known rules that apply to them, from which to construct systems.

- *Compilation.* Differentiating between source and object material. The former is maintained by the designer, the latter is the product, compiled from the source.

- *Linking and binding.* Recognition that complex products have many components and that these need to be assembled in the correct fashion.

- *Configuration management.* A basic ethic that ensures that versions and variants of a product can be recreated.

- *Naming.* Some convention that is recognized and followed by developers to help with the identification of components.

- *Tools.* As well as production tools (those that manipulate the source material), products of any size require tools for test, documentation, conversion etc.

- *Non-functionals.* Recognizing that there is more to design than form and function – speed, scalability and maintainability have to be built in.

- *Structure.* Just as software engineers separate physical and logical design, so media engineers should separate content from structure.

- *Reuse.* Recognizing that there are many generic functions and operations that are best solved once, instead of being almost solved many times.

- *Testing.* It is widely recognized (and poorly practised!) in the software industry that a product that needs to be proved against its specification (verified – bugs removed) and shown to be fit for purpose (validated – user happy).

The way in which these principles apply to Media Engineering will not be the same as found in the software engineers world – one of the messages of the chapter is that the balance we should seek is more towards design and less to production. Nonetheless, we have the foundations for building a method – and this is precisely what we now go on to do.

FURTHER READING

There are thousands of book on software engineering. The list below is representative and covers all of the topics outlined in this chapter in some detail. Some indication of the coverage of each book is given.

Abbott R. *Software Development*, John Wiley & Sons (1986) <u>Compilation, Linking and Binding, Tools</u>

Booch G. *Object Solutions* Addison Wesley (1996) <u>Objects</u>

Budgen D. *Software Design* Addison Wesley (1994) <u>Design Notation</u>

Hetzel W. *The Complete Guide to Software Testing*, QED Information Sciences (1988) <u>Testing</u>

Jacobson I., Christerson M., Jonsson P. & Overgaard G. *Object-Oriented Software Engineering: a Use Case Driven Approach*, Addison Wesley (1993) <u>Use Cases</u>

Leintz B. & Swanson E. *Software Maintenance* Management, Addison Wesley (1980) <u>Configuration Management, Naming</u>

Luce D. & Andrews D. *The Software Lifecycle*, Butterworth Heinemann (1990) <u>The Lifecycle</u>

Norris M. *Survival in the Software Jungle*, Artech House (1995) <u>Non-functionals</u>

Peters L. *Software Design – Methods and techniques*, Yourdon Press (1981) <u>Design Notation</u>

Pressman R. *Software Engineering – A Practitioners Approach*, McGraw Hill (1987) <u>Design Notation, Structure, Reuse Naming</u>

Sommerville I. *Software Engineering*, 4th edition, Addison Wesley (1992) <u>Abstraction, Structure, Reuse</u>

3
DIVA

Give us the tools and we will finish the job.

Winston Churchill

Before diving into detail in this chapter, there are a few things to establish. So far within this book we have argued that there is no established and generally understood engineering discipline which deals with the concerns of designing, developing, delivering and maintaining complex multimedia systems. Furthermore, we can see that this situation is strongly paralleled by the so-called 'software crisis' of the late 1960s and that the problems increasingly being encountered in multimedia have underlying causes that seem very similar to those encountered in the software industry. So it seems reasonable to explore the solution that was eventually evolved for the software crisis as it might, if sufficiently abstracted from the details of software, be equally applicable to the media explosion of the 1990s.

In the present chapter we will begin to test the argument. First we examine some of the evident problems of multimedia systems, as perceived by the authors, and see whether the software engineering principles introduced in the last chapter do indeed offer us a solution.

Not unexpectedly, we find that the principles of software engineering do, after suitable adaptation, translate into useful Media Engineering principles. So the main part of the chapter is given over to explaining the elements of a method to which we have given the umbrella title of Documented Information Visualisation Approach (DIVA). This chapter sets out the principles and, in Chapters 4 and 5, we go on to describe how DIVA can be applied in practice.

3.1   WHY DIVA?

There are many tools on the market that purport to help the designer of an information product. Given this apparent abundance of help, why create a new method? Our own experience of producing large-scale multimedia systems confirms that a set of tools and techniques is needed to address some of the following common problems:

- *Document translation.* Commonly, the implementor of a multimedia system is confronted with a vast set of existing documentation produced by various packages (MS-Word, Pagemaker, WordPerfect, Powerpoint, etc.). Tools are needed to convert these into hypermedia without having to rewrite or redraw large parts of them. In addition, decisions must be made with regard to new material: whether to use a special-purpose multimedia authoring package or to use a conventional tool and perform a translation.

- *Configuration management* (or looking after all the elements of a multimedia publication). Current multimedia technology encourages the fragmenting of information into files that contain a few pages of text, a single picture, a single video sequence or a single sound. Even in quite a small multimedia production the number of individual files can grow to several hundred. Some tools and techniques are needed to keep track of all these files, to record the relationships between them and to manage the effects of change when individual files are updated or replaced.

- *Validation and testing.* Our own experience is that in a typical multimedia system, the number of 'links' (items of clickable text, buttons, icons, clickable pictures, etc.) exceeds the number of files by a factor of about ten-to-one. So a system with a few hundred files is likely to have a few thousand links. It is important to test that all these links work-it is very off-putting for the consumer of your multimedia masterpiece to click on a link, only to receive a bland system error such as 'Error 404: page not found'. The reader is left with an impression much like that experienced when finding blank pages in the middle of a book. Testing several thousand links, haphazardly, by hand is not feasible: even doing it systematically, working continuously through an eight-hour day you are only likely to cover about 3000 links. At this rate, a medium-sized multimedia system can take over a week of continuous work just to check the links (and would probably cost you your sanity, too). The only sensible answer is to automate the testing process as much as possible.

- *Navigation.* In Chapter 1, we made the case that the main limitation (perhaps the only limitation) of multimedia systems is navigation. One of the key measures in developing Media Engineering has been the extent to which it minimises this constraint.

- *Orientation.* Anyone who has 'surfed' the World Wide Web will know that a few clicks of the mouse can take you into a maze of interconnected pages. So how do you find out where you are, where you want to go and how to get there?

- *Metrics and estimation.* If you are planning to produce your own multimedia system, how long will it take you and how many people will you need to work on the job? Conversely, if you are paying someone else to produce your multimedia system, how much should they be charging you and how do you know if you are getting value for money?

Current market offerings may look appealing but they do not really tackle the base problem of complexity. Even if they did, there is no engineering framework into which they fit. This should come as no great surprise. Early software engineering tools (such as compilers and editors) were similar – they helped with one aspect of production but did little to support systematic development.

3.2 WILL SOFTWARE ENGINEERING REALLY HELP?

Many attractive ideas look less appealing when you get close up. Before going on, we should play devil's advocate for a moment. After all, a quick examination of the tools and techniques of software engineering suggests that they are rather specific, not only to the software field, but also to particular applications. For example, one of the earliest, most complete, and now most mature of the development methodologies was SSADM. Even a cursory examination of this method and its practitioners shows that not only is it specifically aimed at software applications, but it also assumes that the software is built around a database management system and, further, that it is most applicable to a breed of computers that live in a half-glazed room, tended by computer operators, quite remote from (and indeed never even seen by) the people who program them.

Similarly, many of the comparable software methodologies such as Yourdon, MASCOT and IEF are all very specific to particular and comparatively narrow branches of software application. Oh Dear!

So, have we gone down a dead end? Given that software engineering has developed into these rather specific and narrow branches, what hope does it offer to us as a solution to the media explosion?

The argument presented in this book is not that software engineering provides us with a complete, ready-made, packaged solution that we can simply pick up off the shelf and start using: if things were that simple, this book would hardly be needed. What we *do* argue, however, is that because of the similarity of the problems inherent in software engineering and Media Engineering, the underlying principles on which software engineering are based should form the basis of a new set of methodologies that apply to Media Engineering.

Hence, in this chapter, we do not focus on a particular software engineering method. Instead, we take the fundamental principles which were teased out in Chapter 2 and attempt to match them to the newer (but similar) issues of Media Engineering.

So what are the abstraction principles that you need to produce large-scale Multimedia systems? We now move on and start to develop a systematic approach to Media Engineering that draws on the software engineering ideas that we have already explained.

3.3   DIVA—KEY CONCEPTS

The DIVA method provides a systematic approach which aims, if not actually to solve the problems that we set out a couple of sections ago, at least to keep them under control. Although the techniques are relatively new to multimedia they are, as you may have guessed, all based on tried and tested software engineering approaches developed over the last two decades.

Let's start to explain DIVA by putting forward a few definitions that we'll be needing to cope with the development of information products.

- *Discrimination.* Many of the problems experienced in building multimedia systems relate to the interaction between *content* and *structure*. If the two become mixed up, there can be unwanted interactions when (inevitable) changes are made.

  The principle of *discrimination* requires that structure and content be separated. This may seem to deny a basic property of multimedia (namely that links can be inserted anywhere in text or pictures). However, it will be shown that such a separation can largely (though not completely) be maintained without compromising the inherent properties and advantages of multimedia. What is paramount is that the designer understands the distinction between content and structure and applies appropriate levels of resource to each.

- *Encapsulation.* This concept describes how elements of content are divided into small manageable items which are, as far as possible, independent of other elements. This division into small, independent units is obvious in a publication such as an encyclopaedia, where each article represents a discrete information object. It is less obvious in some other types of multimedia, but can be applied to good effect in almost all cases as will be demonstrated later. The importance of encapsulation is that it allows:

  —the clear identification of self-contained items that can be configuration managed. Each information object can be edited, changed or enhanced without impact on the remainder of the multimedia system.

  —the management of items of *content* quite separately from the *structure* of the information. Thus we support one of our other key principles – that of discrimination. As far as possible, each information object contains either structure or content but not both.

- *Information Object.* This is an identifiable multimedia item. In practice, it is likely to be a single disk file containing a self-contained set of information. This might consist of a few pages of text on a single subject, a single picture, a single video clip or a sound. Software engineering is concerned with the management of 'modules' of computer software; an information object is an analogous module of multimedia material. It is the smallest item that is managed: it must have a unique name and an identifiable place where it is stored; it must have attributes such as a 'creation date', a 'last modified date' and a 'version number'. The use of these attributes – which we have already argued for in 'configuration management' etc in the previous chapter – will be explained in detail later.

- *Polycontiguity.* It is a fundamental principle that there are *multiple navigation paths* through the same body of information. This principle is described as *Polycontiguity*. The author of a conventional book usually writes it on the basis that there is a single path through it (starting in the top left corner of the first page and running through linearly to the bottom, right corner of the last page). The flow of ideas and arguments follows a linear sequential format. However, the author of a multimedia system must anticipate that people will follow complex threads of interconnection through the material. In order to match the cogency of a conventional book, the author must not only *be aware*

Table 3.1

Overview	Y/N
Guidelines	Y/N
Company standard	Y/N
Checklist	Y/N
Tools	Y/N
Methods	Y/N
Examples	Y/N
Detail	Y/N
Navigation	Y/N

that people will use multimedia in this way but must *design the system* with this in mind.

- *Staples.* Information objects need to be identified in some way in order to distinguish whether they are part of the content or part of the structure. It is also useful to have some way of identifying attributes not apparent to the end user. Examples of such attributes are the identification of some items as 'overview' material and others as 'reference' material.

  In DIVA, information objects can be tagged (or *stapled*) with the set of attributes (or *staples*) that relate to them. This set of attributes needs to be defined and is dependent on the particular multimedia application. In practice, the number of staples should be kept to a manageable number. By way of illustration, Table 3.1 shows an example set of staples relating to a multimedia project concerned with software development.Each information object would have a different profile of items from the general-purpose list in the table.

  By stapling each information object in this way, it becomes possible to automate the picking out, for example, of all the overview material, all of the company standards or all the checklists.

  Exactly *how* information objects are stapled will be covered in a later section.

So much for the ideas. The next thing is to suggest where and when they can be used to good effect. We now revisit the twelve principles explained in the last chapter and suggest how they might play a useful role in support of Media Engineering.

3.4 DIVA – PRINCIPLES

Each of the software engineering principles introduced in Chapter 2 has its counterparts in Media Engineering. In this section we examine each of these principles and indicate the part it plays in the DIVA method.

3.4.1 Abstraction

Abstraction (or the neglecting of detail that is unimportant at a particular stage of the process) is inherent in much of the DIVA method. For example, much of the *system* design is accomplished by considering the system to be composed of nothing more than pages and links. For the purposes of the system design, page content and graphical design can, for example, be neglected or, more realistically, can be tackled in a parallel and only loosely connected design activity.

Abstraction is, however, not dealt with as an explicit topic. Rather, it will be found to be a continuing theme throughout the method.

3.4.2 Lifecycle

It has already been noted that all engineering disciplines begin with a recognition of specific craft skills. Before moving on to be a commercial concern, mechanical engineering thrived on the skills of the carpenter and the blacksmith. Likewise, software engineering grew out of the skills of the programmer. In general, as an engineering discipline matures, the area of concern grows to encompass not just the craft skill, but the whole end-to-end task from an original idea, through design and development, to installation and maintenance. The tools of the mechanical engineer started with the hammer and anvil, moved on to the slide rule and then to the spreadsheet.

The lifecycle, is firstly a recognition that the whole end-to-end task – not just the creative (fun, sexy) bit – must be brought under control. Hence we propose a simple lifecycle for Media Engineering.

A second reason for considering the whole process from concept to maintenance and withdrawal is that it yields a systematic approach – it defines what steps you take and the order you take them in, together with the criteria for completion of each stage. Furthermore, it becomes more obvious how you might trade off the cost, quality and timescale aspects of product development.

Figure 3.1 illustrates the proposed Media Engineering lifecycle.

Needless to say, this is based on a software engineering lifecycle, one originally attributed to Grady Booch [OOD]. For our purposes, the various phases are:

- *Conceptualization.* This is the phase in which the multimedia system

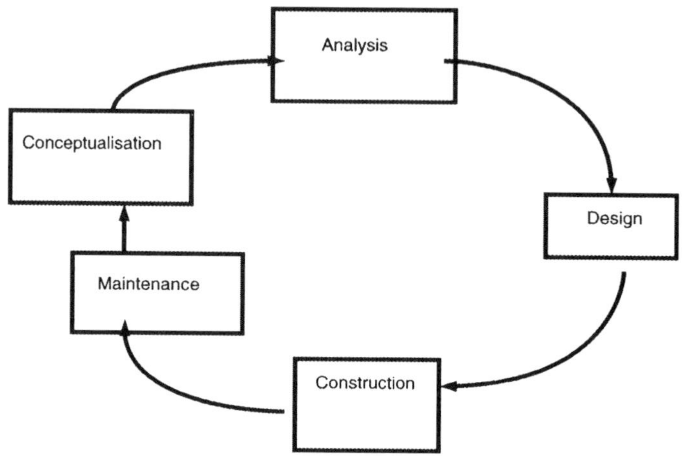

Figure 3.1
Media engineering lifecycle

is conceived and its top level requirements are identified and prioritized. The output of this phase is a top-level description of the media project, together with the set of prioritized requirements.

- *Analysis.* In this phase, the requirements are developed through the use of use cases and prototyping (more of this later). The specific activities of this phase are:
  —Establish use cases that describe some of the main behaviours of the system as perceived by the user. The focus is on how the user is likely to react with the product.
  —Develop a top-level system design that describes the overall structure of the system. This should give an overall picture of the product.
  —In parallel, develop some 'prototype' graphics for the page design. An early view of what is in the designer's mind is often very revealing.
  —prototype the system: at least some example pages and some of the novel aspects of the system.

- *Design.* Refine the design from the top-level structure into a detailed logical design. This step should highlight any issues that are likely to arise during implementation.

- *Construction.* This phase is a detailed process in its own right and is described in detail in Chapter 4. In essence, it involves designing and implementing the system down to the detailed page level. This includes:
  —page compilation;
  —linking;
  —graphic design;

—testing.
Despite the fact that the bulk of available time is usually vested in this phase, it is by no means the most important. If attention is not paid to its predecessors, it will often be time and effort in vain. In the case of a large system, it is easy to dive into the detail of page design, only to become overwhelmed by complexity.

- *Maintenance.*   Multimedia systems, once produced, do not remain unchanged forever. Changes will be needed, for example:
  —to correct any errors;
  —to improve it in response to user feedback;
  —to update it with new information;
  —to develop and extend the scope of a successful system;
  —to take advantage of technological advances.

The various stages in the lifecycle model described above are used throughout the rest of this book. The lifecycle is somewhat idealized. In reality, there is a considerable amount of overlap and iteration between the stages. Even so, it provides a valuable framework within which a group of people can work.

3.4.3 Design notation

A notation is a way of writing down or drawing a design. This is something that is currently completely lacking from the field of Media Engineering. If you approached most designers of a web site and asked them to describe their design, they could probably describe quite clearly the elements of the *graphical* design but would have some difficulty explaining the *information* design, including such items as the way that pages are linked together.

Indeed many sites have not been designed at all. The 'designer' has begun by linking a few pages together and then just grown the site by a process of accretion – many sites display all the worst signs of having been created in this way. Even the best may only display consistency and usability because a principal designer has been able to hold the complete picture in their head whilst implementing the system. For most of us this is too great an intellectual challenge and, furthermore, we require some confidence that the site can continue to grow, evolve and be maintained even if the original designer moves on to other tasks. Without the architect's plans for a house it is difficult to plan a new extension. To be able to write down or draw the design, we need a notation.

One of the innovations that software engineering brought to the software industry was the ability to describe and specify software designs in terms of specification languages, either verbal or pictorial. Many different notations for software have been devised, embodying varying degrees of formality and various areas of application. Although much of the early emphasis was on truly formal languages that had a strict mathematical basis (and hence were quite analogous to the notations used, for example, in mechanical engineering), more long-term impact has probably been achieved by less rigorous but more accessible techniques such as entity–relationship notation, data flow diagrams, message sequence charts and object models.

For a notation to be useful it must fulfil some desirable criteria.

- *Abstraction* (again). Sorry to labour this one but it is fundamental. Abstraction is the technique of ignoring some of the less important details so that the main details of the structure can be manipulated. It allows the designer to see the wood for the trees. Without abstraction, the notation suffers from the problems of the 1:1 scale map of the country: although the detail is perfect, when you spread it out it covers the whole country.

- *Completeness.* There is little merit in a notation that doesn't allow you to express ideas relevant to the design you are working on. The notation should be adequate for recording essential features. It should really help you to reason about your ideas – a good notation will help you to check what it is that you have written down for desirable properties.

- *Unambiguity.* A notation should mean the same thing to different readers. It should also mean the same thing to the same person at different times. If you cannot determine what is meant by each symbol or collection of symbols then there is little value in the notation. This does not necessarily mean that a formal syntax and semantics has to be in place, simply that the notation proves to be clear in its interpretation by its users.

There are most likely some others but this set contains the major ones for our purposes.

Media Engineering notation

When designing a media system, the major items that must be documented are the 'pages' of information and the 'links' between them. We have chosen to focus our notation on the links rather than the pages: links are the things that allow users to browse and surf but they are also the cause of runaway complexity.

When undertaking detailed page design, one might claim that there are many types of link (or just one!). However, this book is concerned largely with designing at the system level rather than the page level. We claim that there are a few useful ways of categorising links at this level which help us simplify the way we describe and document the design. Firstly there are two main categories of links which we refer to as *transitive* and *constructional* (rather than 'intransitive' – we wouldn't want to introduce negative connotations).

A *transitive link* is the kind that is visible to the user: it is activated by clicking on an element of hypertext or a button or some other object and, as a result, some change of context occurs, with a new page of information being presented to the user. This is the kind of link that everyone would think of as a link.

A *constructional link* is a link that is employed to construct a page from various information objects. Multimedia pages typically contain a variety of information objects: images, text, sound, and video. Languages such as HTML create such pages by embedding links to the various information objects. Although these links, when implemented as HTML, look much like transitive links, their function is quite different. In fact the user will not even be aware that these links exist – unless they fail to work.

In general, the system design concentrates on the transitive links, although the physical design will have to include all links.

Transitive links, in turn consist of three major categories: *local*, *unstructured* and *structured* links.

- *Local links.* Local links are those whose scope is limited to a particular 'page', i.e. they are links to a named anchor within the page. The design of these links can be left until late in the design process because they have no impact on the overall integrity of the system as a whole. An example is a Worldwide Web page that begins with a contents list that links to subsequent sections lower down on the same page.

- *Unstructured links.* An unstructured link takes the user from a source location in the information space to a destination which has no structural relationship to the source. In printed documents, a footnote or a bibliography reference constitutes an unstructured link. If the reader is following a structured piece of information, following such a link takes them into a completely unrelated area from which their only choices are either to undertake a simple backtrack to their starting point or else to follow some completely new information thread.

  An unstructured link is a thread that leads to an information cul-de-sac. It is rather like a 'go to' in a programming language, although it has a more auspicious place in the discipline of Media Engineering than the humble 'go to' has found in software engineering.

Some examples of unstructured links are:

—links from an index into the main text;

—links from a search engine into the text;

—links from the text to a bibliography or glossary;

—some of the cross references between topics.

- *Structured links.*   These are links between related pieces of information within a structure that is discernible to the user. Generally, following a structured link takes the user into an area from which they can return directly or via other pieces of related information, whilst retaining some context of 'where they are' in the information web. For instance a menu bar that is common to a whole set of pages would provide an implementation of structured links.

The distinction between structured and unstructured links is useful and should be clearly made during the design stage. It is the structured links that should be the main focus of the design activity: they define the overall structure of the multimedia system. They must be designed so that when following them, the user is provided with enough contextual information to understand where they are going and how they might find their way back. In general, the structured links must be tackled at an early stage of design and the unstructured links can be added at a later stage as they do not significantly impact the overall shape of the system.

When selecting a notation, our focus is on techniques that will allow us to document structured links.

3.4.4   Use cases

The concept of use cases, originally developed by the software engineering guru Ivar Jacobson [UCDA], describes the behaviour of the parts of a system in terms of their responses to particular actions taken by 'actors' who might be human users or other system components.

In the case of Media Engineering, the same degrees of complexity do not arise because the behaviour of systems is much more limited than their software engineering counterparts: the repertoire of behaviours of software systems is potentially limitless; that for media systems is mainly concerned with transitions from one information context to another (i.e. following a link between pages).

Despite the differences between software and media systems, there is still a worthwhile role for the technique of describing the system in terms of its expected behaviour, from the user's point of view. A set of use cases can:

- provide a simple way of documenting system requirements;

- focus on particular areas for early prototyping;

- provide something against which the completed system can be tested.

The generation of use cases is not difficult but is hampered by not always having a known audience. Nonetheless, they should be constructed as part of the rationale for the information product, early in the lifecycle. After all, you do need some form of requirements to design and test against!

3.4.5 Objects

In DIVA, we have introduced the concept of information objects, which are encapsulated multimedia items whose interfaces are defined in terms of their links and anchors. In doing so, we inherit a body of established thinking that needs only to be specialized to our particular application. We will, however, not labour the analogy with object-oriented software engineering.

3.4.6 Compilation

During the Media Engineering process, content is converted from a *source* format (often a word processor document) to an *object* format which can be handled by the multimedia system. For a WWW server, for example, the object format is usually an HTML file. In the DIVA approach, material for conversion is divided up into *information objects* (IOs) at the earliest stage in the process.

Hence, if a large word processor document is to be converted to hypertext, it should first be divided up into a number of *source IOs* (i.e. documents still in WP format but fragmented into the elements that will finally appear in the multimedia system. Each *source IO* must then be processed to produce an *object IO*. Much of the DIVA method concerns the processes for automating that conversion as far as possible.

3.4.7 Linking and binding

Linking (or binding) is the process of creating links between pages so that

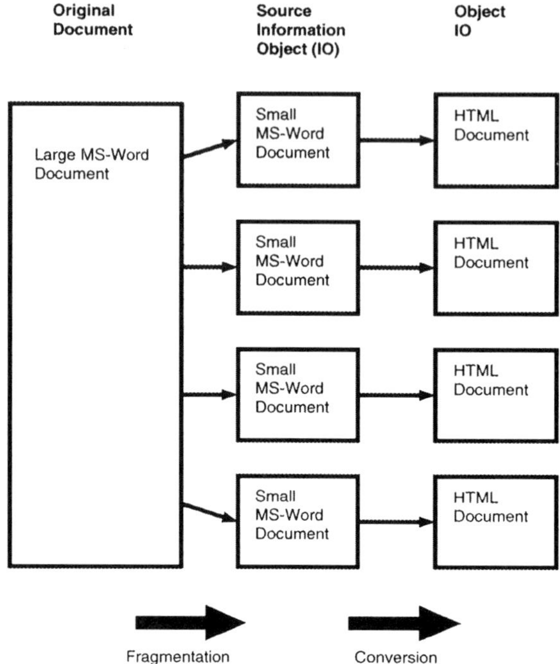

Figure 3.2
The build process in media engineering

by clicking on 'hot text' or on a picture or icon the user can cause a new page to be loaded. We refer to the page on which the link is encountered as the *origin* page and the page that is loaded as a result as the *destination* page. Options exist for linking to be implemented at a number of 'epochs' during the development process. The main options are:

Static linking

This is the most obvious way of creating links. The links are 'hard coded' directly into origin pages when they are authored. For example, consider the following fragment of HTML:

```
...
Click <A HREF=''http://www.norwest.com/index. html''>here</A>
to access our home page.
...
```

This construction will be familiar to those conversant with HTML as presenting the word "here" as a piece of hypertext that, if clicked on, will take the user to a particular destination. The full URL of the destination is written into the HTML page and is inextricably bound up with the information content of the page.

Advantages of static linking are:

- No specialized tools are needed. The links are 'hard-coded' into the hypertext.

Disadvantages of static linking are:

- The structure of the whole system needs to be known at the time that pages are created. This is because the links must contain the directory path, filename and paragraph name within the destination file.

- Changes to the structure are extremely difficult to implement because there is no easy way of knowing the impact on existing links. If, for example, a page is moved from one directory to another on your hypertext server, you will have to search through all pages that could possibly have links to that destination page and update them appropriately. Then, inevitably, you will have to retest the entire system.

Symbolic linking

With this approach, instead of writing the actual links into pages, a symbol is inserted in its place. At some later epoch of the development process, these symbols are translated into the real links. This is exactly like the process of linking employed in conventional software engineering, where a 'procedure' in one module is invoked, by name, from another module of software. A software tool, the 'linker' turns the symbolic name into a real location in the computer's memory.

Advantages of symbolic linking of hypertext are:

- Decisions about the precise structure can be left until late in the development process.

- The structure can subsequently be changed and the system rebuilt by conducting a new linking operation which can, in principle, be fully automated.

Disadvantages of symbolic linking are:

- A specialist symbolic linking tool is needed. These are not yet readily available.
- For small scale systems, the approach can appear cumbersome as it is necessary to perform some processing in between modifying a page and viewing the results.

Run-time linking.

The extreme of late linking is to perform the translation from a symbol to a real link at the time when the link is executed.

An example of this approach is to use a relational database (RDBMS) package to hold hypertext pages. A relational database conventionally holds related items of data (all the items of data relating to each customer of a company for instance) in a manageable form, with the relationships between data items taking the form of tables that are quite separate from the data content. A relational database can equally be used to hold the pages of a hypertext system and to use its tabular structure to produce the appropriate page when a particular link is activated.

Advantages of run-time linking are:

- Links can be wholly table-driven, making them completely separate from the content and simple to change.

Disadvantages of run-time linking are:

- A specialist server such as an RDBMS package or a custom application are needed rather than a general-purpose WWW server.

- The process of resolving links at run-time involves significantly more processing overhead than is incurred by a conventional WWW server.

- RDBMS packages are currently not very efficient (in terms of utiliz-ation of storage space) when storing large text documents.

A similar effect can be achieved without a commercial database applica-tion, as long as you are prepared to write your own custom program (or CGI script) to reside on the server. The program must be activated by clicking on a link and must respond by outputting an HTTP 'location directive', probably read from a lookup table.

Best approach to linking

In spite of the disadvantages, we expect that, long-term, the industry will move towards the third of these approaches (run-time linking) in parallel to a similar trend towards run-time binding in the software industry. The current practice, however, is overwhelmingly to use the first approach of static linking.

In the DIVA approach, we recommend the middle approach, at least for the present, and we advocate using *symbolic links* rather than *absolute links* – another idea from experience with software development. It is easier to maintain a product when you don't have to alter a whole raft of references scattered thoughout the product.

As noted above, commercial tools have not yet fully caught up with the need for symbolic linking. However, our experience is that even if all the symbols have to be converted to absolute links by hand, this is less error prone than hard-coding them at the outset. In spite of the lack of commercial tools, the essentials of symbolic linking are well understood from the software industry; a basic 'translator' of symbolic links to absolute links is a relatively simple piece of software: the authors have used a very simple one written by themselves in the Perl scripting language. Others are available in the public domain.

3.4.8   Configuration management

The *configuration* in this sense is the complete set of information objects that make up a particular multimedia system, together with all the relationships between them. In an HTTP server, it is the totality of the pages, images, sounds, video files and all the links between them. It also includes the directory structure that all these files reside in.

The *management* part means keeping all these things under control so that, for instance:

- We know the total set of items that must be present, and where they must be located for the system to be complete and to function correctly: we know how to build the product.

- As the system evolves through a number of versions, we know precisely which information objects belong to which versions.

- If we make any change to any information object within the system, we understand the impact that it will have on the system as a whole, and we know which parts will need to be tested to ensure that the system works correctly.

- If an accidental change is made, we know how to return the system to its intended state. In software parlance, a baseline is established.
- If multiple changes are made (e.g. by separate team members) the changes cannot interact with one another to give unpredictable results.

What happens if I don't bother about configuration management?

In the case of systems that exhibit poor configuration management, some (or all) of the following symptoms are likely to arise. None of these is hypothetical: all have been observed on real servers and in real information products – some from accessing people's web sites as a user; others from working with site managers. Some examples are:

- A web site is being redesigned and the users find a mixture of pages relating to the old and new design.

- When you look through the server file structure there seem to be a lot of redundant files. Some look like old versions of current pages: others look like test versions that have never been brought into service. However, you cannot tell for sure which ones are actually in use so you daren't delete them just in case they are important.

- You want to remove a page from your web site (or move it or rename it) but you have no way of knowing where it is referenced from within the several thousand other pages on the site.

- You introduce a new toolbar for all the major pages but somehow there are always some pages that want to use the old toolbar.

- The search engine finds pages that the users are unable to find. [In one particular system, on entering the keywords "Windows 95" into the search engine it came back with a reference to a page and quoted the found text as "Dave, can you get rid of this old version of the Windows 95 page." Although users could see this reference, they could not access the page itself – and it took us over a month to clear the problem completely. Since then, problems of this kind are described generically as "Dave bugs" within the company.]

- Users frequently experience error messages that tell them that something is amiss (e.g. "404 page not found") but have no detail on why the problem has arisen nor what they can do about it.

- Somebody puts a file called 'index.html' in the wrong directory, completely overwriting a different file of the same name. When the whole assembly is exercised it doesn't work . . . and you don't know how to fix the problem.
- Two people both thought they would update the site at the same time. They both did a good job but now nothing works.

- Suddenly the web site is all screwed up and half the links don't go anywhere. No-one will admit that they were to blame so it's difficult to find exactly what has gone wrong.

- You include lots of links to the pages on someone else's site, only to find that they have suddenly changed the name of their top level directory and all your links are now wrong.

- The site has been running successfully for months and must be due for some updates but no-one can really remember how it all fits together or where the original instructions were put.

In fact you know you've got problems if your colleagues say things like "it works well enough that the users won't notice the problems. Don't bugger about with it any more or you'll only make it worse."

Media Engineering approach

Once again, these problems are not beyond our means to solve, and Media Engineering can come to the rescue, if applied sensibly. All these problems have direct parallels in the software industry and the software engineering solutions can be brought to bear, either directly or by analogy, on the Media Engineering problem. However, there is no one single piece of technology that will solve all the problems: in practice, a combination of tools and techniques is needed.

These can be summarized as:

- some simple rules of thumb – little more than common sense (but still often neglected);

- some procedural approaches – ways of working that minimise the problems;

- some automated tools, either borrowed from software engineering or specific to Media Engineering.

Details of these tools and techniques evolve over the next few chapters. The next item in this catalogue of principles – naming – is a vital part of good configuration management.

3.4.9 Naming

We have taken the approach of giving a 'logical' name to every entity (page, link, anchor, etc.) as we design it. By a 'logical' name, we mean a name that we record in the design documentation but will not necessarily translate into, say, a 'real' filename in the finished system. There are a number of reasons for doing this:

- Real filenames can be excessively restrictive (e.g. if the system must be

DOS-compatible). At the design stage, it is more important to use 'meaningful' names than DOS-compliant names.

- During design, it is desirable that all names are unique. When the system is fully implemented, the uniqueness may only be required within a limited context: filenames within a particular directory, or anchor names within a particular page. It may, for example, be perfectly sensible to have a large number of files, all with the 'real' name index.html, but located in different directories.

- It is possible that a single logical entity may, in reality, be constructed from several physical files (e.g. a page, as seen by the user, may consist of a combination of an HTML file and several GIF files).

One last point to mention is that common naming conventions go a long way to helping keep control. If all files of a particular type (e.g. an image) have a standard name (e.g. file_number.gif), chances of accidental use are reduced.

3.4.10 Tools

At the time of writing, a number of tools are available that have been developed specifically for the media engineering market: e.g. Adobe Sitemill, Microsoft Frontpage, and others. However, none of them fully meets the requirements of Media Engineering, either in its whole-lifecycle approach or in managing scale.

A recent Forrester report on WWW tools concludes that 'current Web development tools are woefully primitive.' Having interviewed 52 Webmasters, they report that 'Webmasters . . . rely on basic HTML editors like BBEdit' (a simple text editor with some HTML enhancements).

Our recommendation is to employ a range of tools, including some of these media-specific tools, as well as some borrowed from software engineering. Some more detail is given in Chapter 4.

One of the problems with authoring tools is that they lag significantly behind the browser market. The maturity cycle for hypertext development is shown in Table 3.2.

Hence, features that already seem quite mature from a browser user's perspective may not yet be supported at all by authoring tools. At the time of writing, such a lag exists for some of the market leading tools in areas such as the support for tables, client-side image maps and frames. By the time you read this book, those particular examples will, no doubt, have been absorbed into mainstream tools but, already, browser vendors will

Table 3.2

Stage	Time
New feature conceived by browser vendor	0
HTML tags defined	1–5 days
Feature appears in browser product	1–3 months
Accepted by industry	3–6 months
Supported by tools	6–12 months
Set in standards	12 months +

be surging ahead with some new set of features that will, in turn, take time to find their way into the tools market.

3.4.11   Non-functionals

It was only after the basics of notation etc. were sorted out that software engineering shifted the focus from purely the functional aspects of systems, to include also the non-functionals such as performance, availability, reliability and security. These issues are equally important to Media Engineering and are covered in some detail in Chapter 5.

3.4.12   Structure

There are several issues of structure that are important to Media Engineering:

- *Decomposition and reassembly* (i.e. breaking the problem down without losing sight of the overall picture and whilst retaining relationships between the bits).

- *Discrimination* (separation of content and structure). A previous section of this chapter introduced the notion that in engineered media systems, the structure of information should be kept separate from its content. We now consider how this is achieved in practice.

At first sight it may seem strange to attempt this separation: on the face of it, the mixture of structure and content seems an inherent part of technologies such as the WWW and other hypermedia. We are all familiar with pages containing 'hypertext' that links to other material; similarly, we expect that every page will include navigation bars and buttons that will lead us to other pages. However, whilst the technology certainly allows for this sort of usage, the result can often be a complete jumble of

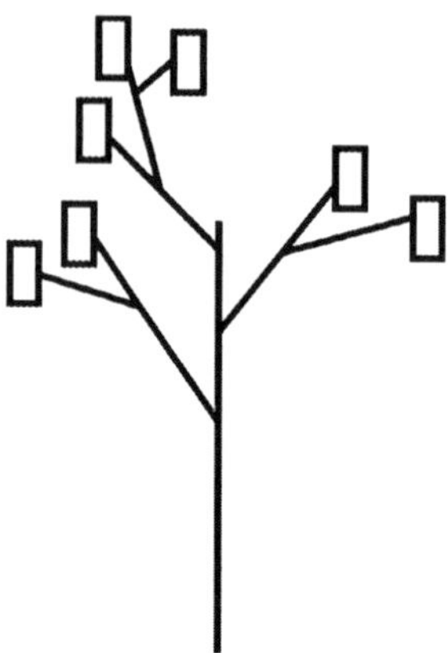

Figure 3.3
The hypermedia tree

links – especially if the media system is large and complex. In practice, the technology can also be used in a more subtle way to create navigable and manageable systems.

If we intend to separate structure and content, we may view our hypermedia system as a tree structure, as shown in Figure 3.3. Here, the trunk and branches of the tree represent the structure, whilst the leaves represent the information content.

The advantages of designing the content and structure separately and only bringing them together during implementation are:

- Changing the details of the content need not alter the structure. This means that the two skill sets that we introduced in Chapter 2 and illustrated in Figure 2.3 can operate in tandem.

- A number of different structures can be applied to the same content to provide (for example) different views onto the same base information for different users. This supports the principle that we have named 'polycontiguity'.

The separation of content and structure is vital. Without it, maintenance and update can be (to say the least) somewhat fraught.

3.4.13   Re-use

One example of re-use is that of 'post-processing'. This is not an essential step but has proved very useful in practice. Typically, the structure of a hypertext page is something like:

Standard header and menu bars

Main body of page

Standard footer

The standard header and footer may be common to many pages (or all pages) within a particular hypertext system and serve the purpose of providing a familiar point of reference (e.g. for navigation) to the user whilst also 'branding' the page as being part of a coherent whole.

Rewriting the hypertext for these standard elements in every page is undesirable for several reasons:

- the amount of work involved;

- the scope for accidentally introducing variations which may confuse the user;

- the difficulty of updating every page if you simply want to change the 'brand image';

- the scope for replicating an untested error onto every page of your hypertext system.

This last reason is one which the authors encountered in practice: a standard footer included contact details for a help desk for users of the system. Only when this had been cut and pasted to every page of our system did we realize that there was an error in these details. Fixing the problem entailed re-editing every page.

As a solution to these problems we have used a 'post-processor' which will add in text from a standard header or footer file and insert it into the hypertext for a particular page.

In common with many of the other ideas in this book, the approach is taken directly from software engineering practice where 'include files' are a standard part of software authoring.

Some HTTP servers will perform this function at run-time. For instance, the NCSA server will process documents whose names end in .shtml rather than .html, and will check for server-side include commands [HOO]. Other server side approaches to 'include' files can perform badly. This is because the server may spend its time parsing evey file that it is asked to transmit, looking for 'include' statements. It is well worth checking your server documentation before adopting this approach!

The authors have adopted a different approach which consists of inserting 'include' statements into the source files and then using a text processing tool to replace these statements with the contents of particular files. The tool used was a very simple home-built tool implemented in Perl, but the same could be achieved using almost any text processing tool including word processor macro languages. There are also some commercial tools available that will perform this function – a shareware tool called GMTL is also available over the Internet [GMTL].

3.4.14 Testing

For those who have not been involved in the development of a large hypertext system, it might appear that testing is simply a matter of taking each page of hypertext as it is produced, and viewing it with a hypertext browser to check that it 'looks right'. This level of testing is, at best, the equivalent of 'unit testing' in software engineering: it may verify that the individual item works correctly but does not validate the complete system.

In general, testing will consist of:

- unit tests (i.e. page tests) which check the syntax and behaviour of each page or information object;

- system tests which check the integrity of the whole system (i.e. that links go where they should);

- use cases, which ensure that the product behaves as a user might expect;

- acceptance testing, the final testing by the customers and/or users to establish fitness for purpose.

Each of the above principles has direct bearing on the techniques that follow and will be illustrated further in the practical examples. Also, the rules of thumb and checklists collected together in Chapter 5 and Appendix 1 respectively are based on these principles.

3.5 SUMMARY

We started this chapter by exploring just how much benefit and guidance the Media Engineer can derive from the experience of the software engineer. As our story unfolds, it becomes clear that many of the problems encountered in practice in multimedia systems are analogous to well-known problems in software engineering.

Given this piece of encouragement, we proceed to project the principles introduced in Chapter 2 into the Media Engineering world. In doing so, we find a comforting match and start to derive some useful guidelines. In particular, some of the fundamental requirements in building information products become clear – there is a need to

- separate structure from content;

- specify a notation that supports this;

- manage and automate the product build process.

In the short term, we can apply some simple techniques and rules of thumb (based on software engineering experience and best practice) to do just this. This is what the next chapter is all about.

Doing this alleviates some of the worst problems of Media Engineering but in the long term, application of the principles of software engineering will have to result in the development of industrial strength media engineering tools. That is some way off, though. The good news is that we seem to have started off in the right direction.

REFERENCES

[GMTL]	GMTL Reference Page http://www.pobox.com/~gihan/gmtl_ref.html
[HOO]	http://hoohoo.ncsa.uiuc.edu/
[OOD]	Booch G. *Object-oriented Analysis and Design with Applications*, Benjamin/Cummings (1994).
[UCDA]	Jacobson I., Christerson M., Jonsson P. & Overgaard G. *Object-oriented Software Engineering. A Use Case Driven Approach*, Addison Wesley (1993)

4
Theory into Action

There's nothing so practical as a really good theory.

Ludwig Boltzmann

This chapter provides a step-by-step guide to the use of the DIVA method in practice. The previous chapter described the key concepts and some of the alternatives. Now we interpret these in the context of the set of tools and techniques which are realistically available to the Media Engineer.

This chapter is structured around the lifecycle phases outlined in Chapter 3, namely:

- conceptualization

- analysis

- design

- construction

- maintenance

As noted earlier, although the lifecycle is presented as though it has very clear stages, in practice there can be overlap and even some iteration between stages. We cannot do much about this, so we present each stage in its turn. Needless to say, in practice, some interpretation is necessary.

4.1 CONCEPTUALIZATION

This is the stage of deciding what you are going to do, agreeing it with your customers and suppliers and writing it down for future reference (so that you can, for example, measure your success in achieving it at a later stage). During this stage you should accomplish the following:

- Define the scope of your multimedia production.

- State (or get your customer to state) the key requirements.

- Make some basic choices about how it will be delivered to your public.

- Estimate the overall size and complexity of the task in hand.

- Undertake some simple project planning of resources, timescales and costs.

The definition and documentation of all these items serves two purposes: the first is to provide clarity to all who work on the project and throughout the stages of the project to ensure that the original vision and purpose is not lost along the way; the second is to describe the success criteria against which the project will be measured when it is completed.

We shall describe each of these tasks in turn.

4.1.1 Definition of scope

It is desirable to produce, early on in the project, a simple statement of what the project consists of. Such a scope statement should include:

- A mission statement which concisely summarizes (probably in a single sentence) the intention of this project. The purpose of this is to provide a clear statement of the central purpose of the project in a form that is readily understood by everyone working on the project (customers, suppliers and all contributors).

- A subject scope statement which can take the form of a set of bullet points listing the main things that are included within the project and those that are excluded. The aim of this is to provide, as clearly as possible, a dividing line between this project and the rest of the world. This is for a number of reasons: firstly, it is easy for poorly scoped projects to grow out of hand; conversely it is easy to miss important areas until late in the project lifecycle; finally, it is important to distinguish this multimedia work from any others being conducted.

- A statement of the target audience. Who is this aimed at? This will affect many things: the depth of coverage; the complexity of language and grammar; the style. In order to give an impression of the required style, it may be useful to liken it to one of the well-known newspapers or journals (*Times* style or *Sun* style, for example).

4.1.2 Key requirements

At this stage, a statement should be made of any key requirements – particularly those that could be show-stoppers at a later stage. Requirements should be expressed as simply and unambiguously as possible and it is general practice to distinguish 'mandatory' requirements from 'desirable' requirements. With multimedia projects it is preferable to concentrate on the real show-stoppers and to leave more detailed requirements until the next lifecycle phase. Requirements should include both functional requirements (e.g. 'Every page must include a link back to the home page') and non-functionals ('All information should be accessible by three mouse clicks or less'). Indeed, in Media Engineering, the distinction between functional and non-functional requirements is so hazy that it is probably not worth labouring.

An example set of key requirements might look like Table 4.1.

Although we have only considered two priorities of requirement (Mandatory and Desirable), other approaches to prioritizing requirements can be adopted (e.g. listing them in priority order). Normally the list of prioritized requirements should be agreed by all parties (e.g. customers and suppliers) and should be signed off by them. Current practice favours techniques such as workshops, which include customers, suppliers and end users 'brainstorming' the requirements (e.g. writing them on post-its and sticking them on a wall), grouping what they come up with and agreeing priorities.

Table 4.1

The entire system must fit on a single CD	Mandatory
A glossary of terms should be available on screen at all times	Desirable
All pages must include a link back to the home page	Mandatory
etc.	

4.1.3 Basic delivery choices

The main choices within the scope that we are discussing are those relating to delivery by World Wide Web and Internet technologies versus delivery by CD ROM. Although these technologies are converging, there are still sufficient differences that this choice needs to be understood at an early stage of the project.

Assumptions about viewing technology need also to be made at this stage. For example, in the case of WWW browsers, different products support different functions. This may be dependent on the browser supplier (Netscape, Microsoft, NCSA, etc.), the version of the product employed (Netscape, for example, have produced several very different

Table 4.2

Browser support	MSW
HTML V1	Must
Tables	Must
CGI forms	Must
Quicktime movies	Should
Frames	Wont
Scripting	Wont

versions of their product in less than a year), and the platform on which it will run (PC, Macintosh, etc.).

Assumptions about the client platform will need to include some consideration of the graphics and colour capabilities. A multimedia production authored on a 24–bit colour machine will look very different on a 16–colour PC (yes, we do mean 16–colour, not 16–bit colour. Such machines are not that old!).

Similar choices will need to made with regard to CD ROM productions: in particular the supported platform and its assumed capabilities. However, the CD ROM author at least has the choice of viewing technology under closer control. Taking, therefore, the more difficult case of WWW material, the author must make some basic decisions about which browser features are assumed to be present: for example what are the assumptions regarding support for:

- frames

- scripting languages (e.g. JavaScript)

- support for Active-X and Java

- image maps (e.g. client-side image maps)

- sound and video support

- support for proprietary formats including Adobe Acrobat and Macromedia Shockwave.

Usually, there is some trade-off between desirable features and size of potential user base: extensive use of video footage, for example, can create a more impressive product but may only work on the most high-performance and best-equipped PCs. It is suggested that a 'policy statement' on the support for different client technologies is formulated. This summarizes your assumptions about the end-user PC environment and can take the form of a set of statements categorizing those facilities that the user *must have* (in order to use your product at all), *should have* (to view some of the 'bells and whistles' of your product), and *won't have* (so are not required for your product). Typically, the 'should haves' are limited to optional extras such as sound and video that enhances material available in other forms and these should typically represent no more than 20% of the whole product.

For example, Table 4.2 summarizes assumptions about a particular WWW product.

In the case of the 'shoulds', it is desirable to design-in alternative viewing options when you get to the design stage. For example, if image maps are a 'should' a simple menu alternative can be provided for those browsers which do not support image maps.

Another approach to the problem of browser diversity is simply to make a decision about which browser(s) will be supported. For example, one might decide that a particular system will only be guaranteed to work when viewed using Netscape 3.0 on a PC platform. Such decisions simplify design and testing but limit the potential market.

A final area of assumptions about delivery choices relates to network capabilities. For example, a system that will only be viewed via a company's high speed LAN can exploit options that are unrealistic if accessed over a 14.4 kbit/s modem link.

4.1.4 Estimate of size and complexity

At this stage of a project there are many unknowns but it is still important to *estimate* the scale and complexity of the task. The following is a list of things that should be assessed:

- The number of text files. A multimedia work that takes the form of an encyclopaedia is likely to have at least one text file for each 'article' or subject covered. In WWW terms, each 'page' is a separate file. The total number of files gives quite a good measure of the overall complexity of the project.

- The number of hypertext links. This is the other major yardstick of complexity.

- The number of graphics files, i.e. the number of pictures and drawings.

- The number of sound files.

- The number of video sequences.

- The number of image maps.

- The number of items of client-side application functionality (such as JavaScripts)

Also at this stage, it is necessary to estimate the amount of 'branding' material that will be required:

- customized graphics

- buttons and icons

- banners

- backgrounds.

4.1.5 Project planning

Estimating of costs and timescales is notoriously difficult within the software industry and early experience with Media Engineering indicates that the situation is likely to be no better in this industry. However, the authors have used the following technique to provide an outline estimate of the work involved in a number of planned multimedia tasks.

- *Assumptions.* The following assumptions are made:
  —The formula excludes the time taken to author original material.
  —All material has already been produced and is ready for hypertexting.
  —Only minimal use of sound and video has been made.
  —No scripting or mobile code (e.g. Java) is employed.

- *The formula.* Number of text pages $= t$
  Number of pictures $= p$
  Number of links $= l$
  Page rate $= r_1$
  Link rate $= r_2$
  Required effort (in work-days) $= w$

$$w = (t + p)/r_1 + l/r_2$$

  In this formula, we use $r_1 = 6$ and $r_2 = 30$, or to put it in words:
  —add up the number of text pages and pictures and divide the total by 6;
  —add up the total number of links and divide by 30;
  —add the resulting two numbers together and this is the number of work-days needed.

  So, for example, a simple WWW system consisting of about 6 pages and 30 links could be built, debugged, tested and installed in about two days.

- *Modifications to the formula.*
  —If the source material is in a 'raw' form that was intended for some other purpose (e.g. you are converting a 100–page word processor document) the constant r_1 should be reduced to a value of 4.
  —Add one day for every two video items (excluding the production of the video itself).
  —Add one day for every four image maps (excluding the production of the pictures).

We must emphasize that this formula is only an outline guide and the true time requirements will depend on many factors, not least the experience of the people engaged in the work. Nevertheless, the formula provides a useful starting point for planning and, at the very least, discourages over-ambitious developments which grow to a level of complexity at which they have to be abandoned.

4.2   ANALYSIS

During this lifecycle phase we accomplish the following

- Develop 'use cases' describing scenarios for how the product may be used in practice.

- Storyboarding.

- Prototype the top-level screens.

- Undertake a top-level logical design of the system.

4.2.1   Use cases

Compared with their software engineering counterparts, the Media Engineering use cases are rather pale companions. Nevertheless, they serve a useful purpose in clarifying more detailed requirements.
The main objectives are:

- to outline a set of scenarios that are representative of the way that the system will be used in practice;
- for each scenario, to describe the behaviour of the system in the face of various actions by the user.

For example, in a particular multimedia project, we defined a number of scenarios, of which one was summarized as:
'The user enters a keyword and can locate all pages that contain the keyword.'

Table 4.3

Use case number	UC1	
Use case title	Keyword search	
Preconditions	User is accessing a page that includes the SEARCH button	
User action	System response	Event response number
User clicks SEARCH button in current window (window x)	System opens a new window including a search field, OK and CANCEL buttons and simple instructions	ER1
User fills in SEARCH field and clicks OK	Search window disappears. A new window appears with a list of lines of text containing the keyword	ER2
User clicks on one of the lines of text	The page which includes the selected text is displayed in window x, which is brought to the front of the screen. The list window remains visible in the background	ER3
Alternative events		
User clicks CANCEL	The search window disappears and the user is returned to window x	AER2

The use case is summarized in the Table 4.3

Particularly in such cases as this example, where a number of things may be accessible on the screen at one time (e.g. various windows or frames), the use case includes enough detail to tell when new items will appear or disappear, which are 'at the front' on the screen, and so on.

4.2.2 Storyboarding

The end user usually knows what they want to see in the final product. They would typically express their ideas in a combination of page layout, links, graphical design and logical sequences. An example is given in Figure 4.1.

In effect, this gives the Media Engineer a storyboard on which to base the design of the information product. In the example shown, the informal notation can be readily mapped into DIVA concepts for subsequent development. A dialogue is needed to understand whether links that are shown are structured or unstructured, what key performance parameters, what needs to be on the screen at the same time etc. The checklist in Appendix 1 helps in this part of our Media Engineering process.

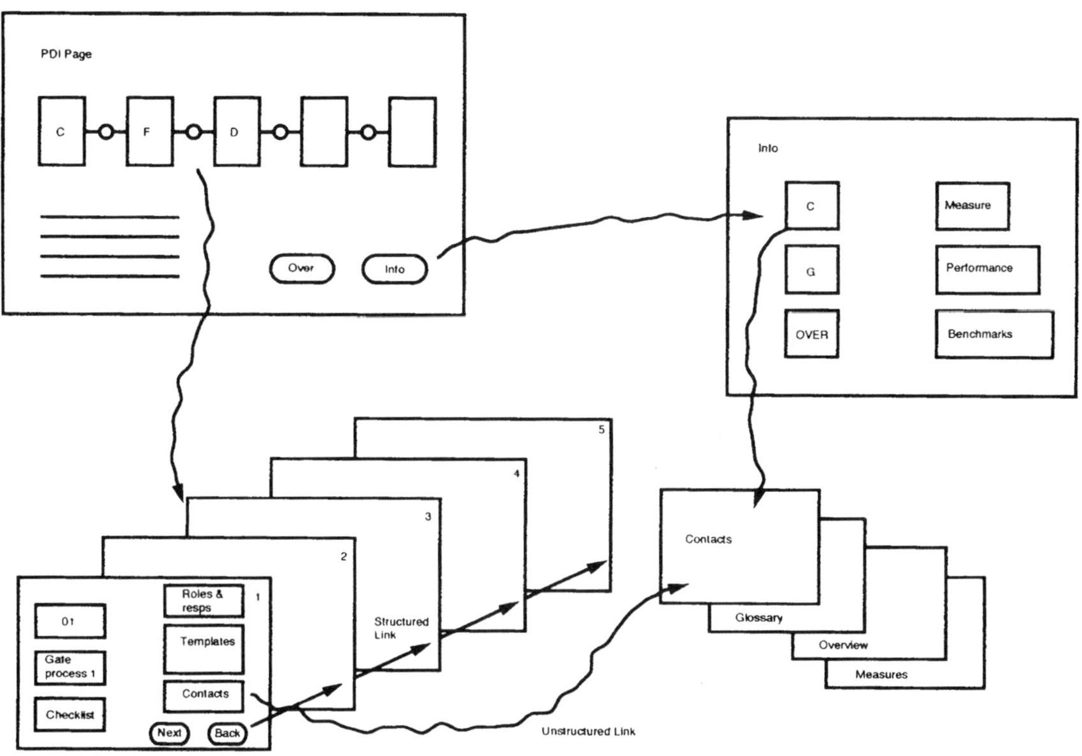

Figure 4.1
Example storyboard

In the diagram, the user shows their home page (top left) as a sequence of information objects that combine to tell the story they want. Immediately below this is one of a number of possible invocations of traversing the information objects. Part of the media engineer's job at this stage is to determine exactly what the required paths are (rather like the tours described in Appendix 3) and to form the initial ideas on where the main structured links are and what the main types of information objects are. Later on, this will all tranlsate into staples and links. For now the aim is to understand how the user's storyboard might translate into an information product.

4.2.3   Prototype the top-level screens

Prototyping is important because the media industry in general is focused on the visual appearance of a product far more than a technical specification of its characteristics. Hence, if you wish to explain to a customer what requirements you intend to satisfy with your product, this can most readily be accomplished by demonstrating a few top-level screens rather than providing a list of features.

Some of the things you should be considering at this point are:

- Is there some overall 'metaphor' that provides a structure to your product? For example, some multimedia encyclopaedias employ a 'museum' metaphor in which the user moves from room to room and exhibit to exhibit; others retain a simple 'book' metaphor.

- What are the top level options available to the user (i.e. the menu of options available from the home page)? These might include various subject categories, use of an index, use of a search tool and access to a glossary, for example.

- Overall design features: navigation 'palettes'; buttons that are common to every page; guided tours.

Prototyping is also a useful way of animating both the storyboard and some of the key use cases, firstly to check that they are really what is required, secondly to check whether they are usable by 'real' end users and, thirdly, to check that they are feasible to implement.

4.2.4   Top level logical design

When discussing the design of media systems, we distinguish between the logical system design, the physical system design and the page design. We distinguish these terms as follows:

- The *logical system design* describes the system in terms of the links between information objects. These links may be implemented as buttons, hypertext or imagemaps. The logical design thus describes the structure that will be perceived by the user.
- The *physical system design* describes the structure of the system as a series of files, directories and applications. It does not show the links that may exist between these items. In a World Wide Web system it describes essentially the file structure of the server.

- The *page design* is, of course, the design of an actual page of information. This may include a number of design areas:
  —design of the page content (i.e. the information content);
  —the graphic design of images on the page;
  —the realization of the links from the logical design in terms of buttons and hypertext;

—the construction of the page from a number of information objects;
—the use of formatting features such as columns, font sizes and tables;
—the design of scripts (e.g. the use of Javascript) to enhance the function and appearance of the page.

When designing a site that is anything more than a trivial size, it is important, at this stage, to document a top-level logical design. The more detailed logical design, together with the physical design and page design, are left until later (other than for the purposes of prototyping). The top-level logical design needs to fulfil the following functions:

- providing a simple shared view that can be common to team members, customers, contractors, etc.;

- providing a basis for some decomposition of the job into manageable segments;

- providing an estimate of the complexity (and hence the timescale and cost of the development).

This level of design is far from rigorous and can be documented with boxes and arrows. At this point we begin to consider the different types of link that were introduced in Chapter 2: *Structured links* (which are an inherent part of the structure of the system and retain some context when followed by the user) and *unstructured links* (the Media Engineering equivalent of a 'goto' statement which takes the user into some completely unrelated context). The third category of links (constructional links) do not feature at this level of design.

Figure 4.2 shows the top level design that was built by the authors for a hypertext system of technical computing standards for internal use within a company. Here, a 'box' represents a grouping of related pages which, because of the nature of the content, have been further grouped into 'levels'. In this example, one of the smaller boxes would contain anything between 1 and 50 HTML pages (our average was about 20).

We have used bold, double-ended arrows to signify structured links and normal single-ended arrows to signify unstructured links.

The 'levels' represent the following:

- *Access pages.* The top level pages that will be visited first by the user. These include the home page itself, together with help pages and search pages.

- *Overview pages.* This particular system is designed to have a few pages that provide an overview and summary of the total contents.

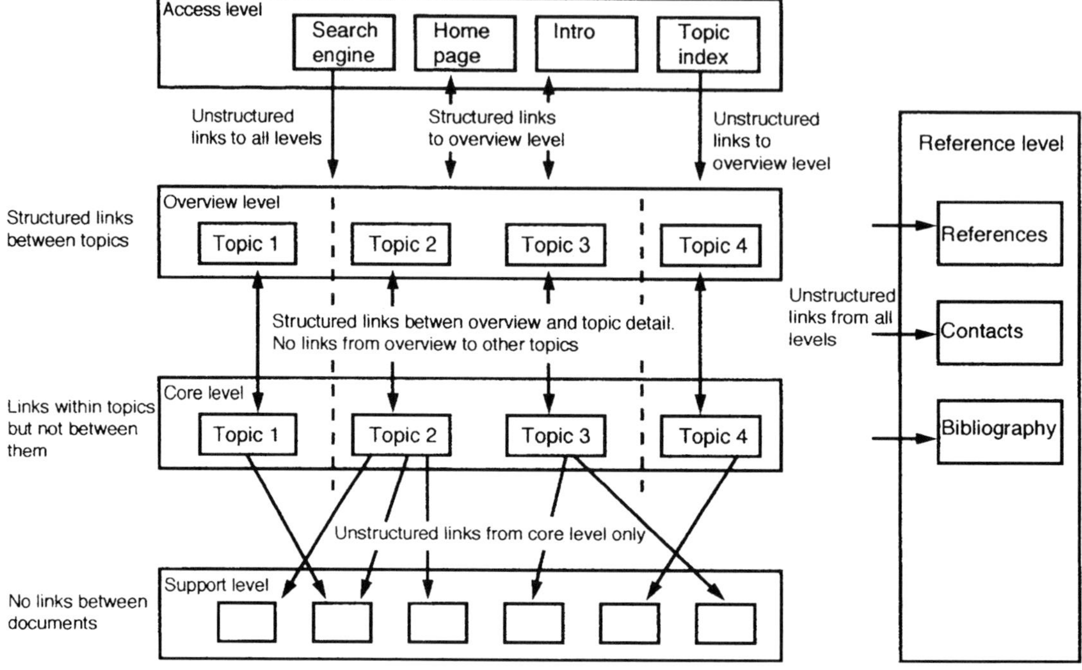

Figure 4.2
An example of top level system design

There are then overviews of each of the four main topics covered.

- *Core pages.* Each major topic has a set of pages relating to that technical area.
- *Reference pages.* There is a set of reference material including a glossary and various external references which are divided into those relating to printed works and those referring to other on-line material.

- *Support pages.* These form a set of (almost) stand-alone documents that provide supporting reference material.

This simple decomposition of the hypertext system into its main elements (the five levels) is useful for several reasons:

- Providing a more detailed understanding of the content of the final system. In systems of this kind, the issue of maintaining a shared understanding between all participants is a recurring theme and is often a critical success factor.

- Providing a structure for dividing up work between authors and other contributors. Tasks such as authoring, conversion and testing may have to be undertaken by a team rather than an individual. A simple decomposition such as that shown in the figure provides a useful way of dividing the work. For example, separate authors can work on each of the main topics with some understanding of how their material will be integrated into the whole.

- As a possible graphical representation for the construction of navigation aids. The figure itself could be employed as an image map that is incorporated into the finished system. More likely, the structure of the figure may suggest a more appropriate visual metaphor that will finally be used for navigation. Perhaps, a visual metaphor could take the form of a study desk with three large volumes on it, representing the three main topics, with a fourth, marked 'reference' standing beside them. A single sheet of paper on the desk could be marked 'overview' and a set of library catalogue drawers marked 'access'.

- As a potential structure for directories and files when the physical design is undertaken. We may, for example, decide to design the physical structure around a main directory containing a separate directory for each of the main boxes in the figure.

It can be seen from the figure that some design decisions have already been made at this stage. Each technical topic is divided into an overview section and a core detail section. The overviews will be linked together and to their respective detailed sections. However, no cross-linking is shown at the detailed level. In reality, this decision was taken to limit the complexity of the system for the sake of both the implementors and for the end users.

4.3 DESIGN

During the design stage it is necessary to:

- complete and document the logical design through functional decomposition;

- complete the physical design;

- document the mapping between the logical and physical designs;

- undertake generic page designs.

4.3.1 Decomposition of the logical design

The top level design can be broken down by a process of functional decomposition, to the point where individual pages are shown in the design. The approach we have adopted is summarized as follows:

- Focus on documenting links rather than pages.

- Begin with the complete system and document any structured links that are common to *all* pages in the system.

- Decompose into functional blocks and again document structured links that are common to all pages in the block

- Decompose down to the page level, until structured links specific to the page have been documented.

- Document unstructured links and local links quite separately during the page design stage.

In our notation, we use the following conventions:

- *Box icon.* (Figure 4.3). This represents a component which is some collection of pages or other media objects. It could be the whole system or some decomposed part of it (e.g. one of the 'levels' in our earlier top-level design). The component is given a unique logical name.

- *Page icon.* (Figure 4.4). This represents a single hypertext page. The page is given a unique logical name which is written beside it. The name should give some clue as to the function of the page but is a *logical* name which is not necessarily the same as the ultimate filename of the page. Also, a page may be constructed from a number of information objects and will probably consist of a number of 'real' files, together with the necessary constructional links.

- *Arrow icon.* (Figure 4.5). This represents a link. Again it is given a logical name which is written in the box. The name should give some indication of how the link will appear to the user who clicks it (e.g. a button name or piece of hypertext but, again, the exact mapping to a physical realization is left until later.

- *Anchor icon.* (Figure 4.6). An anchor is a destination for a link. The name of the anchor denotes an item within an information object.

For example, using the previous example the first stage of logical design might look as shown in Figure 4.7. Here we have decided that every page in the whole system will have a link to home, search, topic index and

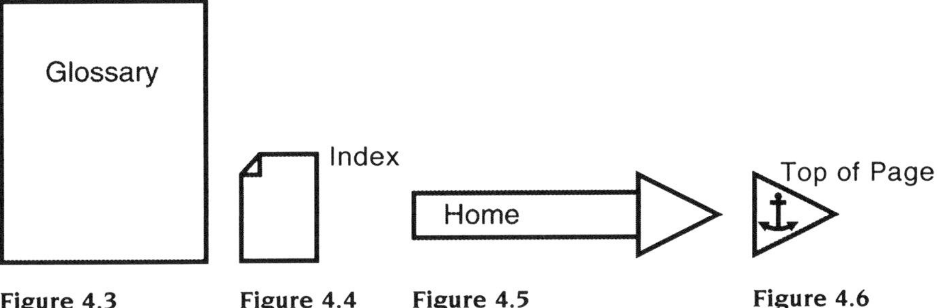

| **Figure 4.3** | **Figure 4.4** | **Figure 4.5** | **Figure 4.6** |

glossary pages. In the case of the glossary page, the link terminated on an anchor with the logical name 'top'.

If we decompose the system into its main boxes, each of these will have some generic links. For instance, those for the overview level are as shown in Figure 4.8. This shows that all of the overview pages have links to the Overview__index page and Core__index page as well as the general links to home, search, topic index and glossary pages that are common to all pages.

Decomposing the overview level, it consists of the overview index plus sections on each of the technical topics. One such technical topic, Topic 1, in the figure, is actually 'Computer operating systems' (Figure 4.9).

All pages in his section have a link to the section introduction. The operating systems section itself is structured as a number of 'pages' as shown in Figure 4.10.

We have now completed the design, down to the page level. It is important to note that, as we decompose the system, we are only documenting the links that are specific to this level of decomposition. Hence the total number of links for an individual page is built up cumulatively (i.e. some specified here, others inherited from earlier work).

If we take the page that we have named Operating__Systems__Intro as an example, it includes links to all the following pages:

Home
Search
Topic__index   } (in common with all pages)
Glossary__index index

Overview__index } (in common with all overview documents)
Core__index

Operating__systems__intro   (in common with all computer OS pages)

Mainframe__OS
Server__OS   } (specific to this page)
Desktop__OS

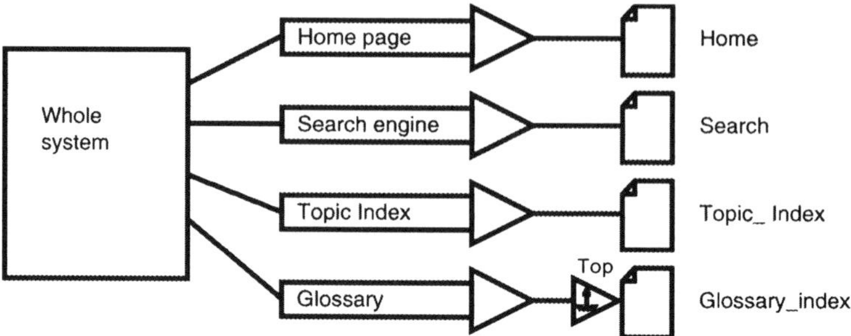

Figure 4.7
Logical design—first step

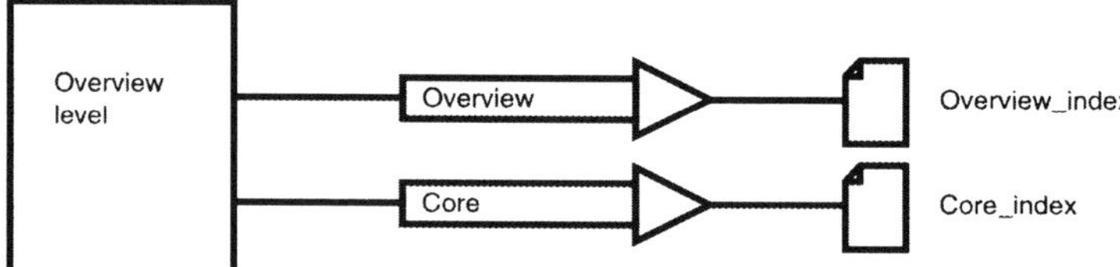

Figure 4.8
Links particular to the overview level

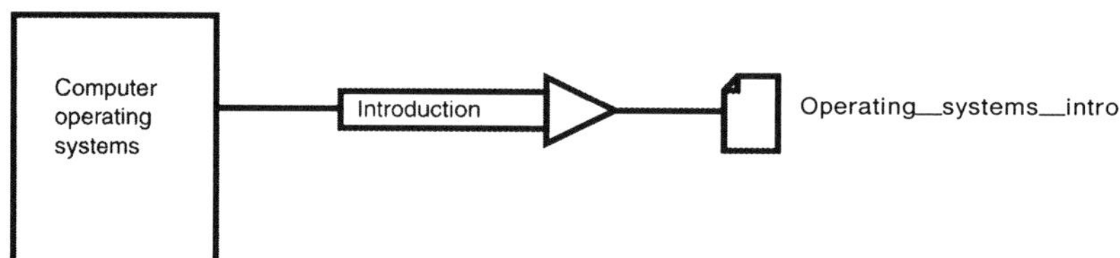

Figure 4.9
Logical design at the topic level

We could draw an inheritance hierarchy at this point (as is done, in software engineering for object-oriented designs) but this would be labouring a simple point!

The link to itself may seem strange, but this is quite common if the intention (as with this set of pages) is to have a common navigation bar for each main area of documentation.

4.3.2   The physical design

Currently, we have reached the stage of creating a logical design. We have created:

- a logical structure that will represent the main view of the documents as seen by the end user;

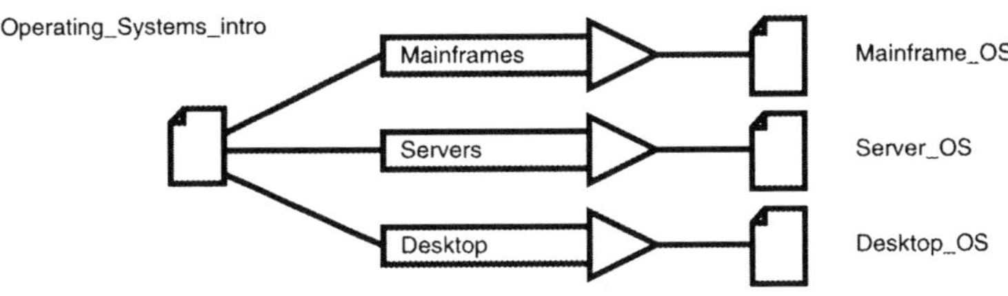

Figure 4.10
Decomposition to page level

- a logical name for every link;

- a logical name for every page;

- where links connect with anchors embedded within pages, a logical name for every anchor.

Next we need to document the physical structure of files and directories and convert the links into relative or absolute URLs. We do this in two steps: Firstly, we create a skeletal structure which includes all the directories and the main pages. Secondly, we add into it the additional information objects such as graphics, sound and video. So, addressing the first of these stages, we may choose a physical structure that broadly reflects the logical structure, e.g. that shown in Figure 4.11.

Here, the lines between items represent the physical containment of files and directories within directories. They need bear no relation to the hypermedia links between items. Having undertaken this decomposition into topics, sub-topics and individual files, the result should be a complete list of files that will be produced, together with the directory structure into which they will be inserted.

4.3.3 Mapping between logical and physical structures

This task includes two main elements:

- the mapping between logical names and physical names;

- the consideration of constructional links that assemble a 'page' (as seen by the user) from a number of media objects.

The two tasks are documented together in Table 4.4.

As a practical detail, it is useful to maintain this table in an electronic form such as a spreadsheet so that extra fields can be added to aid in

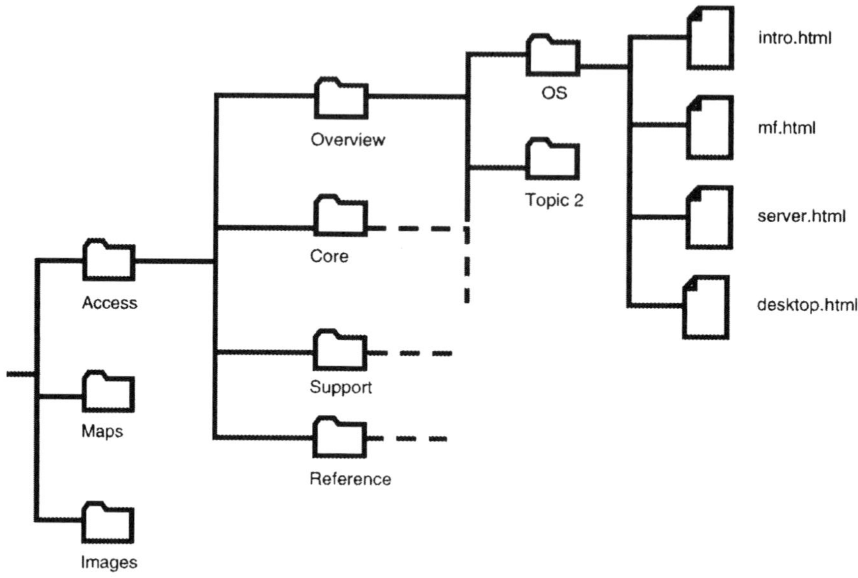

Figure 4.11
Physical design

managing the production (author's name, required-by date, actual
delivery date). In particular, the table can be used as a configuration
management tool (see later section) if a column for version numbers is
added.

Maintaining this mapping is, in practice, a non-trivial job. For large
products some form of automation should be investigated.

4.3.4   Page design

Although page design is not the focus for this book, it is worth noting that
this is the point where the 'generic' page design work is crystallized.
Probably, prototypes will have been produced during the previous
lifecycle phase, but now is the time for the bulk of the work to be done. In
particular, this includes:

- 'branding' graphics;

- buttons, palettes and icons that will implement the structured links;

- stylistic decisions;

- graphical navigation tools.

Table 4.4

Logical page name	Directory path	File name	Notes
Home	/ACCESS/	INDEX.HTM	
	/IMAGES/	MSTHD.GIF	Masthead for home page
	/IMAGES/	PALLET.GIF	Menu bar
	/MAPS/	PALLET.MAP	Map file for clickable menu bar
Overview_index	/ACCESS/OVER/	INDEX.HTM	
	/IMAGES/	OVERBT.GIF	Overview button bar
	/MAPS/	OVERBT.MAP	Map file for overview button bar
etc.			

4.4 CONSTRUCTION

During this lifecycle phase, we undertake the following:

- write or convert source material;
- build in links and anchors;
- use post processing if desired;
- undertake the main configuration management tasks;
- test.

4.4.1 Write or convert the material

Here we are referring not to the creative craft of writing material but rather the *process* of authoring and the *tools* that support that process. The main options open to the author are:

1. Use a simple text editor and write the material directly in hypertext (e.g. HTML). This is a very common means of producing WWW pages. The following is an example of a short hypertext page which has been written in this way:

```
<HTML>
<HEAD>
<TITLE>Example WWW page</TITLE>
</HEAD>
<BODY>
<CENTER>
```

```
<H1>Example WWW page</H1>
</CENTER>
<H2>Introduction</H2>
```

This page is intended to illustrate some of the key concepts of HTML markup.

```
<H2>Examples</H2>
```

A hypertext page may include a number of formatting features such as:

```
<UL>
<LI>Headings.
<LI>Bullet lists (such as this one) and numbered lists.
<LI>Tables
<LI>Graphics
<LI>Hypertext links
</UL>
```

More information can be found by clicking

```
<A HREF=''HTTP://www.abc.def:8080/introduction/help.html''>
here</A>.
<HR>
</BODY>
</HTML>
```

Figure 4.12 shows what appears when this is rendered by a browser. It should be fairly clear how the HTML relates to items on the screen. For instance, the <HR> tag produces the horizontal rule that you see. For those not familiar with HTML, an overview is included in Appendix 2.

Although this is a common approach to authoring, it suffers from several disadvantages:

(a) The author has to be acquainted with the hypertext language (HTML). From the example it is clear that the language is somewhat cryptic and wrestling with its syntax is unlikely to facilitate the flow of creative ideas onto the page.

(b) There is enormous scope for error. Even for those who are well-versed in hypertext it is easy to make either individual errors (such as writing <CENTRE> instead of <CENTER>) or errors caused by a lack of matching of tags (for example, starting a heading with <H1> and forgetting to finish it with a matching </H1>. Not only is there scope for errors, but when they do occur, they are difficult and time-consuming to find and correct.

(c) Lack of future-proofing. Markup languages are developing at a

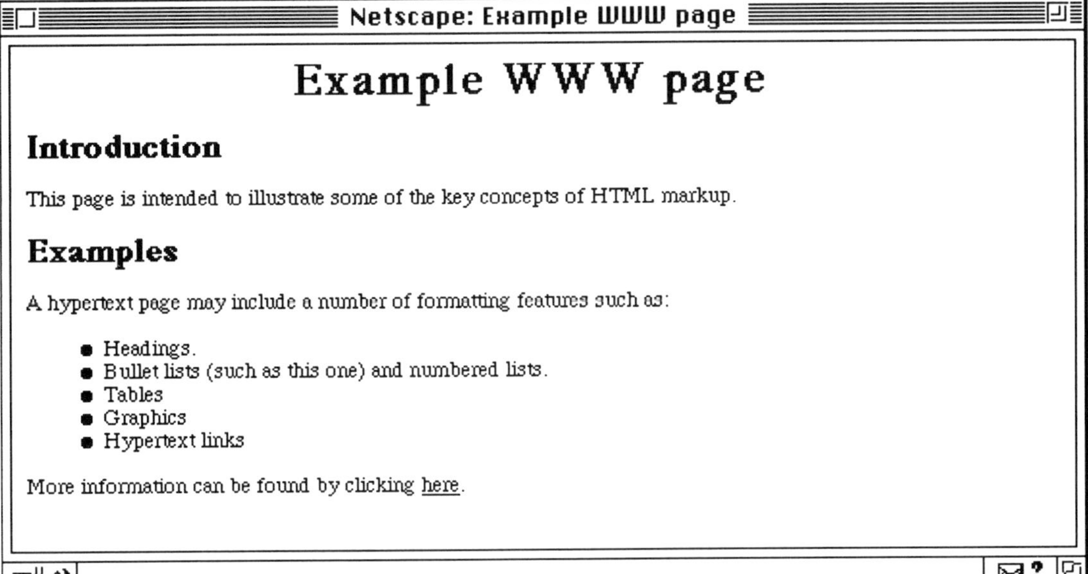

Figure 4.12
Example html rendition

rapid rate as browser suppliers add more and more features to their products which can only be activated by new additions to the hypertext language. Updating hand-written hypertext to take advantage of these developments is not feasible.

(d) Links are 'hard-coded' into the hypertext. In the above example, one line reads:

```
More information can be found by clicking
<A HREF=''HTTP://www.abc.def:8080/introduction/help.html''>
here</A>
```

This provides a hypertext link to a particular destination page that will be reached if the user clicks on the word 'here'. However, the exact location and name of the destination page must be known at the time when the link text is written. It follows that the exact structure of the hypertext system must be known before the pages can be written.

(e) Changes are difficult to control. Firstly, when editing the content it is easy to make inadvertent changes to the structure (e.g. by accidentally deleting part of a hypertext tag); secondly, it is difficult to make changes to the structure without undertaking a major editing operation on the content pages.

2) Use a text editor with hypertext features such as HoTMetaL. These will insert the hypertext tags at the press of a button (or click of a mouse) and generally offer a preview mode that shows how the finished page will look when viewed by a browser. This has the advantages that only limited knowledge of the markup language is needed and the scope for making errors is much reduced. However, it still suffers from some of the other problems associated with in-line hypertexting.

3. Use a fully WYSIWYG editor such as Adobe Pagemill or Microsoft FrontPage. This is a good approach which overcomes many of the problems. The only arguments against it are that products of this kind are not generally aimed at medium to large jobs (they work well with 20 to 50 pages but less so with 200 plus) and they don't help much with the conversion of existing material.

    Also, as noted in Chapter 3, the production cycle for tools is slower than the innovation cycle for hypertext features. The browser vendors are inventing new hypertext tags faster than the tools vendors can provide the facilities to implement them.

4. Write pages using your favourite word processor and then translate to hypertext. At the time of writing, this is recommended as the most practical approach for medium to large hypertext systems. Converters are available as add-ons for many popular word-processing packages (e.g. Internet Assistant for Microsoft Word or the HTML 'filter' provided with Clarisworks). Alternatively, 'batch' conversion programs can be used such as RTFtoHTML which converts files saved in RTF format (Rich Text Format invented by Microsoft and available as a 'save as' option in a number of popular word processors) into HTML.

The advantages of this strategy are:

- the vagaries of hypertext markup are not visible to the author. This makes life easier and reduces error.

- there is no new application to learn. Material is written using your existing favourite package.

- files are maintained as standard word processor files. As the hypertext languages include richer features, these can be taken advantage of by converting documents through updated filters rather than having to rewrite the documents.

Currently most hypertext writers use simple text editors and hypertext markup is generated largely by hand.

The authors have used a range of approaches, including the use of simple text editors (such as the Unix utility 'vi'), word processor add-ons such as Microsoft Internet Assistant, and integrated authoring tools such as Adobe Pagemill. To some extent, Media Engineers are likely to pursue their personal preferences, but the authors recommendation would be to use simple conversion tools such the Internet Assistant extension to Microsoft Word or the shareware 'RTFtoHTML' (which takes a word processed document and converts it to HTML). See Appendix 2 for more detail on this.

Some popular word processors (such as Microsoft Word) allow the definition of templates and styles that facilitate conversion. The files generated by this process should be the physical manifestations of the files that we listed during the previous stage. If any changes are made during this part of the lifecycle, it is important to go back and change the design documentation accordingly.

In addition to simple text conversion, it is necessary to convert pictures and other media types. A discussion of some of the tools that are available for doing this sort of work is included in Appendix 2.

4.4.2 Creating links

A link has an origin and a destination (a head and a tail). Each tail end can be reached from any number of head ends, but each head can have only one tail. The destination can be just the name of a file (and its directory path) or can be a label within the file. The destination is usually known as an 'anchor'.

Chapter 3 identified a number of options for generating links: hard-coding them into the hypertext; inserting them into the hypertext symbolically and then using a text substitution tool to convert them into 'real' links; or using a drag-and-drop editing tool that inserts them automatically. The authors have used all methods successfully. Our software engineering inclinations have encouraged us to adopt the middle of these options although, currently, tool support is virtually non-existent. Our preferred approach to this problem has been to insert the link in symbolic form into the original word-processed source document. A necessary feature of a symbolic link is that the symbol must be readily identifiable within the text: that is, it must not look just like any other piece of text. The two forms of symbols that we have used are as follows:

- ##Symbol_name#link text##   The symbol for a hypertext link

- $$Symbol_name$$ The destination of a hypertext link (anchor)

We then used a simple text substitution tool (written in Perl script) which would translate the symbolic names into real anchor names and URLs in the source text, using a manually prepared look-up table to accomplish the translation. This is accomplished at the linking stage, after our word-processed documents have been converted to HTML.

By this stage, all the pages will have been written and the absolute structure of the hypertext system will be known. The process is as follows:

- Ensure that the physical structure of the hypertext system is completely defined. This includes naming all files and directories, and having a clear plan of which files go in which directories.

- Draw up a translation table for symbolic links. In general, these define two things: the destination file path name plus (optionally) the named paragraph within the file. Supposing we have symbols help1, introduction and intro_para3, the translation table might look like:

Symbol	File	Paragraph name
help1	/main/help/help.html	help1
introduction	/main/intro.html	
intro_para3	/main/intro.html	para3

- Perform the translations. Our translation tool will translate, for example, `$$intro-para3$$` into the name ``para3'' and will translate the hypertext link `##intro-para3#see introduction##` into `<A HREF=''/main/intro.html#para3''>see introduction </A>`

It is emphasized that the significant consideration is the use of symbolic links: less important is the precise syntax. The syntax described here is the one that is used by the authors – it was chosen on the basis that symbols are easily identified and that they pass through unmodified by the word-processor-to-hypertext translation process. Our Perl-based tool simply parsed the hypertext file and then used the translation table to convert them to 'real' links.

4.4.3 Post-processing

As noted in Chapter 2, post processing of files provides a means for reusing shared files. In our case, we inserted lines into our source information objects of the form:

```
#include ''xyzzy.txt''
```

This line would pass unscathed through the HTML conversion process and our linking process. We then wrote a simple text processor (in Perl script, as usual) which would scan through the resulting files, find any `#include` lines and replace them with the entire contents of the named file. Some commercial tools are available for performing this function, such as the Orb product [ORB] and GTML [GTML].

4.4.4 Configuration management

In Chapter 3 we discussed some of the issues of configuration management and the types of problem that can arise if it is not given due consideration. Strictly, configuration management is not a subject that is limited to one phase of the lifecycle: it permeates all the activities of media engineering. However, the time when it becomes a major part of one's activities is during the implementation phase when there are many files being created, stored and modified (sometimes by a whole team of media engineers).

Although configuration management of software engineering is well-understood, there is, unfortunately, no one single piece of technology that will solve all the problems: in practice, a combination of tools and techniques is needed.

Firstly there are some rules of thumb that are little more than common sense.

1. Enforce complete separation between the development site and the live site. Clearly, you are asking for trouble if you tinker with a web site whilst it is in use. This separation does not mean that development and live sites must be in different buildings or located on different machines. The important thing is just to ensure that the users can't see the development files and the developers cannot touch the live files.
2. The design should be documented. We have covered the details of how to do this in earlier sections. This is the point where that documentation begins to pay real dividends.
3. The files should all be backed up regularly and backups should be clearly marked to show which 'snapshot' of the system development they represent.

Then there are some simple procedural rules that should help:

1. Every page should include a version number. In HTML this can be inserted into the page as meta-information, using a META tag. For example, the following HTML fragment illustrates META tags in the header of an HTML file.

```
<HTML>
<HEAD>
<TITLE>Computing Handbook</TITLE>
<META NAME=''Author'' CONTENT=''Mark Norris''>
<META NAME=''Version'' CONTENT=''07''>

</HEAD>
<BODY>

. . .
```

HTML Version 2.0 [HTML] allows the definition of META tags that consist of a name/content pair whose purpose is to 'document the content, quality and features of a data set, indicating its fitness for use.' Within a META tag, the NAME part is user-defined and, in this case, we have defined two named tags: "Author" and "Version". The values assigned to these are "Mark Norris" and "07" respectively.

In software engineering it is common practice, not to use simple integers for version numbers, but to adopt decimal numbers (e.g. Version 1.03). (In the author's opinion this is simply a scam for obfuscating the number of versions that it takes before software works properly). The form of numbering is up to the house style of the developer and numbers like 1,2,3, . . . work equally well. All that matters is to include a number and to increment it *every* time a page is changed or updated and back up accordingly.

2. For a particular 'release' of a web site, the design documentation should define all the files and their locations. In addition, the software configuration should include a list of the version numbers of all the files. This 'snapshot' of all the file versions fully defines the released configuration.

There are a number of other things that can be addressed by procedure or by the use of particular software tools:

1. Preventing several team members from editing the same file at the same time. This can be achieved in a number of ways, ranging from a simple office whiteboard on which people write up the name of any file they are currently editing, through to the types of configuration management tool that are commonly used by software developers. These generally operate a library function and require the software (or media) engineer to 'book out' particular files for editing and then 'book them in' again afterwards. Only one person can book out a file at any one time and version numbers may be added automatically. Some of these tools have problems in dealing with multimedia systems. For example:

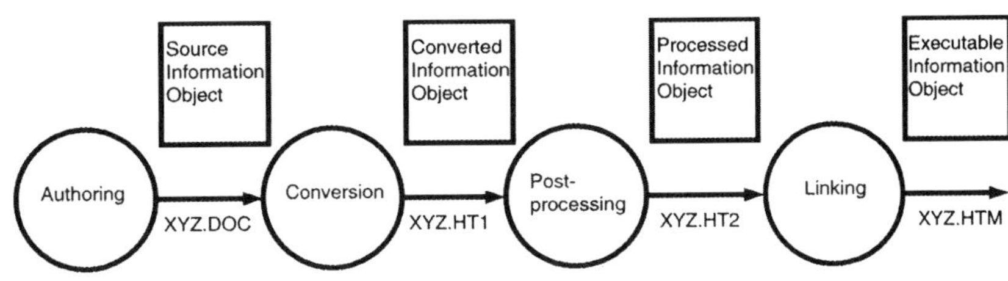

Figure 4.13

(a) they may not cope with the full range of file types (GIFs, JPEGs, etc.) that make up a multimedia configuration;

(b) they may not cope with duplicate filenames. WWW systems frequently include several files called 'index.html' which, in the final system, are distinguished by the directory in which they are located rather than by their names.

2. Link checkers that check for inaccessible files. The situation may arise (perhaps after the system has gone live) when it is noticed that there are some files which do not appear to take any part in the multimedia system. Tools such as Adobe Sitemill are effective at checking for inaccessible files, allowing the Webmaster to remove them safely without fear of problems.

As you progress through the production lifecycle for your multimedia creation, you will generate a range of different files. It is essential to decide on a consistent naming convention for all the files so that they can be easily distinguished. Figure 4.13 illustrates the main process steps in production of an example WWW hypertext system and shows a naming convention which has been applied to the files at the various stages. This is, in effect, a build model for information products; the dual of the software engineering build process shown in Figure 2.4.

Table 4.5 explains the naming convention.

4.4.5 Testing

Chapter 3 identified the need for several levels of testing, including unit testing (or page testing) and system testing.

The unit test *should* include the following:

- Checking that the *syntax* of the hypertext is correct (e.g. 'correct' HTML has been used). Although a simple visual check using a browser sounds a perfectly reasonable way of conducting this test, in practice,

Table 4.5

File type	File name extension	Explanation
Source IO	.DOC	In this example, source material has been authored with a word processor such as Microsoft Word.
Converted IO	.HT1	The DOC files have been converted to hypertext, eg using a tool such as RTFtoHTML or Internet Assistant. However, the resulting file is not yet a fully usable HTML file: it still includes post-processor commands and symbolic links.
Processed IO	.HT2	After post-processing, the post processor commands (notably #include statements) have been translated.
Linked IO	.HTM	After linking, all the symbolic names have been converted into links and anchors. The file is now a fully usable HTML file

some browsers are more fussy than others about the strict interpretation of the hypertext standards. For example, consider the following fragment of HTML:

```
<A HREF=''xyx.html>
```

This is clearly incorrect as there is no closing quotation mark after the filename. Some browsers (e.g. Netscape 2.0) will recognize this as an error; whilst others (e.g. Netscape 1.2) attempt to do the 'right thing' even though the hypertext is flawed. They therefore treat this as though the offending quotation mark was in place. Which of these browsers is 'right' remains a moot point: what is clear is that a page that appears error-free when tested with one, may exhibit errors when viewed with the other.

Because of this lack of certainty in the accuracy of hypertext (particularly in cases where it may be viewed via a range of browsers outside the author's control) it is useful to apply a 'static testing tool' to the hypertext. Such a tool simply checks the correctness of the syntax of every hypertext page. A number of tools are available that will perform this function (e.g. weblint [WL] and htmlchek [CHK]: also some of the integrated tools such as Adobe Sitemill will do it.

- Checking that the *semantics* of the hypertext correspond with the author's intentions. This can only be achieved by viewing the hypertext with a browser and checking that it conforms to the expected appearance.

In hypertext terms, a *system test* requires the following:

- verifying that every link works correctly. Every link should take the user to a recognizable destination and not generate a generic systems error (the infamous error 404 widely seen on WWW);

- verifying that every embedded image loads correctly;

- verifying that other embedded multimedia objects (sound samples, video clips or animations) load correctly;

- verifying that imagemaps (clickable images) work correctly;

- verifying that all agreed requirements have been met. This should refer back to a table of requirement, such as the one shown in Table 4.1;

- verifying that all use cases have been implemented correctly.

For some of these items it is possible to use an automatic test engine that will follow links and determine those for which destination files are missing, for example. Again, Adobe Pagemill and a number of others will accomplish this.

4.5 MAINTENANCE

HTTP servers are remarkably robust and many systems can be operated as 'one man and a dog' operations (in which the dog is there only to stop the man tinkering with the server, and the man is there to feed the dog). Nevertheless, the lifecycle does not terminate when the system goes live. Change is inevitable and ongoing care and maintenance has to be planned in advance.

If the DIVA techniques proposed in this chapter have been adopted, the maintenance and evolution should be relatively trouble free. The main things to ensure at this stage are that good practice continues to be maintained. For example:

- Post delivery changes should not be made directly on the 'live' machine. A replica of the live system should be maintained in a development environment and all maintenance changes should be implemented and tested on that before uploading to the live machine.

- Any changes should be reflected into the documentation, not just made *ad hoc*.

- Configuration management practices that were adopted during production should be continued into the maintenance phase.

In the case of material distributed on CD-ROM there is very little that can be done between major releases. However, in the case of WWW servers, there are a few issues that are specific to the maintenance phase:

4.5.1   Logging of server usage

Regular analysis of server logs can reveal a great deal of useful information:

- Errors and failures are logged and can provide essential information on problems with the server.

- Log files provide management information on the usage of the service: how many users, how many accesses, etc.

- By looking at the hit rate for the whole set of pages, redundant (i.e. never accessed) pages can be identified and dealt with.

- Server downtime can be logged and compared with any stated requirements for availability.

It is common practice to add a page access counter to every WWW page. There are three principal arguments against this:

- A separate program is run by the server every time a page is accessed, putting unnecessary load on the server.

- If users access the server via a proxy, it is unable to cache the page correctly.

- It can look very poor in the early stages when the numbers are very low.

- Page authors may be tempted to cheat and start the counter at a high initial number.

4.5.2   Monitoring remote links

Most servers include links to other WWW servers, elsewhere in the world. If one of these is removed from service, your customers will click its link and fail to access it. They perceive this as a failure of *your* server. Remote links should be kept to a manageable number and checked from time to time to ensure that they have not disappeared or relocated.

4.5.3   Customer feedback

It is customary to provide a feedback form on Web pages. Use of this by customers results in occasional e-mails (or log files) with suggestions for improvements. In order to handle these professionally, it is necessary to implement some simple process for dealing with them. In the simplest case this consists of:

- Log the suggestion.

- Decide how to handle it.

- Log the decision.
- Implement any changes.

- Inform the originator.

This process can be expanded, to taste, if, for example, the logging, decision-making and implementation are all done by different people.

4.6 SUMMARY

This chapter has gone through the DIVA lifecycle step by step. At each stage we have amplified the tasks that need to be carried out and indicated how these can best be accomplished in practical Media Engineering. In the absence of comprehensive tool support from the industry, we have tried to major on practical guidance and rules of thumb based on our own Media Engineering experience. Support materials for this chapter are provided in the checklists included in Appendix 1 and the technical guides in Appendix 2. In addition, the next two chapters add practical weight to the procedural guidance and design options given here.

REFERENCES

[CHK]   http://uts.cc.utexas.edu/~churchh/htmlchek.html
[GMTL]   GMTL Reference Page http://www.pobox.com/~gihan/gmtl_ref.html
[HTML]   Berners-Lee T., Connolly D. *Hypertext Markup Language 2.0*, RFC 1866, November (1995)
[ORB]   http://www.cinenet.net/users/cberry/orbinfo.html
[WL]   http://www.khoros.unm.edu/staff/neilb/weblint.html

5
Practice Makes Perfect

Good judgement comes from experience. And experience comes from bad judgment.

Fred Brooks

The method presented in the main text of this book has been developed partly through a transfer of established ideas from another discipline, partly through invention and partly through trial and error. The last ingredient is a significant one. Isambard Kingdom Brunel used much the same approach in developing bridges – and he remarked, when one fell down, that everyone should be grateful as he was planning to build more to that same formula.

One of the lessons from trial and error – other people's as well as one's own – is that you need to take a balanced approach. A product is usually only as good as it's weakest part. Inattention to one area often leads to a cost, time or quality penalty later on (that is, if there is a later on). Measures that can be taken to reduce the likelihood of oversights omissions and errors are always worthwhile.

A general lesson learned by many is to document what has worked in the past (as well as what didn't) and to learn from the experience next time around. Past experience doesn't always help with the current problem but many issues do come up time and again and can be resolved in much the same way.

In Chapter 4 we described the process of Media Engineering through the use of a lifecycle. However, this is not the whole story. Just as it is perfectly possible to use all the tools and techniques of software engineering and still produce software that is poorly designed and unusable, so with Media Engineering, the DIVA method, alone, is no guarantee of perfect results. If poor materials are passed through a perfectly-designed process, the results will still be poor.

This chapter describes some of the issues of using DIVA in practice which will assist the Media Engineer in putting the best possible material through the process. In effect, this is the collection of our learning points on Media Engineering.

5.1 GOOD PRACTICE IN ESTABLISHING REQUIREMENTS

In Chapter 4, we described the requirements phase of the Media Engineering project. However, we gave little guidance on what is a *good* set of requirements. At risk of dodging the issue again in this chapter, rather than list the requirements (which, after all, are specific to your project) we at least list some of the questions that you should be asking to establish requirements. These are:

- *What do you want to say, and who do you want to say it to?* This is the fundamental question which needs to be answered in the 'mission statement' for the project. It implies clarity in the proposed content and scope of the job and its intended audience.

- *Why will the audience find it of interest?* This is the 'so what?' test. Surfing the Internet it is very easy to find sites that have been produced with great loving care by their authors but are of no interest to anyone else.

- *How can you make your message tightly focused and captivating in its delivery?* Sophisticated multimedia can be used to add clarity and insight to your information; if poorly used, they can add distraction and obfuscation.

- *What effect do you want your message to have and how is that best achieved?* How does your message relate to existing messages? Unlike any other medium the very nature of on-line products gives the producer tremendous opportunities to use related products – such as World Wide Web sites – in support of their own. However, this is not without its pitfalls. At the time of writing, one UK on-line newspaper has obtained a temporary injunction preventing a rival on-line publication from providing links to its stories.

- *What process and legal issues do you need to consider?* Most companies have some form of internal information security policy, for example, which may require approval for publication, and security clearance for sensitive information. Legalities such as copyright, intellectual property and trademarks must be adhered to.

- *Is the level of security or privacy clear?*   If the product is built for a restricted audience, will they know if the material is restricted? A suggested marking hierarchy would be as follows: in confidence; in commercial confidence; not to be shown outside team/group/company, unrestricted).

  As a general guide, mechanisms such as simple firewalls and access controls based on source IP addresses are adequate for information that is 'not to be shown outside the company' – that is, information that is not for outside viewing but would not cause great embarrassment nor give away key technical or business secrets if it was retrieved by a determined hacker. For higher levels of privacy, stronger security mechanisms (including data encryption, secure sockets and site certification) should be used.

- *Is the source of information known?*   An information product will usually bring together many disparate contributions. Just as you would want the design and build of the product to be cogent and uniform, so the user will want to know about the quality of materials used. A list of sources should be kept – if for no other reason than to help with configuration management.

- *Must text-only browsers be supported?*   Images contain a lot of data and can take a long time to transmit to the user's screen – especially when the user is accessing the World Wide Web via a slow speed dial-up link. To speed up their access to information, people with only slow-speed access will probably disable the display of graphics until they have found the information they are interested in. One should also be aware that some users employ text-only browsers (such as Lynx) and that some users of the Internet are blind.

This final factor may lead to the requirement that your WWW pages should be meaningful when displayed without the graphics. This can be achieved by, for instance, providing alternative text in your HTML file as a part of each image specification, e.g.:

```
< IMG HEIGHT=100 WIDTH=200 ALT=``Home page'' SRC=``homepage.gif''>
```

where the ALT tag enables clients without graphics to see a description of the potential image.

The above line includes the specification for the size of the image. In some browsers this will significantly speed up the display of text on the page, whilst the pictures are still loading. Although it is impossible to get an exact match, it is common sense to ensure that the length of the 'alt' text is not excessive for the size of space available.

It is worth making sure that alternative text communicates well without the graphics. It shouldn't be simply a dull description of the graphic, but should replicate in text form any hypertext links made from the graphics.

5.2 LINKING STRATEGIES AND SYSTEM STRUCTURE

One of the design issues that is independent of the process concerns structuring the information through the linking of pages. There are various approaches to the way that 'pages' of a multimedia work can be linked together. In practice, most WWW sites are some combination of these.

5.2.1 Linear (book style)

Each page is linked to the next. The intention is that the reader will read through linearly from beginning to end. Typically, each page has a 'back' and 'forward' button (Figure 5.1).

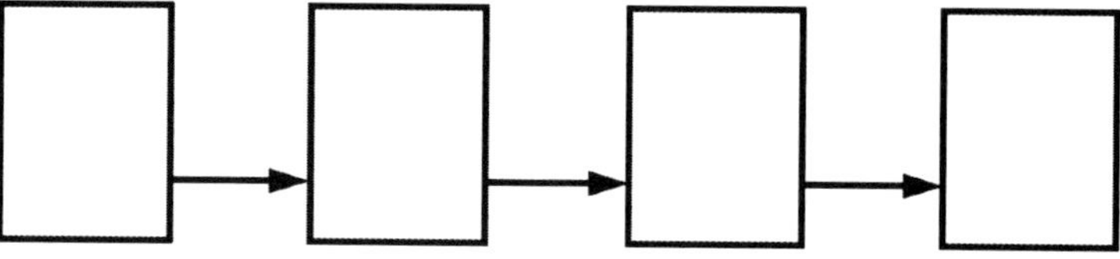

Figure 5.1
Linear linking

5.2.2 Hierarchical (menu style)

Here, each page contains a menu of options which takes the reader on to a page with yet another menu of options (Figure 5.2). This approach was common in early page-based information systems such as Teletext and Prestel.

5.2.3 Network

Here, pages are linked in an arbitrary way to form a network. Typically, the links are 'unstructured' in the sense introduced in Chapter 4. This is illustrated in Figure 5.3.

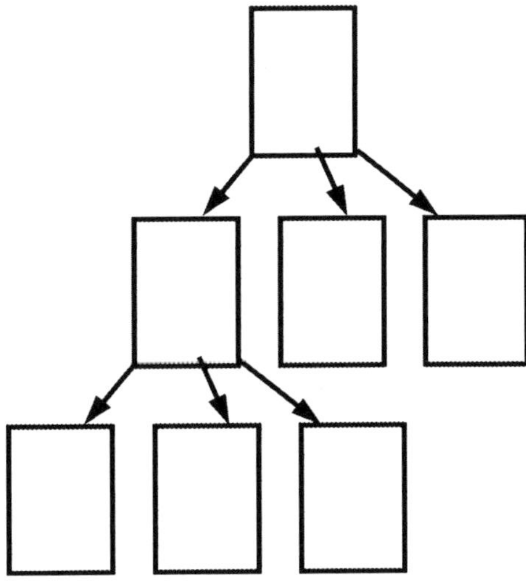

Figure 5.2
Hierarchical linking

5.2.4   Tour style

The last of these, 'tour style' is not widely seen yet but offers considerable value and has been used successfully by the authors. The principles are:

- The main hypertext pages are written with minimal hypertext linking.

- Separate hypertext material is produced to thread these pages together

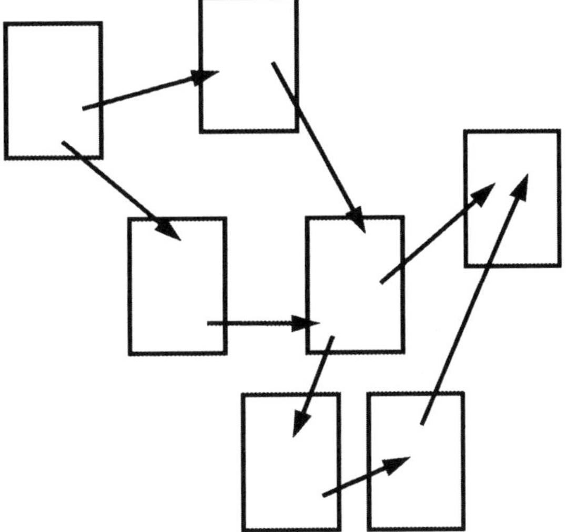

Figure 5.3
Network Linking

in different ways (Figure 5.4). The same page may participate in any number of different tours.

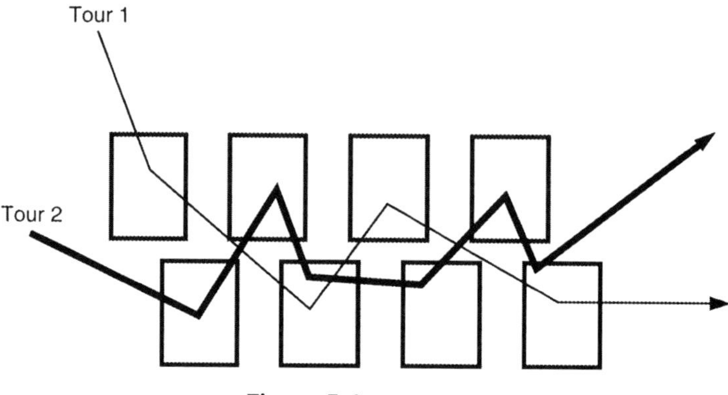

Figure 5.4
Tour-style linking

The tour structure can be achieved in a number of ways which require different sets of facilities from the browser. All these amount to separating the *structure* of the hypertext from the *content*: i.e. employing the principle of *discrimination* introduced in Chapter 3. Discrimination, as exploited for tours and other structural approaches, is described in the next section.

5.2.5   Other structures

There are probably other structures – some hybrids of this basic set and some we simply have yet to encounter. The collection explained here has proved a useful set for a wide range of products.

5.3   DISCRIMINATION – SEPARATION OF STRUCTURE FROM CONTENT

Previous sections of this book have introduced the notion that in engineered media systems, the structure of information should be kept separate from it content. We now consider how this is achieved in practice.

The following sections demonstrate some of the practical ways that separation of structure and content can be achieved. Each represents a certain degree of trade-off between the ease of implementation and the usability. After considering these options we offer some discussion of these trade-offs and offer some pragmatic advice.

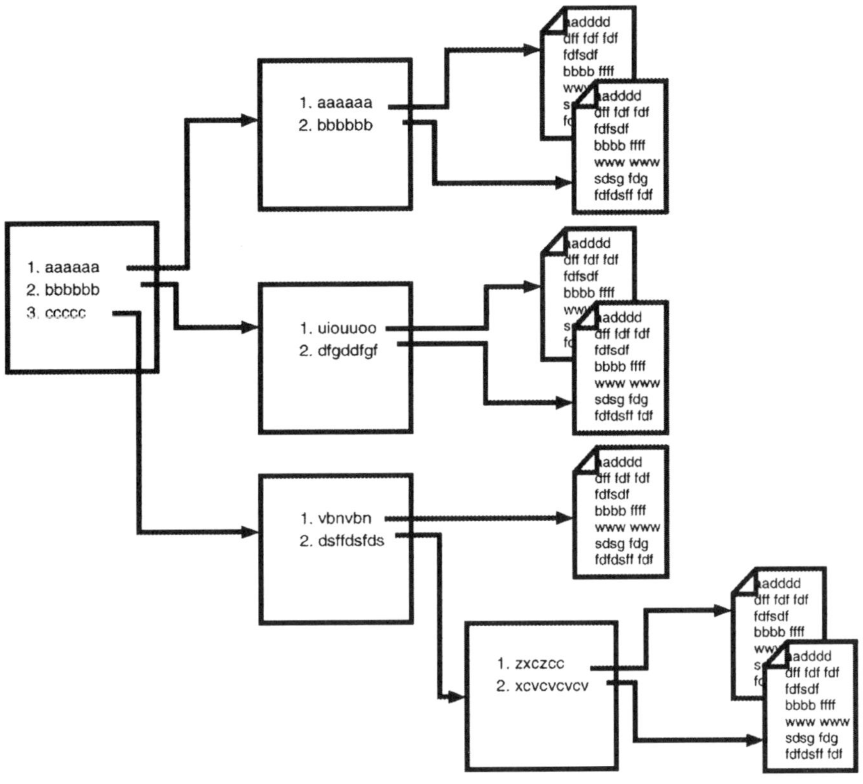

Figure 5.5
Linked Menus

5.3.1 Simple menu pages

When discussing structure in Chapter 3, we drew a tree picture (Figure 3.3) which illustrated how we might consider a medium to consist of a structure (the trunk and branches) separate from the information (the leaves). Such a system could be viewed as a hierarchical structure (Figure 5.2) and could be implemented through a set of linked menus (Figure 5.5).

Here we have imposed a discipline on our media design which may be summarized in the following rules:

- We divide the design into two types of 'pages' those that function as menus, or navigation items and those that contain information.
- Menu pages may contain both links to other menus and links to information pages.

- Information pages do not contain links.

As drawn in the figure, the structure is a 'simply-connected tree': there are no cross links between menu pages. However, such cross links can be introduced without prejudicing the simplicity of the structure, although, when designing a system, there is much to be said for completing a preliminary design using only a simply connected structure and then adding the cross links as a later refinement. That is, design the structured links first, and then add the unstructured links.

Also, the information pages, in practice, will contain some links although the simplicity of the structure can be preserved if information pages only have links:

- local to the context of the page (e.g. a list of topics at the top of the page with hypertext links to sections within the page);

- a return link to the menu page from which the information page was linked;

- a 'home' link to the root of the information tree.

In this section we have treated 'menu pages' as though they were simply a numbered list of destinations. However, in practice, they can be implemented in a number of ways including 'clickable' pictures (image maps), button bars and any other hypertext navigation object.

The attraction of implementing this kind of system is that it is simple to do, works with any browser and achieves our stated aim of retaining a good separation between content and structure. The weakness, however is that there are no direct links between information pages: a user who wishes to follow a thread of information must navigate to the first page then backtrack to a menu before reading the next page, and so on.

The 'guided tours' described in the previous section can readily be implemented using this approach, with the menu acting as a 'contents list' for the pages that make up the tour. As each page is read, it is necessary to return to the contents page to pick up the link to the next page of the tour.

5.3.2   Menus in frames

In order to overcome the usability weaknesses of the option of Section 5.3.1, hypertext systems can exploit the 'frames' feature of the current generation of web browsers or equivalent mechanisms in other media systems. Two sorts of frame are commonly implemented:

- *Basic frames* divide the browser window into a number of separate areas in a 'tiled formation'. Each area, or frame can be the target for different hypertext pages but the frames remain in relatively fixed

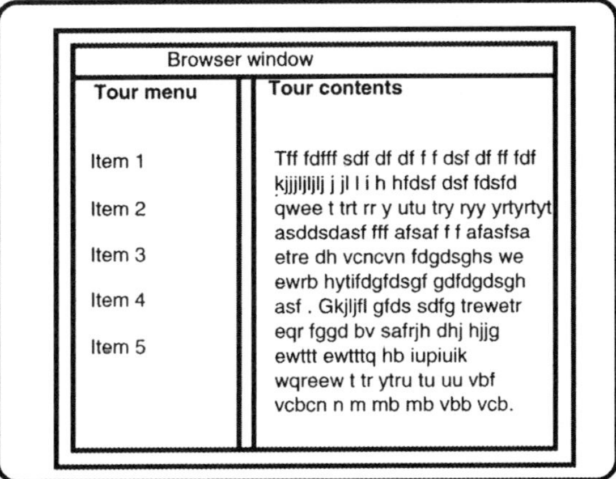

Figure 5.6
Menus in frames

positions on the screen and may not, for example, overlap.

- *Floating frames* behave as completely separate browser windows that can be moved around the computer screen independently and may overlap with other frames.

For the purposes of designing the hypertext structure, the kind of frames system employed is not important although, clearly, it will have an impact on the actual screen design and visual representation.

By using frames, the designer can ensure that both navigation pages and information pages are simultaneously accessible to the user. The design may then be partitioned into the pages which will appear in the 'navigation frame' and those to be displayed in the information frame. This is illustrated in Figure 5.6.

Again, this approach can be used to implement 'guided tours', with the tour items listed in one frame and the information pages appearing in another.

5.3.3   Programmable buttons

The advent of scripting languages such as JavaScript and programming languages such as Java have led to the possibility that a navigation object such as a button or a piece of hypertext may be 'intelligent' so that instead of simply having a static connection to another page, it may run a simple program and be context sensitive. A button, embedded in a page may for example run a JavaScript which retrieves from the server a table which, in turn, points to the destination. Hence, the structure is not embedded in the buttons but is embedded in the table.

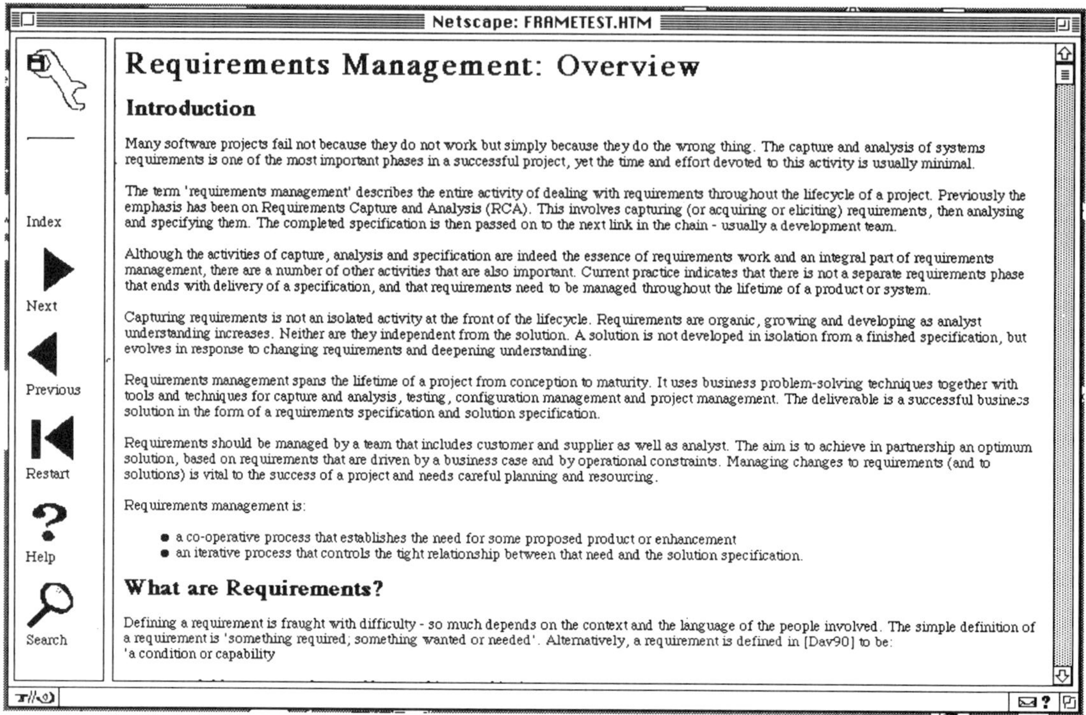

Figure 5.7
Example screen using programmable buttons

Once again, this approach can be used to implement a guided tour. A simple way to accomplish this is to use two frames, one containing the information pages and the other containing the tour navigation buttons to provide context sensitive navigation. Here, the navigation buttons are specific to the tour and not to the page which is currently being displayed. Figure 5.7 illustrates a page from a guided tour of software engineering. The 'intelligent buttons' for moving back, forwards, etc., use Javascript to select the appropriate next page from a table that is specific to the tour.

In some cases, intelligent buttons need to retain 'state' information relating to the client. For example, the button may need to know which guided tour is currently in use. Typically, this would be achieved using the 'Magic Cookie' feature of a WWW browser – see Section 5.5 for more information on cookies.

5.3.4 CGI scripts

Just as Java and JavaScript allow the option of buttons which display intelligence at the client end of a WWW system, so CGI scripts can be used to provide similar intelligence at the server end. Hence, clicking a button does not directly load a page, but, rather, executes a CGI script which determines (from a table) which page should be loaded next.

The script will typically output the following to your HTTP server:

```
Location: http://www.norwest.com/services/brochure.html
```

which would cause your browser to load the right page.

5.3.5 Full database engines

Rather than simply allowing the HTTP server to extract pages from the server's standard filing system, an alternative approach is to use a commercial database package such as Oracle to hold the pages and the tables that represent the relationships between them. Hence the intelligence concerning which page should be loaded next can be built into the database.

5.4 GUIDED TOURS EXAMPLE

To illustrate the various approaches to separation of content from structure, we take a simple example. The example is chosen to be about the simplest case that displays all the characteristics of a content/structure-separated system – however, it is so simple that it would be unlikely to be implemented in any of these ways in reality.

WWW is to be used to document a financial approval system for project expenditure for a large corporation. The company's existing documentation system can be shown as a flow chart which references different documents according to the nature of the project that is to be approved. The flow chart is shown in Figure 5.8.

This process includes different procedures for business case preparation, sign-off and project management (quality file) according to such factors as the overall cost of the proposed project and its level of capital expenditure.

Different users of this documentation system will wish to reference different sets of documents according to these criteria. By employing hypermedia, the appropriate documents can be selected for the user.

The aim of the hypertext system is to lead users through the appropriate documents for their own particular cicumstances.

We examine how this could be implemented using the various approaches:

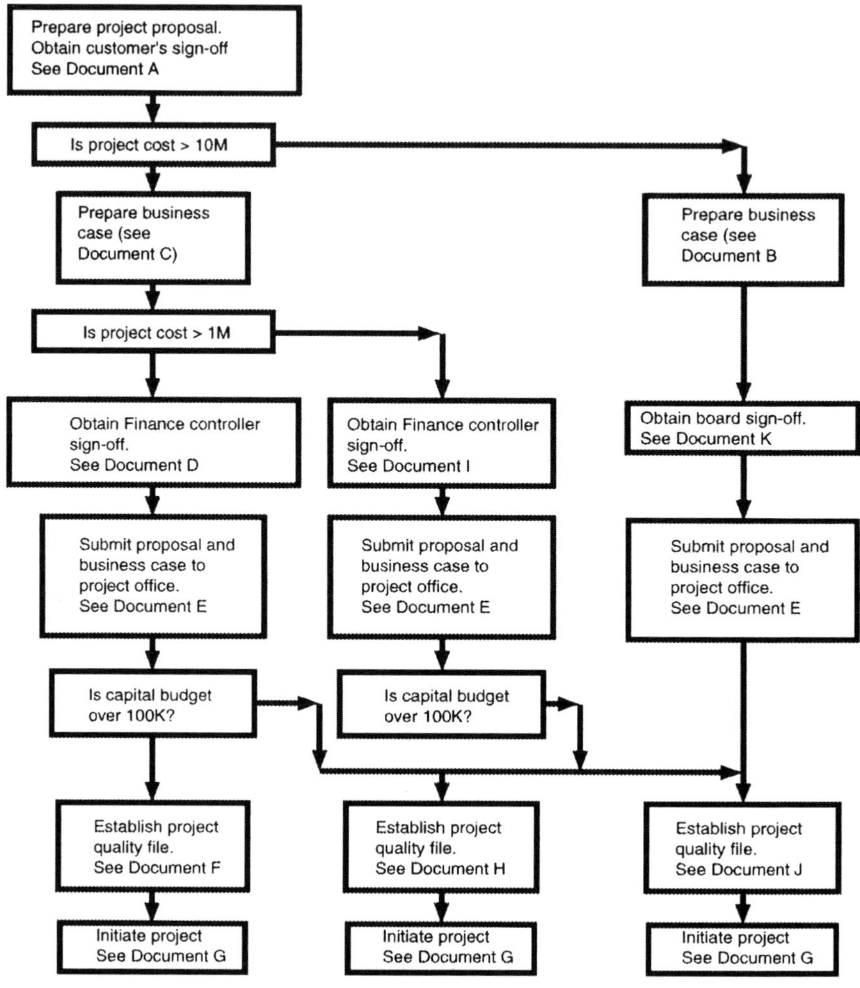

Figure 5.8
Example process

5.4.1 Simple menus

Here we have decided to implement a single top level menu that allows the users to select the type of project they are engaged in: projects over 10M etc. A sub-menu page then describes the steps they must undertake to obtain financial concurrence. These sub-menus point to the actual reference documents that describe the process steps. To use the system, the user first selects the required type of project then steps through the items in the sub-menu, retrieving each of the reference documents and

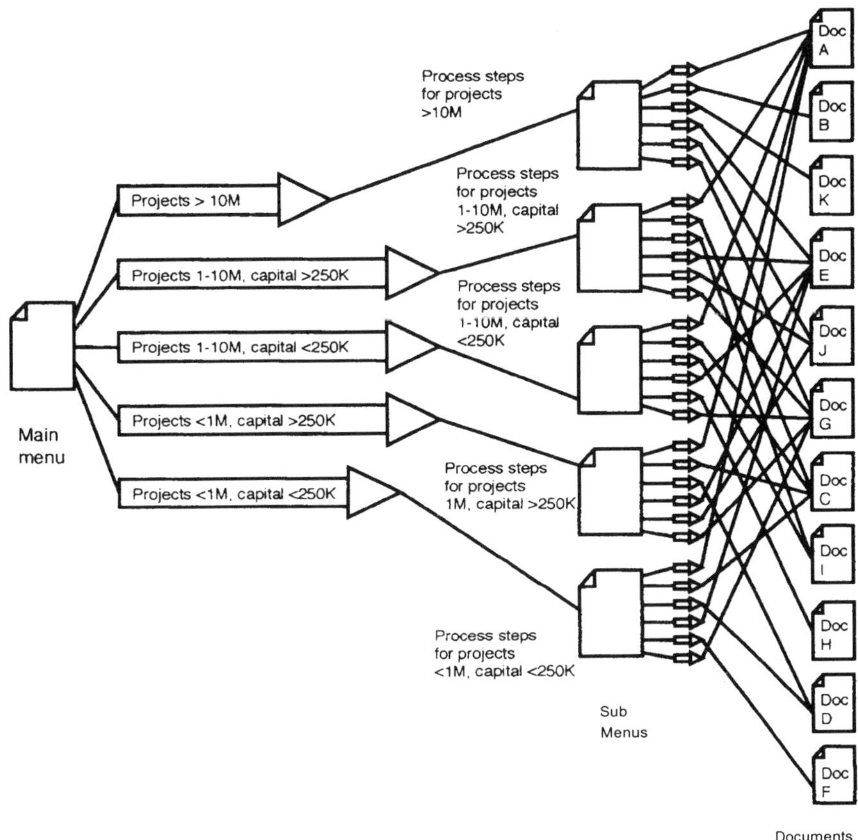

Figure 5.9
Simple menus design

returning to the sub-menu to find the link to the next one. The structure of
the hypertext is shown in Figure 5.9.

5.4.2   Frames approach

Here the same hypertext structure is employed (as per Figure 5.9) but the
navigation screens – the menus – always appear in one frame and the
information documents appear in the other, see Figure 5.10.

The left-hand frame would remain visible at all times and as the user
clicked on particular items, the detailed information would appear in the
right hand frame. A further example of this way of using frames is
illustrated in the next chapter, where navigation information is kept in
one frame and detailed technical guidance in another.

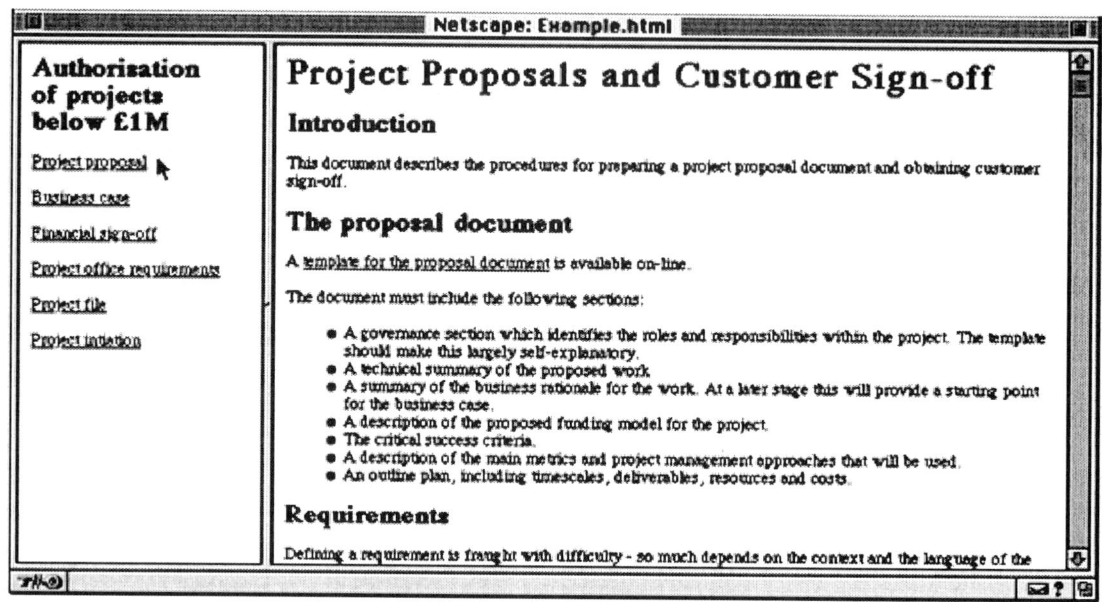

Figure 5.10
Frames-based design

5.4.3 Programmable buttons

Using programmable buttons it is possible to redefine the sequence of pages according to the user's requirements, hence providing customized 'guided tours' for the various kinds of user. The system must configure itself to offer five different tours corresponding to the five different project types. The design of each of these is illustrated in Figure 5.11.

The function of the 'Next' button is clearly dependent on the particular tour that the user has embarked upon. This differs from the usual 'stateless' nature of WWW systems. Somehow the 'state' information of which tour the user is engaged in must be preserved as they move from page to page. This can be implemented fairly simply in JavaScript. We provide a detailed worked example in Appendix 3 for anyone who wishes to implement this facility (or anyone who doubts the essential simplicity of the approach).

5.4.4 CGI scripts

Essentially this approach achieves the same effect as option 3, except that this time, the 'intelligence' is retained at the server end rather than being sent to the client. Once again, the issue is how to retain the state

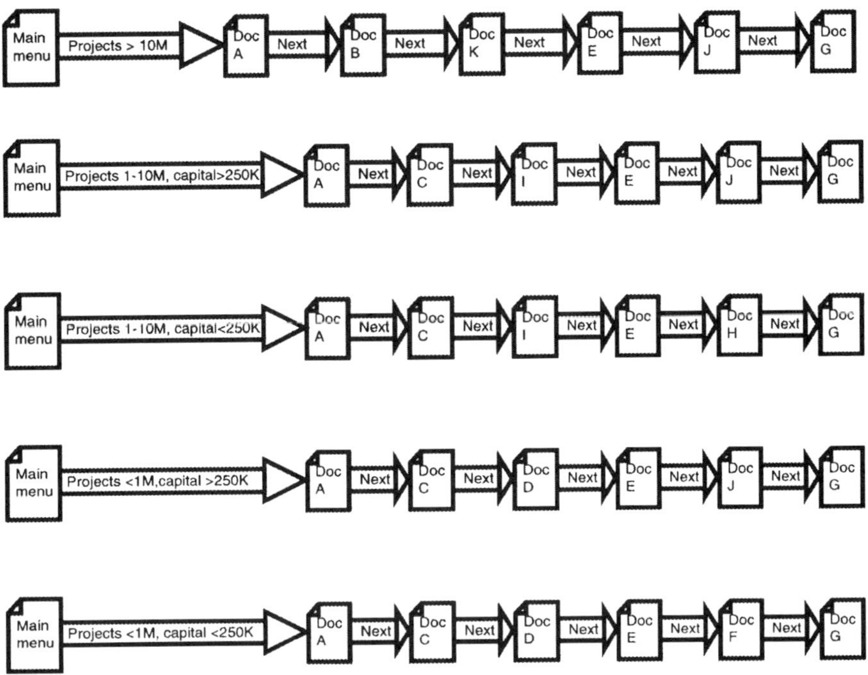

Figure 5.11
Design for programmable buttons approach

information between page accesses. This is either done by retaining a server file that tracks what the particular user has accessed, or else uses the cookie feature of browsers to retain the state information at the client end. An alternative way of passing the state information to the client is to use 'hidden fields' in a form.

5.5 MAGIC COOKIES

When building guided tours or in other cases of polycontiguity, we have noted the need to retain 'state' information about the client. This might include such data as:

- which tour is currently in progress;
- which pages have been visited previously;
- what role the user is playing (e.g. in a system where different users have different views of the documentation);
- Which of a set of preferences the user has selected.

One approach to this problem is to make use of the 'magic cookie' feature available in most browsers. The cookie is a file of name/value pairs which is held on the client PC and accessed by the browser. A server CGI script or a client JavaScript can create new items in this name/value list, can change the values and can read back the values. Additional features allow the cookie to relate only to a particular web server (or directory path within the server) and allow the cookies to expire after a certain time period.

It is beyond the scope of this book to go into the details of CGI scripting and JavaScripting. However, for those familiar with the JavaScript, it is straightforward to make use of the cookie feature: for example a JavaScript might define a cookie whose name was 'Tour' and set it to values such as 'Overview tour', 'Express tour', 'Project manager's tour', etc. This is done by a JavaScript statement such as:

```
<SCRIPT>
document.cookie=''Tour=Express;   expires=Tuesday,   19—Nov-1996
10:10:00 GMT''
......
</SCRIPT>
```

This statement is included at the start of the first page of the tour. As the user moves on to subsequent pages, the intelligent buttons are able to determine which tour is currently in progress by accessing the document.cookie variable.

When reading the tour details from the cookie file, you should remember that, in general, there could be a whole list of cookies and so your script should search the list for the 'Tour' cookie. As an illustration, the following JavaScript fragment searches through the document.cookie string and prints out the value of the Tour cookie:

```
var value_end=0
var clength = document.cookie.length
var i = 0
while (i <clength) {
var j = i + 5
if (document.cookie.substring(i, j) == ''Tour='') {
value_end = document.cookie.indexOf ('';'', j)
if (value_end == -1) value_end = document.cookie.length
document.write(document.cookie.substring(j, value_end))
}
i++
}
```

5.6   GOOD PRACTICE WHEN CREATING LINKS

In addition to the technicalities of generating links, there are some stylistic guidelines that should be adopted:

1. Don't pepper links throughout a section of text. This is generally poor practice because it results in a conflict between the use of the paragraph as a logical thread of argument and that of a list of possible destinations. For example

   The <u>woollen industry</u> was the most important factor in the <u>growth of Ipswich</u> as a <u>port</u> within mediaeval <u>Suffolk</u>: the <u>demise of that industry</u> led to a decline in prosperity <u>which continued through into the twentieth century</u>.

2. Do not repeatedly use the word 'here' as the source for links. The problem in this case is that the link text really tells you nothing about the destination, e.g.

   Click <u>here</u> to find out about the woollen industry.
   Click <u>here</u> for more information.
   Click <u>here</u> to continue.

3. Do not use long, convoluted text as link text:
   <u>More information about the Mediaeval woollen industry in general, and its impact on Suffolk towns, in particular, can be found by clicking on this sentence.</u>

4. Do use lists of topics as links. For example:

   Further information is available on the following topics:
   (a)<u>General information about the woollen industry</u>
   (b)<u>Growth of Ipswich</u>
   (c)<u>Ipswich as a port</u>
   (d)<u>Suffolk in the middle ages</u>
   (e)<u>The demise of the woollen industry</u>
   (f)<u>Ipswich from mediaeval times to the present</u>

In this example, the list of topics serves as a menu of further options.

5.7 GOOD PRACTICE IN PAGE DESIGN

5.7.1 Conversion from original word processor documents

Some general dos and donts are:

- Do use in-built styles that can be readily translated to hypertext (Heading 1, Heading 2, etc.)

- Do make use of formatting options such as bold and italic.

- Don't use different fonts and font sizes. The use of different fonts and font sizes does not translate well through the hypertexting process. Web browsers usually allow users to configure their own choice of font so authors have only minimal control of this aspect of the visual appearance of the final product.

- Don't use indenting. Indenting can be an effective way of showing the structure of a printed document. However, hypertext systems, including HTML, don't have facilities for indenting text.

- Don't make assumptions about page or screen width. Browsers will normally reformat paragraphs of text to suit the user's screen size. There is no way for the author to know how this will appear.

- Don't use 'whitespace' characters for formatting. These include multiple space characters, tabs and carriage returns. Although they can be used to create a particular formatting effect on screen in a word processor application, the results are usually very disappointing when this has been translated into hypertext.

- Don't use multi-column text.

- Don't use large or complex pictures or those for which fine detail is important. Pictures will have to be converted to a bit-map format in which some detail is lost. Furthermore, they will end up being displayed on a screen over which you have very little control.

5.7.2 Provision of feedback facilities

It is important to make it easy for people to contact the providers of information, e.g. by providing an author's name on the home page as a hypertext link to their e-mail address or similar. To help maintainability, it is usually better to do this to a general point of contact, e.g. `<A HREF=''mailto:server_administrator@info.com''>` rather than a specific one `<A HREF=''mailto:fredsmith@info.com''>`.

Alternatively, a feedback form can be provided as a server-based CGI application. A number of these are available in the public domain for different server platforms. Essentially, the user fills in an on-line form and the details are logged in a log file.

5.7.3 Clarity of information status

Details of the last date on which a page was updated should be displayed when pages are being updated frequently. This information could be included on the credits page. As an option it can be included within the footer of the home page. Other things that help in managing the information base would be the name and e-mail address of the owner of the information (the person who will be responsible for keeping it up to date), any 'don't use before' or 'don't use after' markings.

Frequently there is substantially more enthusiasm and time available for setting up a new information service than there is for maintaining it over a period of time. A cursory surf of the Internet will find any number of pages which are undoubtedly out of date. The 'don't use after' marking is a good discipline for ensuring that the review period for the information is made public: always a strong encouragement for acting to keep it up to date (or removing it). Alternatively (or additionally), date information may be included in META tags within pages and a server-based application can periodically check for those that have reached their sell-by dates and flag this to the Webmaster.

By way of example, here is how you would use META tags to include date information on a page.

```
<HTML>
<HEAD>
<META NAME = ''date'' CONTENT = ''25 Nov 1996''>
<META NAME = ''review date'' CONTENT = ''25 Feb 1997''>
```

5.7.4 Is page size appropriate?

The speed of response when the user requests the download of a World Wide Web page is determined by the speed of the slowest link in the communication path between the user and the information server and by the amount of information contained in the page. The 'size' of pages should therefore be limited – especially in the case of pages that are used solely for navigation around an information base. Most users won't mind waiting for useful information, but they are likely to object to waiting for pages that only point to other pages.

The size of a World Wide Web page is a combination of the amount of text and the number and size (bytes) of any graphics. As a rule of thumb, the total amount of data to be transmitted should not exceed 50 Kbytes (unless prior warning of a 'large' page is given).

Traditionally, people have been constrained to A4 or some other physical page limit. A page of on-line information can be any length and the 'right' size depends a great deal on content and the relation to different parts of the document. The only real advice is to do whatever makes the information easiest to find and read. Always be prepared to experiment and change the structure of your pages if necessary. Perhaps the only guide here is to ensure that key material and information is correctly visible within a 640 × 480 window. As a rule of thumb, it is worth limiting the width of your pages to 500 pixels wide, so that they print properly on an A4 sheet of paper.

One thing to bear in mind is that there is a trade-off between the ease of finding something on any particular page and the ease of keeping track of where you are within the site as a whole. Whatever page size you do decide upon, try to give the user some means of anticipating how far they need to scroll on any particular page. And always provide 'return to top' and 'home' buttons).

5.7.5   Is navigation intuitive?

Unlike conventional publishing, hypertext allows the user to find their own route through complex information by using links. This puts the onus on you to consider exactly how you are going to help them to get the best from the product. Possibly the most important point to remember is that you cannot predict what the user will do. They may go straight to a section buried deep within the structure, missing out altogether any introduction or guidance material. This has evident disadvantages if they by-pass information that may be critical to their understanding, so some guards have to be put in place.

First, the user should be encouraged to read information in a logical sequence. Second, if they choose to ignore the guided tours, feature stories and editorials, it should be fairly clear how they get back from whichever part of the product they have chosen to go to.

5.7.6   Is the structure explicit?

Is there an overview of everything available. This enables a user to get a full picture of the product or service in one go, and this can help to make even the most complex of structures understandable. An easy way to achieve this is to use the titles or icons used on the opening page throughout. Ideally this should be restricted to no more than six sections, one of which should be a link to a full contents listing for complex sites. The structure should relate logically in some way to the content of the service itself – this will make it easier for users to predict the structure and to keep track of where they are.

Most structures will have some form of hierarchy, with pages that are likely to be more popular with users at a higher rather than a lower level.

5.7.7   How much graphics should be used?

Images can greatly enhance the appeal of a document. At the same time, they can detract from its usability. In general they should be as small in terms of memory size as possible. The size a graphic takes in memory depends on three factors:

1 the actual dimensions – the width and height of the image;

2 the complexity of the image. A complex photographic image in a great many colours takes up far more space than a line image in a few colours;

3 the compression technique employed. The difference between image formats such as GIF and JPEG is explained in Appendix 2.

From the user's perspective, it is not so much the size of the graphic that is important, but rather the time it takes to load: and this is dependent on the network speed. Hence the Media Engineer should consider the size of graphics in relation to the anticipated network speed accessible to users (over a 14.4 Kbit/s link, average transfer speeds are typically around 1200 bytes/s, so a 40 Kbyte image will take over 30 s to load).

A general principle should be to use graphics for information not decoration – users are liable to get irritated rather than edified by the over-use of 'gratuitous graphics'. When they are included, it is worth choosing a preferred format. For photographic images containing lots of colours JPEG is much the best option – and the files can be successfully compressed to reasonable sizes without unduly degrading the quality of the image. For graphics containing relatively few colours, the GIF format is quite all right. As a rule of thumb: GIF – under 40 Kbytes; JPEG – over 40 Kbytes).

It is worth noting that the LZW data compression algorithm (used for all GIFs) encodes the image row by row and looks for repeated horizontal patterns. Hence, the smallest GIFs result from images with long horizontal sequences of the same colour. Hence, all things being equal, you should try to use horizontal bands of colour rather than vertical ones.

In addition, the LZW algorithm is not particularly good for encoding plain black and white images.

If JPEGs are used, it is worth remembering that conversion to the JPEG format always involves some loss of detail. Although this is usually minor, if a JPEG image is repeatedly edited, the results are cumulative. Hence, if a JPEG needs re-editing, it is preferable to go back to the original image (e.g. a TIFF file), then edit it and reconvert it.

On the other hand, conversion to GIF loses colour information – GIFs can never display more than 256 colours. One of the worst things that you can do is to convert your image to a GIF and then convert the GIF to a JPEG.

5.7.8   Are images re-used?

Images are usually cached by the browser – that is, once the image has been downloaded a copy of it is kept. This means that multiple copies of a single graphic are displayed much more quickly than a lot of different graphics.

Users will therefore see a faster response if the same graphic is repeated as, say, the bullet for a list, rather than if a differently designed graphic is used for each bullet.

It is good practice to store all the general purpose graphic images in a single file on the server. This ensures that multiple copies of bullet graphics, and the like, do not proliferate through the directory structure. Hence browsers will always refer to the same copy of the graphic, irrespective of which page it is displayed on.

5.7.9   Is the first page inviting?

The opening page of an information product acts rather like the front cover of a magazine. It should be inviting, functional and fit for purpose. Typically it should contain a number of elements:

1 brand identity and privacy marking;

2 image(s) that graphically reinforce the objectives of the product and its brand;

3 description of sections – between four and six is good;

4 navigation bar that introduces the icons that should be used throughout the product. The usual set would include; search, home, index, feedback and perhaps a few others;

5 a footer with source and status information.

5.7.10   Are all links valid?

Hypertext links should always lead to other pages, and hopefully each link should be a logical development of the storyline that has been built into the product. Inevitably, this will be tested by users – people are very adept at surfing, trying new links just to see where they go. So care should be taken not to make the effect of activation of a hypertext link into an irretrievable action. There are several guidelines here:

1 With elements of your directory path inevitably changing over time, hypertext links between files within a supplied directory or directory tree should be specified using relative, rather than absolute addressing.
2 Be wary of using hypertext links to other sites which may be replaced or updated, leaving your link inoperable.

3 Links to large files (e.g., large graphics and video), to 'unusual' information (e.g., VRML files), or to potentially 'volatile' sites (e.g., sites not always available) should be clearly identified through inclusion of a graphic, explanatory text, and (where appropriate) an indication of the size of the data being referenced. For example:[Image] – QuickTime[TM] movie (8MB)

A final guideline is to use a commercial tool to check links – it is not a job to be tackled by hand.

5.7.11 Will the user see what was intended?

There are many different (usually) older versions of browsers that sit on a variety of different computers with different resolutions, sizes, colour capability and so on. This is the good reason for using a basic standard such as HTML, rather than a particular browser product.

In addition, across the range of available browsers (e.g., Netscape, Mosaic, Microsoft Internet Explorer, etc.), there are differences in the level of implementation of the HTML text-encoding language and in the way that some HTML syntax is interpreted. What is more, these differences are compounded by subtle variations between implementations of the same client when running on different platforms (Windows, Macintosh, Sun, etc.).

In order to deal with this you may opt to explicitly target information design for display on one client (usually Netscape as it dominates the browser market). This is a viable strategy but does leave you at risk should the selected browser become less popular in the market. Whatever approach is taken, the risk of having to rework an information product should be recognized.

5.8 GOOD PRACTICE WITH LEGAL ISSUES

First some caveats. The present authors are engineers, not lawyers, and would regard the details of legal considerations as being outside the scope of this book. Furthermore, many of the legal issues regarding the Internet, in particular, are unclear, as they have never been tested in the law courts. To make matters worse, the Internet crosses international boundaries and hence is not the domain of a single legal jurisdiction. Nevertheless, there are some obvious issues that should be considered.

5.8.1   Copyright issues

You cannot publish material for which you do not own the copyright or the intellectual property rights unless you have the legal owner's permission in writing. Infringement is an easy mistake to make and potentially costly to resolve. Sound advice is, as always, simple: if you don't own it, don't publish it. This goes for images as well as anything else – some images, such as those from photo-libraries, are licensed for each application separately. Additional usage would infringe copyright.

Some clipart and on-line public domain graphics libraries are copyright free under certain conditions of use. The advice here is to check the small print very carefully!

5.8.2   Acknowledgement of trademarks

Always acknowledge third party trademarks and copyright credits. This is generally done by inclusion of the [™], Æ or © mark, with a full credit included within the credits page or within the relevant page footer. The exact wording for this can be obtained from the owner(s) of the product, service or information that you have used. Ensure that you submit your intention to the owner(s) in writing, and receive written confirmation of their acceptance in return.

5.8.3   Proprietary buttons

Some companies allow other sites to copy particular buttons for links to the company's site. For example, Netscape offer a button with a link to the current version of their Navigator product for download. Although copies of these can be seen in many places, if you choose to use them, access the owner's site and check for any conditions of usage before sticking them on your pages. For instance it may be a requirement that you simply include a (constructional) link from your page to the master copy of the graphic rather than taking your own private copy. Irrespective of conditions of usage, it is courtesy to check periodically that you are still using the current version.

5.8.4 Are adequate warranties in place?

Even if your document is published for local consumption, there is always the possibility that someone will pass on a print-out of the content. It is important that the last page (credits page) carries the products and services disclaimers if you refer to product or service related information.

5.9 MAINTENANCE AND DELIVERY ISSUES

5.9.1 Is maintenance catered for?

Much of the motivation behind Media Engineering has been to provide techniques that allow information products to be systematically built and kept. A large part of the thinking has been to cater for change. In particular products on the World Wide Web are expected to change quickly. And there is nothing worse than a site with information that is evidently out of date or not operating properly. The currency of information and references to other sites need to be planned as part of the product development – apart from anything else, knowing that you will have to effect change focuses the mind on including adequate mechanisms for finding and updating items. Keeping it constantly updated, will encourage users to make a point of returning regularly.

5.9.2 Are product delivery standards established?

Following the spirit of software engineering development, there should be a prescribed set of deliverables that constitute an information product. This set should probably include the following:

- a single directory, containing all of the text (usually HTML) files and accompanying graphics, movies, etc.;

- a document that describes the overall structure of the product and any instructions required to build it from the supplied files.

In addition, some conventions should be established before development so that there is consistency of delivery. Notably:

1 Each directory should include a file named index.htm. This should be

the principal page for the information held in that directory (i.e. the home page for the topic at that level).

2 File names should be restricted e.g. to be between one and eight lower case characters long. Valid characters are: a..z, 0..9, -, __.

3 File name extensions should be constrained, e.g. to be three characters long and lower case (e.g. HTML files will use the .htm extension).

Commonly, systems and pages are designed on PCs (or Apple Macs), which treat upper and lower case names as synonymous, and are then uploaded to Unix servers which have case-sensitive file systems. It is a common error that URLs embedded in pages use upper and lower case interchangeably and hence do not work correctly on the target environment. In Unix, 'Index.htm', 'index.htm' and 'index.HTM' are all different files.

5.9.3   Is there a material check?

Is someone responsible for checking that:

1 the material is appropriate to be published on an open channel;

2 the material is appropriate to be published in an electronic form;

3 the material is owned by the information provider publishing it;

4 there is no overlap with existing material;

5 a suitable review date is set;

6 the material conforms to any in-house design guidelines;

7 action can be taken on user feedback – including correcting errors;

8 there is a contact point for enquiries and feedback;

9 some evaluation is made of information usage;

10 obsolete information is removed, as necessary?

5.10   GOOD PRACTICE WITH IMAGE MAPS

Clickable images are one of the exciting new features that were popularized by World Wide Web. Like many others they can be exploited to good effect or can be a source of problems.

5.10.1 Client side image maps

Some, but not all, browsers can support client side image maps. There are several advantages to using them:

- An additional access to the server is not needed when the user clicks on the picture: the translation from the click position to the destination URL is done at the browser. This can be an advantage when network speeds are slow.

- Server side image maps consume more processor resource than plain HTTP accesses.

- The use of client-side image maps facilitates the production of 'stand-alone' WWW systems that do not use a server. For example, the complete website can be installed on a portable PC, together with a browser, and can provide a portable demonstration system without a server.

The main drawback of client side maps is that they are not supported by all browsers. Hence, the recommendation is to use client-side maps but also to provide a server-side map as an alternative.

5.10.2 Absolute URLs

Where server-side imagemaps are used, the URLs of destination pages must be expressed as absolute URLs, rather than relative ones. It is a common fault to forget to change these when a change to the configuration is made (e.g. when transferring a working system from a development machine to a live machine).

5.10.3 Make it clear what is clickable!

By default, browsers will display image maps with a coloured border indicating that they are clickable. Many designers override this feature, perhaps because the blue of the border clashes with other colours used in the picture. In such cases, some clue should be given to the user that the picture is indeed an imagemap (e.g. include a caption that says 'click anywhere on this picture').

5.10.4 Size of image maps

We have already cautioned against the use of over-large graphics. Users are likely to be extremely irritated if they have to scroll from side to side to find the part of the image that they are supposed to click on.

5.10.4 Detail of image maps

As far as possible, it is desirable to keep the clickable regions large enough to be clicked! Avoid, for example, having tiny bullet-type dots that have to be clicked. In practice 10×10 pixels is probably about the minimum.

5.10.5 Text alternatives

In the section on good practice for requirements, we noted that graphics should have text alternatives for people who either do not have graphics-capable browsers or who have chosen to disable the loading of images. In the case of image maps, the provision of a text alternative is essential because, otherwise, there may be parts of your site which are completely unreachable by some of your users. Two approaches to this issue are:

1. Include a small text menu following the graphic. A common convention is for this to be in a small font, with the menu items placed in square brackets. For instance, a button bar at the foot of a page, which includes links for 'Home', 'Index', 'Search' and 'Help' might be followed by a small, one-line menu:
   ```
   [Home] [Index] [Search] [Help]
   ```
2. Include a completely separate version of the page for those with text-only browsers. There should be a clear link to it from the main graphics-rich page.

5.10.6 Image maps versus individual buttons

Frequently, the same functionality can be provided either through the use of an imagemap or through an array of individual buttons. In many cases, the individual buttons can provide an equally good graphic appearance and have the advantages that:

- There is no need for a map file. The selection process is much simpler and will never need a map CGI application to run at the server.

- Text alternatives can easily be provided for each button.

- Different pages can use different selections from the same overall repertoire of buttons. Given the browser caching facility, this can offer much better performance than the situation in which a page-specific button bar is loaded with each new page.

If an array of buttons is used, it may be desirable to use a table construct to place the buttons in appropriate relative positions.

5.11   GOOD PRACTICE WITH COLOURS IN BACKGROUNDS AND IMAGES

5.11.1   Background colours

Background colours are selected using hexadecimal numbers in an HTML tag such as:

```
<BODY BGCOLOR = ''FFFFFF''>
```

The hex number represents the levels of red (r), green (g) and blue (b) in the form 'rrggbb'. For example, FF0000 is primary red, 000000 is black, FFFFFF is white and 808080 is a middle grey.

Finding the right hex number for the colour you require can be simplified if you have a grahics package that allows you to select colours by RGB values. Some on-line colour charts are available (e.g. Doug Jacobson's RGB Triple Colour Chart [RGB].

5.11.2   256 colour PC problems

A large number of PCs will display only 256 colours on the screen. However, some of these colours are used for the Microsoft Windows environment and, when using the Netscape browser, others are specific to the Netscape logo. Hence, the number of colours available for use by embedded GIF images is actually rather less than 256. In the versions of Netscape that run on Windows PCs, the actual colour palette available for displaying images consists only of 216 colours. Furthermore, this palette is predefined, so an image cannot use *any* 216 colours: it must use the 'standard' 216 colours. If an image uses some other colour, Netscape will produce the nearest equivalent by 'dithering' colours from the standard palette. To avoid this, it is useful for the designer to be aware of the 216 standard colours and, wherever possible, to use these for simple images.

Using the hexadecimal rrggbb notation for possible colours, the 216–colour palette only allows each colour to have one of the following hexadecimal values: 00, 33, 66, 99, cc, and ff. Thus a colour denoted by 33cc99 is displayable using the palette, but 30cd98 is not.

It should be noted that although the 216–colour palette works fine on the PC and Mac users of Netscape, it is not guaranteed to give good results for Unix users. This is because, on Unix, Netscape constructs a palette, based on the number of colours available when it is launched (which may be less than 216).

When using a graphics package such as Adobe Photoshop, it is useful to set up a suitable 216 colour palette.

5.11.3   Anti-aliased images

When using graphics packages such as Adobe Photoshop, it is common practice to anti-alias objects against a plain background. This removes the staircase appearance of diagonal lines by blending the edges slightly with the background colour. A common fault arises when authors turn such images into transparent GIFs and they end up being displayed (by accident or design) on a background of different colour. For example, an object anti-aliased against white and then displayed in a grey browser window appears to have a dusting of snow around its edges.

5.11.4   Gamma mismatches

When dealing with a graphics display system, it is usually understood that when the input levels are zero (e.g. rrggbb values are zero), the output is also zero (i.e. black). Also, when the input is at its maximum (e.g. rrggbb = ffffff) the output is white. However, in between these extreme cases, there is generally some non-linear relationship between the levels that are put into the system and those that are seen on the screen. The 'gamma' of a device is a way of characterising that non-linearity between input and output. The formula is:

$$\text{output} = \text{input}^{\text{gamma}}$$

i.e. the output is equal to the input raised to the power gamma. Here, the range of values for both input and output are chosen to be in the range 0 (black) to 1 (white). If the display system was perfectly linear, the value of gamma would be 1.0 – however, display systems are not perfectly linear. A 'raw' monitor has a gamma of about 2.5. Apple Macintoshes use a gamma correction in the computer which corrects it to about 1.25; most PCs, on the other hand, do not employ gamma correction and the effective gamma of the display system is thus around 2.5. Variations in gamma explain why images drawn on one computer may look quite different on another. For example, images that look good on a Mac may appear dark and dingy on a PC. Most good graphics editing packages allow the gamma value to be altered.

5.12 SUMMARY

This chapter is a collection of practical hints, tips and advice in each of the main development areas, from requirements through structure design to product maintenance. It is very much a catalogue of the things that we have found useful in developing an information product; some are there as part of the DIVA approach and some are learned from experience.

This chapter also looks at some of the technical options and preferred solutions for dealing with images, links, colours etc. Again, this is much more personal experience than formal theory, but we've tried to include only the bits that stack up with other people's judgement and intuition.

A little attention to the guidelines provided here can save you from many of the problems that we have encountered.

FURTHER READING

Heid J.   Optimizing web and CD-ROM graphics, *MacWORLD*, May, 129–131 (1996).
[NTN10117] Netscape Technical Note 10117. *Netscape Navigator's Color Palette on Windows. The 216–color Windows palette explained.* Netscape Communications (1995).
[RGB]   http://www.phoenix.net/~jacobson/rgb.html
[WWWS]   Levine R. *Guide to Web Style*, Sun Microsystems.

6
Case Study: the Software Engineer's Library

Scraps of Navigation – that's' my education

Ewan McColl

The ideas of Media Engineering and the DIVA method that supports it were built up over a long period. One of the first real tests of the ideas, principles and techniques that we have grouped together in this book was the development of an Intranet based reference manual. This chapter describes this application of the DIVA method, one that was undertaken by the authors and was managed through to a successful conclusion in less than three months.

Over a number of years, a great deal of manuals, guidelines, 'state of the art reports' and similar documentation has been produced with the aim of promulgating consistent approaches and best practice within BT's software engineering community of about 4000 software professionals. The initial brief for this job was to take the core of this information and turn it into an on-line software engineer's library. The resultant product was for internal consumption within the company rather than being accessible, for example, over the global Internet. Hence both the customer (in the sense of the person who funded the work) and the end users were a relatively known community. One added complication that was thrown in at the outset was that the structure should also be suitable for a variant to be produced as an external product.

Some of the particular challenges that faced us with this task were:

- The source information was in a multitude of different formats (at least four different word processors and three different graphics formats).

- The source information was structured as documents rather than as hypertext. Some of the documents extended to hundreds of pages and could not be converted directly to hypertext 'pages'.

- The resource available for the task was very limited: indeed this was largely done as a 'spare time' activity by the two present authors, aided by a willing vacation student.

Early on in the task, we set ourselves some basic principles and ground rules which we endeavoured to follow throughout the job. These were:

- We would apply the Diva method as rigidly a possible.

- We would use 'tours' as the principal way of structuring the material for the user.

- We would document everything meticulously. This is an inherent part of the method but was seen as particularly important for this job because of its part-time nature and the need to be able to pick up where we left off at any time.

Our key success criterion from day one was to have a sufficiently attractive and useful product to engage a champion for its exploitation within our own organisation. A secondary (but still very important) measure was whether we could find an external agent to take ownership of a variant of the product.

What follows is a step by step account of how we moved towards these objectives. In line with previous chapters, we went through a standard series of process steps in developing the Software Engineers Library – here is the story of each of them.

6.1   CONCEPTUALIZATION

The basic mission and scope were largely defined by the pre-existing source material and hence were easy to document and agree with the internal customer. This also gave basic shape to the external product. For both the internal and external products, there was a clear idea of the effect we wished to have on the user (e.g. a source of respected, reliable information ordered to assist the busy practitioner).

In terms of customer requirements, the technique of use cases was employed to identify at least a testable subset of the functions that the system must perform. These were documented prior to any development and, to a large extent, dictated the tour structure adopted.

Table 6.1

Every page must have a link back to the home page	Mandatory
A glossary of terms should be kept on screen at all times	Desirable
Three clicks to the information	Desirable
etc.	

At the same time that the use cases were written down, a set of key operational requirements was derived (Table 6.1).

In scoping the system we identified over 50 technical topics that would need to be covered: object-orientation, software procurement, project management, testing, and so on. To further clarify the scope, we indicated where the source material for each of these topics would be obtained. In truth, we would have preferred fewer topics but the user steer was for broad coverage.

The delivery choices were less straightforward. First, it was decided to deliver through a WWW route but also to retain the option of publishing on CD-ROM. However, we decided to focus the design decisions on the WWW option and accept that some re-engineering would be necessary for the CD version. At the time of planning, BT was overwhelmingly using Netscape 1.2 for its browser technology but the selection of a corporate browser was the subject of an open tender that was about to be let to the industry. Hence, we not only could not predict the exact technical capabilities of the browser but we also could not even predict which supplier's browser would be in use.

We were very keen to try out our ideas of separating content and structure through techniques such as context-sensitive navigation and we made the decision to assume that by the time our development was complete, the 'standard' BT browser would be able to cope with frames and scripting (or some equivalent functionality). This decision was fortunately borne out in practice. The problems we faced here were rather less than those for which the target audience is unknown: at least we had a pretty clear idea of which browers were being used at the time and the fact that they would all have a common upgrade path, even if the details of the new browser were unknown.

Our browser assumptions were, in summary, as shown in Table 6.2. At this stage, we made an estimate of the size and complexity of the task and concluded that the final system would comprise the items shown in Table 6.3.

Plugging these numbers into the estimation formula in Chapter 4, we arrive at a figure of about 220 work days. Here we reached the first discrepancy between our intuitive guesses of what could be accomplished and the reality of our existing experience that we had formalized in the

Table 6.2

Browser support	MSW
HTML V2.0	Must
Tables	Must
CGI forms	Must
Server-side image maps	Must
Client-side image maps	Should
Quicktime movies	Should
Frames	Must
Java Scripting	Must
Sound	Wont
Proprietary formats	Wont

Table 6.3

HTML files	300
Figures	100
Sound	0
Video	0
Imagemaps	2
Links	3000
Custom icons	10
Custom pictures	2
Banners	5

DIVA method: the task that we had optimistically expected to complete in a couple of months in our 'spare time' now looked as though it was going to take about two years even if we could each devote a whole day a week to it!

At this point, we brought in some extra effort, in the form of our vacation student, to help with the mountains of work that faced us.

6.1.1 Decisions on tools and methods

As already noted, we had decided to adopt a 'pure' DIVA method wherever possible. However, DIVA is not prescriptive about tools and, at this point we made a selection of tools for each of the key areas:

- authoring and editing;

- post-edit link insertion;

- post processing (include files);

- testing;

- configuration management;

- graphics editing, conversion and resizing;

- server scripting;

- file transfers to server;

- browser choice for testing;

- server logging and analysis tool;

- search engine.

We chose a reasonable set, given what was available in a limited time, plus our knowledge of the (internal) user base.

6.2 ANALYSIS

6.2.1 Development of 'use cases'

Use cases were developed for a number of scenarios:

- the user performing a keyword search;

- a user requiring an across-the board introduction to software engineering;

- a user requiring best practice knowledge on one of a number of technical areas;

- and so on – about 20 distinct cases in all.

Once documented, the use cases were put away and not altered. They were pulled out for reference at regular intervals through development.

6.2.2 Storyboard

In conjunction with some enthusiastic users, we quickly covered most of the available wallspace around us with sample graphics, screen layouts and ways of structuring the information. Some of this was rejected (by popular demand) some was generally liked and found its way into subsequent design.

Although scrappy in presentation and variable in format, this was a vital part of getting our ideas straight. It was also useful in managing the expectations of our initial users.

6.2.3 Prototype the top-level screens

Some key features were prototyped to test out the principles and gain customer approval. These included:

- some custom-produced graphics which could be adapted to various purposes;

- the use of frames to implement guided tours;

- the on-screen glossary facility.

The prototypes were installed on a notebook PC and shown to the customers and a number of potential users. We found a customer who, on seeing the prototypes, was willing to champion the product and commit to deploy early versions for test.

The early feedback gained both from the customer and from potential users from this exercise proved invaluable in clarifying the requirements and shaping the design.

6.2.4 Top-level logical design of the system

We envisaged this library as adopting an 'encyclopaedia' style with the bulk of the material taking the form of 'articles' relating to each of the main topics included. As noted earlier, there were over 50 of these technical topics and it seemed natural to base our top level design around them. For ease of reference, we adopted a naming convention that used an alphabetical identifier for each technical topic area. For example:

A	Requirements capture for software projects
B	Software design
C	Software implementation
.	
.	
.	
Z	Software contracts and procurement
AA	Object oriented design
AB	
.	
.	
.	
AZ	Software documentation

There was considerable diversity between these topics. Some were fairly simple with just a few documents. Other proved to be complex products in their own right with much sub-structure.

Our top level design is illustrated in Figure 6.1.

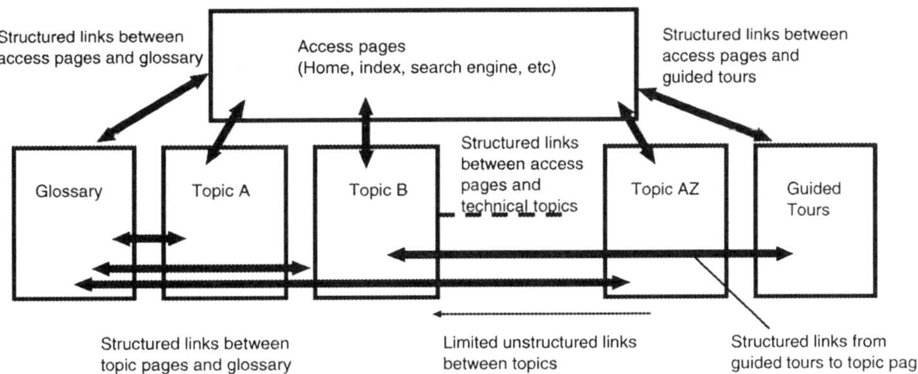

Figure 6.1
Top level design

At this stage, the system was envisaged as consisting of a small set of 'access' pages with links into the 50 technical topics. In addition, there is a glossary which is intended to be an integral part of the system rather than purely an unstructured reference. Also there is a set of guided tours which are implemented through structured links. These are based strongly on the principle of polycontiguity – they provide the user with a variety of different paths through the same base of information. The guided tours are dealt with in detail later.

It was decided that the technical topics would be largely self-contained, with only limited unstructed links between them.

6.3   DESIGN

Having completed a rather informal top level of the design, the next step is to apply the notation described in Chapter 4 to document the system level hypertext links and then decompose the structure into finer levels of detail.

Following the stages described in Chapter 4, the product evolved as follows:

6.3.1   Decomposition of the logical design

We first designed the system-level links – i.e. those that are common to all

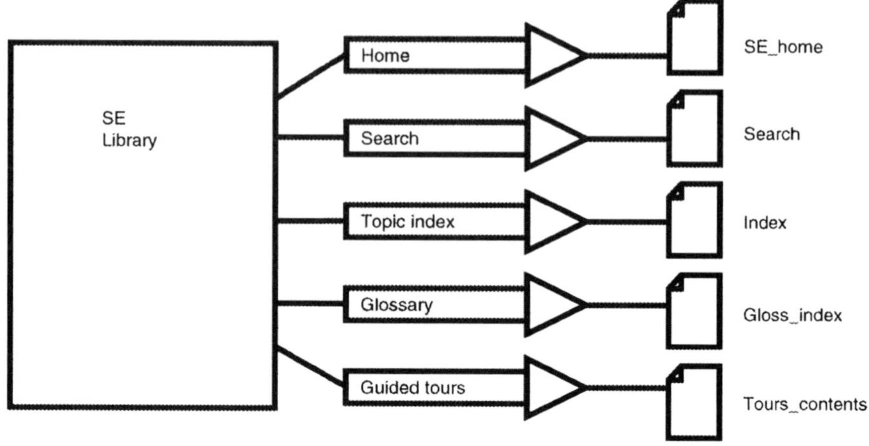

Figure 6.2
System-level links

pages of the system, using the notation described in Chapter 4. This is
shown in Figure 6.2.

This design records the fact that every page of the system will have a
link to the home page, search page, topic index, glossary and guided tours.
At this stage, that decision suggested that these might form a common
button bar – something we were rather pleased about as it fitted with our
intuitive feel.

We now started to decompose the system into its main functional units
before going on to design each one in detail. Our top-level design has
already shown that the system will consist of an 'Access pages' component, together with components for each of the technical topics. The
access pages consist of Home, Search, Index, Glossary and Tours pages.
The design for these is recorded as in Figure 6.3.

The Home page actually has no links from it other than the generic
links that are common to all pages.

The Search page links to a CGI search engine. The main topic index
links to each of the 50 or so topic introductions. The guided tours are left
until later as they will be picking up pages from other areas.

For each of the technical topics shown in the top level design, we chose
to break out into a common format comprising the following main
sections:

1. overview
2. definition

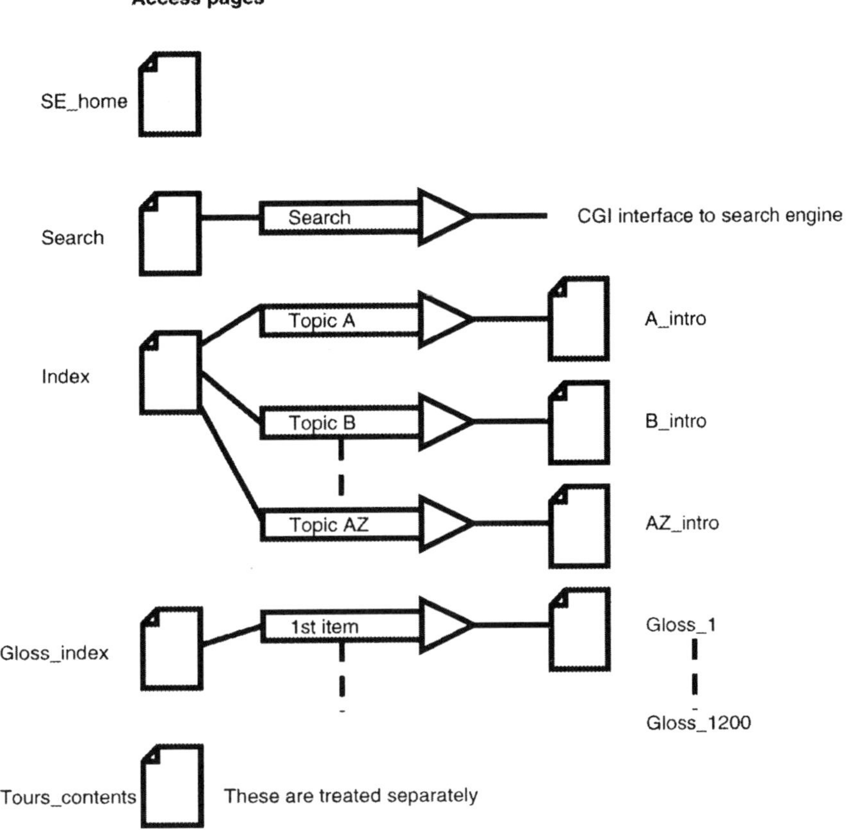

Figure 6.3
Link design for the access pages

3. key features
4. best practice
5. checklists.

Again, this fitted well with the use cases and, from inspection of the available material, seemed reasonably achievable. The chosen section structure is illustrated in Figure 6.4.

For each topic, the link design is as shown in Figure 6.5, i.e. each page within a topic will have a link back to the topic overview.

If we decompose a typical topic, we have the design shown in Figure 6.6.

Thus, each topic consists of a topic introduction which is structured into the following sections:

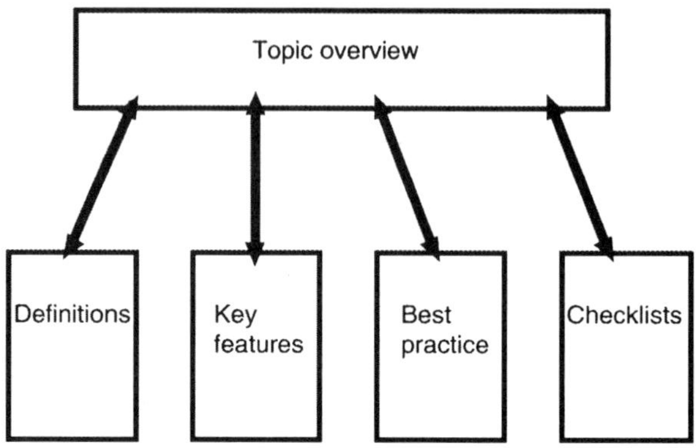

Figure 6.4
Decomposition of topics

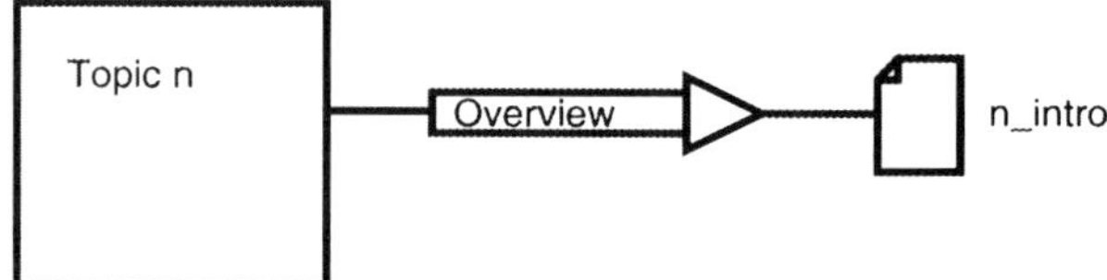

Figure 6.5
Link design for a typical topic

- definitions

- key features

- best practice

- checklists.

Each of these sections has a pointer to a page that contains more detail on the definitions. For instance, the key features under the maintenance topic simply explains the various issues and activities in software maintenance. A deeper level gives detail of how these issues are dealt with and what the steps are in the various activities.

Although this was the 'generic' design for a topic, in practice, some variants were designed to account for topics that include obvious sub-topics; those with large 'key features' sections that had to be split up; those with multiple checklists, etc.

The guided tours were designed separately. They were constructed from a few specially designed pages (generally the first and last page of the tour) with the remainder of pages being drawn from the main body of

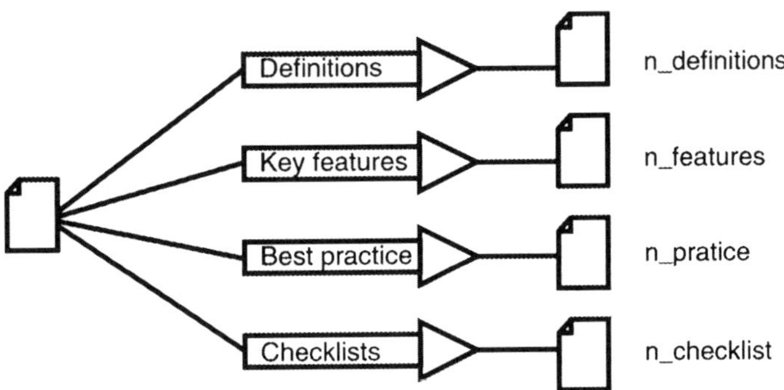

Figure 6.6
Decomposition for a typical topic

pages. A tour is implemented by designing a contents page which includes a structured link to each of the pages of the tour (Figure 6.7).

Here, the page with the logical name 'Tour__1__intro' is a page that is the specific introduction to this tour. Likewise, 'Tour__1__end' is a customized end page. However, the pages A__overview and C__overview (and a whole series of other overviews in the real system) are drawn from the overviews of existing topics.

6.3.2   Complete the physical design

The above piece of design not only gave us a structure for working on the material but also suggested the physical structure of files and directories. This is illustrated in Figure 6.8: a separate directory is defined for each of the major topics; these are grouped, for convenience into six higher-level directories (labelled SE1 to SE6).

6.3.3   Document the mapping between the logical and physical designs

As part of configuration management strategy, we wanted to make sure that the pedigree of all of our source material was known. The catalogue in Table 6.4 formed part of the inventory. This was the record of where text, pictures, build instructions etc. could be located. Version numbers were kept, where appropriate (although at a lower level than shown here).

These records formed the basis for our compatibility and baseline records.

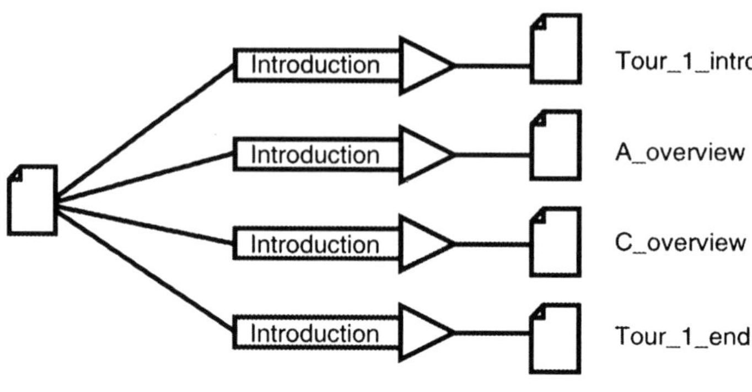

Figure 6.7
Example tour design

6.3.4 Undertake generic page designs

The logical system design already provided some constraints on the page design. For example:

- Every page is to have links to home, search, glossary, tours and index. This is embodied in the final design shown in Figure 6.2.

- Every lower level page in a topic is to have a link to its overview and should follow a standard layout that help the user to know where they are and where they can go – see Figure 6.5.

This led to some early design decisions about the page layout:

- The 'standard' links were provided through a common graphical toolbar that was repeated on every page. As well as being a consistent navigation feature, this bar provided a consistent graphic theme throughout the system.

- The desire to provide a 'structured' link to the glossary proved problematical: it is quite difficult to retain any sort of context for the user whilst diving down into detailed definitions of terms. A dual solution was finally arrived at: in the detailed technical areas, the idea of a structured link to the glossary was abandoned; but in the more 'tutorial' areas, the structure was maintained by placing the glossary in a separate frame.

- Also at this point we designed the page layouts for the guided tour pages which were a particular feature.

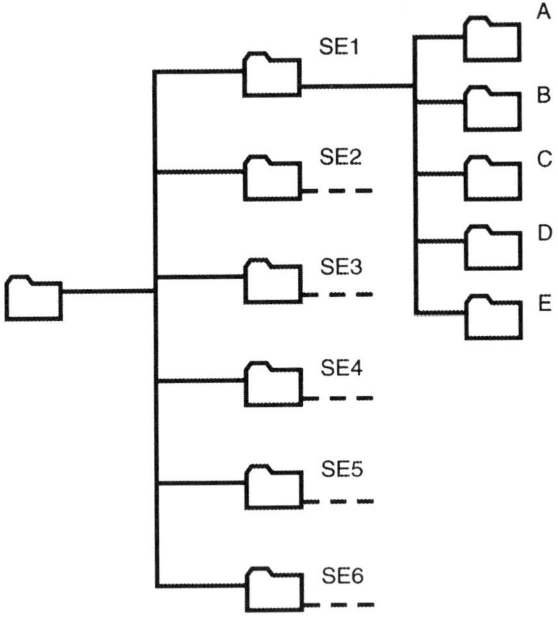

Figure 6.8
Physical design

Table 6.4

Logical page name	Directory Path	File Name	Notes
SE_home	/	index.html	
	/	title.gif	Title for home page
	/	home.gif	Home button
	/	search.gif	Search button
	/	index.gif	Index button
	/	gloss.gif	Glossary button
	/	tours.gif	Tours button
Search	/	search.html	Search screen

6.3.5 Content research and cataloguing

Although not a formal part of the process as we have described it, in practice, this project required the collection of the source material prior to conversion to hypertext. In order to keep track of this task, a substantial catalogue was built up for each of the topic areas, identifying the exact set of sources for the material. This consisted of a spreadsheet that included, for each topic area:

- the topic area;

- the file location where it would be stored when implemented;

- the source of the information (book or manual title, page number, etc.);

- a brief description of the key points of the subject to be covered;

- if the information was available in electronic form (some, particularly some figures, was not and had to be scanned or reconstructued);

- obvious cross links to other topics.

This was useful for the internal Web product, as source information was requested so that readers could assess the credibility and relevance of the advice they were looking at.

6.4 CONSTRUCTION

In its delivered version, the Software Engineer's Library consisted of over a thousand files, was built from over a hundred individual source documents and used over 6M of disk space. In this section, we look at the practicalities of handling this sort of volume.

6.4.1 Write or convert source material.

As already mentioned, virtually all the material already existed before we took on the task of hypertexting. Hence the main job was one of *fragmenting* the material into hypertext pages of a manageable size, and, simultaneously, *reorganizing* it into a common structure (based on the overview, definition, key features, best practice and checklists sequence noted above).

We used a variety of tools in order to assess their relative merits. A significant proportion of the documents were in Microsoft Word format and our preference, as already noted, was to fragment them as source documents and then to convert them to hypertext using an HTML filter. Translation was based on 'styles' and character formatting of the source document.

6.4.2 Build in links and anchors

Again we tried a number of techniques for creating links. As the design was already well documented at the time that the detailed editing of pages was commenced it was feasible to hard-code the links. Nevertheless, we also made use of symbolic linking which had proved effective in other projects.

6.4.3 Use post-processing if desired

The post-processing technique was used to add standard headers and footers to files, for example to add the standard menu bars and common meta-information.

6.4.4 Undertake the main configuration management tasks

We considered using a commercial configuration management tool but in the end relied largely on a procedural approach rather than a tool-based approach. The tools that looked good on the surface proved no substitute for a methodological approach.

Two separate environments were maintained: a development environment and a 'live' environment. The development environment was a well-equipped Apple Macintosh: the live environment, a Unix server. In order to avert file synchronization problems, our approach was to create a complete functional, tested system (i.e. the set of files and directories) in the Apple environment and then to transfer it as a whole to the Unix environment using an FTP-based file transfer utility which would transfer complete directory structures.

Every time significant changes had been made (and tested) in the development environment, the complete structure was uploaded afresh to the live environment (outside office hours). Each of these complete sets of files was treated as a new 'version of the entire system.

6.4.5 Test

The three levels of testing were employed: page testing, system testing and customer acceptance testing.

Tests included:

- Testing with Adobe SiteMill for HTML and link errors. Effective but not enough on its own.
- Testing using an in-house 'web crawler' tool called wwwics that follows all links and reports on the structure that it finds. Again, it helped but was only part of the story.

- Manual testing of pages for intuitively correct behaviour.

- Manual testing of the search engine using keywords that were known to be contained in certain pages.

- Manual testing of the feedback form to ensure that it worked correctly. Initially between ourselves, then across a wider base of 'tame' users and finally for real.

- Manual testing of guided tours – against the design and the use cases.

- Testing against key requirements – against use cases.

Where errors were found, these were logged, appropriate changes were made and re-testing was conducted.

The final stage of testing was customer acceptance testing (CAT testing). For this, the system was transferred to the live server but was protected from general use by a user-name/password protection system. For administrative simplicity, a single user-name and password were shared by all the members of a test panel (this scheme does not offer any auditable level of security: it simply deters the nosy!).

The panel of testers was chosen largely from potential users of the system who were asked to participate and were given a questionnaire (see appendix) together with a more free-form comment form. The CAT test was run for a week on the basis that the testers would undertake their tests in free time during that period: a commitment of about half an hour per tester was a guide to the effort required. This was very much in line with intended purpose for the product – something to which reference would be made frequently but for short periods.

One of the features of the CAT test was to ensure that at least one of the testers was using the worst possible network access that was likely to be encountered in practice. This is a good test for overuse of graphics! Also, there was sufficient variety of end-user equipment to check that they saw something that approximated to our intention.

6.5 MAINTENANCE

6.5.1 Post delivery changes

The configuration management techniques outlined in the previous section were continued into the maintenance phase of the project. Their real value came when changes were needed. Updates to the system are accomplished by a complete upload of a new set of files (even if only a few of them have been altered in practice). This is no great burden and is a safe way of keeping everything in step.

6.5.2   Logging of server usage

Server logs were analysed each month to obtain management information such as:

- number of page accesses in the month;
- number of users who accessed the system during the month;
- number of failures (errors such as 403 and 404 in the server logs);
- most used pages (those to consider promoting in the structure);
- least used pages (those to consider relegating in the structure);
- number of new users (who had not accessed the system in previous months);
- proportion of users who accessed the system on more than one day (repeat users).

The above figures rely on the ability to identify individual users. This was done purely on the basis of the client IP address – an approach that is not completely accurate because:

- People may use each others' machines.
- Hot desking and drop-in centres mean that some machines are used by many people.
- Some buildings use IPX/IP gateways in which a single IP address may be shared by a large number of users.
- Some machines are multi-user.
- Some users access the system via proxy servers.
- Some accesses may be by 'robot PCs' or search engines. We specifically tried to exclude these by filtering out known addresses of search engines from the log files.

In spite of these errors, the log analysis provided sufficient information for some valuable conclusions to be drawn and for useful modifications to be made to the early version.

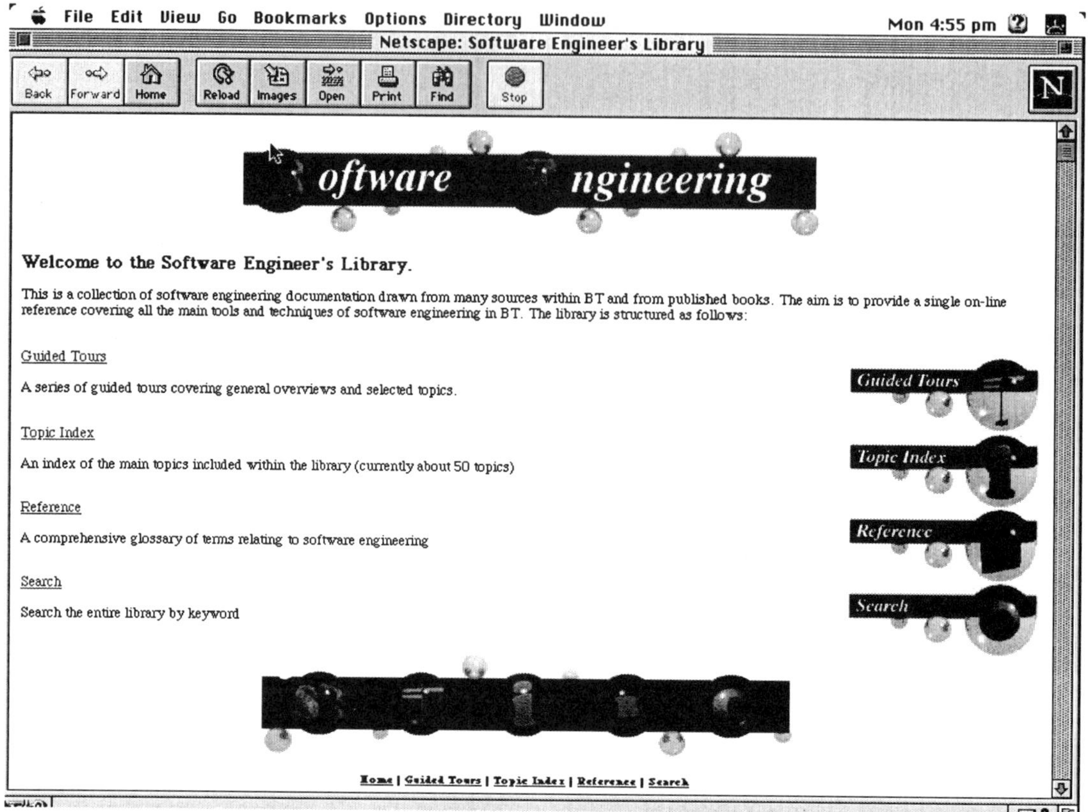

Figure 6.9
Software engineer's library home page

6.6 THE PROOF OF THE PUDDING

The Software Engineer's Library was completed successfully in September 1996. Figure 6.9 shows the home page.

One obvious feature is the toolbar which implements the structured links to home, tours, index, reference and search facilities. This toolbar is repeated on every page of the system.

Figure 6.10 shows a page from the guided tours.

This page includes three frames:

- The main right-hand frame displays the current information page – in this case the Software Design Overview.

- The top left frame holds the contents list for the tour. Clicking on each of these items in turn brings up the relevant page in the main right-hand

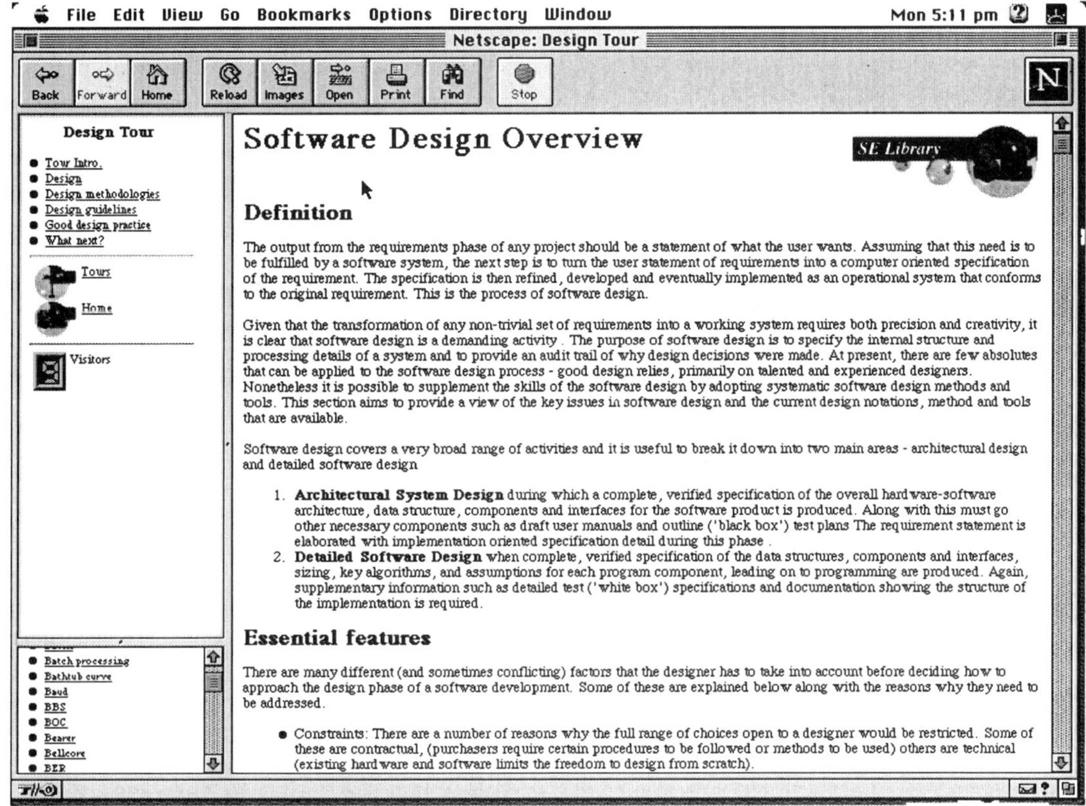

Figure 6.10
Guided tour for software design

frame. This frame also includes buttons for returning to the Tour Contents and Main Home Page.

- The bottom left frame contains the glossary of terms. This is kept on screen during the tour and allows the user to find and click on any uncertain terms.

A measure of the effectiveness of the design process for the library is that its ownership mirrors its inherent structure – nominees own the content in specific topics and manage the level of unstructured linking to other topics.

6.7 SUMMARY

The first version of the DIVA method was built from our intuition and experience of developing information products. It was subsequently modified in the light of application and this chapter has shown how it has been used to produce one particular product – the Software Engineer's Library.

Our conclusion from experience of using the DIVA method has been that it provides a good framework within which to work and contributed to a successful result in a short timescale. Some of the key points made here are that:

- The emphasis on documenting the design and implementation at all stages is amply justified.

- The approach does nothing to stifle the creative side of page design.

- Once started, the method seems to work itself.

- Handover from implementation to maintenance can be painless.

- The process is not an unnecessary burden: on the contrary and contributes to an on-time delivery.

7
Needles and Haystacks

Where is the wisdom we have lost in knowledge?
Where is the knowledge lost in information?

T. S. Eliot (Choruses from The Rock)

In the first few chapters of this book, we built our basic ideas on media engineering by looking at what software engineers had done some thirty years before us. To close, we find that there is one further lesson to be learned from the world of software engineering. This is that the most effective tools in building effective systems are not always the well-founded methods, tools, techniques and theories that support the discipline.

It is often the rules of thumb, borne of experience, that set an endeavour in the right direction. In the authors' experience, the software engineering fraternity rarely apply all of the rigorous analytical methods available. That is not to say that projects proceed in a completely haphazard way: in practice it is the experience of key designers and project managers that guide development. And they apply intuition to balance the need to deliver more, faster with sound engineering principles. Hence the proliferation of books labelled as 'idiots guide', 'cook book' and the like which often outsell more formal texts.

In this spirit, we start this chapter with our ten golden rules for media engineering. These are the simple truths that persist, the basic touchstone to be borne in mind for any project.

7.1   TEN GOLDEN RULES

It was George Bernard Shaw who said that the golden rule is that there are no golden rules. We have found that media engineering does not fit this pattern. There are specific issues that should be attended to. This list reflects both the authors' intuition and the principles embedded in DIVA.

7.1.1   Ultimate purpose

What is it that you hope to gain through designing this information product? Is it a piece of long-term infrastructure (e.g. an on-line reference manual), a shorter-term utility (e.g. advertising or awareness information) or is it a temporary thrill (e.g. some glossy graphics to show what can be done)? Whatever the reason, the purpose should drive the process!

The rationale for the information product impacts on the technical options chosen and the overall approach taken. Information may be infinitely malleable and intangible, but it can be costly or time consuming not to consider the success criteria early on. And it is not so much the costs of over-engineering that matter here, but those of under-engineering. An information product that is not fit for purpose, like any defective product, is a liability that can cost out of all proportion to its original value. The key points are:

- *Define success.*   This can be number of hits per day for an advert, number of repeat visits, number of leads, orders etc from your page, design awards, level of user admiration, a perception of being one up on the competition, savings on paper, etc. And have some sort of measure – it doesn't have to be precise; an approximate answer to the right question is better than an exact answer to the wrong one.

- *Plan accordingly.*   If you just want to get there first – use anyone. If you are building an information product that will form an integral part of your business, a reliable and trusted supplier should be sought or you could set up a formally controlled in-house unit.

- *Budget accordingly.*   If it is a bit of publicity, then pay for it off the advertising budget. If the aim is to provide an on-line quality management system, then you pay as for any quality initiative. If it is a service or product for someone else, it should pay for itself or be part of the product line.

7.1.2 Who is in the audience?

The appeal of information, like beauty, is in the eye of the beholder. A structure that suits one person or set of people may not please another. It is easy to assume that an audience is thinking along the same lines as yourself and end up confusing the user. On the other hand, it can be unnecessarily tedious to spell out every last detail and assumption.

In truth, you are unlikely to know exactly who your audience consists of – anyone can go and buy a compact disk or view some Web pages.

What can be done is to assume the typical user and build for them – if nothing else, the rationale for the product should give some clue as to the profile of a typical user. This is where use cases then come into their own. As well as giving some touchstone for content, they also help to guide the type of language that should be used, the sorts of images that are most appropriate and the way in which the finished article is likely to be used.

7.1.3 How will you know when you're done?

Or to put it another way, how do you judge when the product is good enough

This is always going to be something of a value judgement but there are a number of essential features. For one thing, it should contain and make accessible all of the intended content. It is always worth checking the final article against the initial bill of goods that it was intended to include. Even if the two do not match, there should be some record that omissions/inclusions were intentional. One of the features of the notation developed in Chapter 4 is that it gives a basis for testing the information product against its specification.

You're never really done. The World Wide Web, in particular, is a living beast and that is why some of these guidelines are here – to help the warm satisfaction of the first release percolate through to subsequent updates.

Change should be planned from day one. Additions should be prioritized and put in as planned upgrades, rather than being added piecemeal. Also, it can be a good idea to use a first release to establish acceptance – user feedback on what they want can be easy to collect and invaluable to have. So make feedback easy (e.g. with counters and forms for Web pages). Find out what they really like, and what is wrong, missing or simply annoying.

7.1.4 Keep the content and the structure separate

As a general rule, you should design the structure of the product first and then drop the information in. And then the thing to guard against is trying to cram more and more into an existing structure. You lose cogency very quickly as a mix of structured and unstructured links are added.

As maintenance and flexibility become more important, the need to design the structure separately from the content becomes more of an issue. This is one of the basic tenets of DIVA.

7.1.5 Three clicks to the information

The complexity of the structure should reflect purpose. The authors frequently hear that the golden rule is three clicks to the information. This only tells half of the story.

Some measure of hierarchy needs to be built in to any information product But if we are talking about one that has the sole purpose of selling goods, then the structure should be considerably flatter than that for a reference material.

A phrase oft used by software engineers about design options is horses for courses. So it is here – an update on applications technology may be best delivered by publishing a simple, logical, flat structure that is well indexed. On the other hand, product design standards may require a much deeper and more complex hierarchy.

Rather than 'three clicks to the information', the rule should be 'no more than three clicks to the information'. And in some cases, one click should get you there.

7.1.6 Media Engineering is different

It has a lot in common with the design of Web pages, the production of documents, but requires a balance of literary and technical techniques. The information should not be treated or presented as it is on paper, the technology should not be exercised unless in pursuance of a goal determined by the information product.

This having been said, you should aim to take as much care and time over writing on-line documentation as you would over writing a conventional document. You still need to think about all the same things: document structure, use of headings and sub-headings, contents, perhaps an index if it's a large document, use of spell-check and grammar-check facilities, plan of layout and consideration of the appropriateness of illustrations or photographs.

Furthermore, you should be subject to some form of quality assurance process – a formal review if the page is part of a prominent service, or an informal one if it is for local use. At the very least, you should try it out on a panel of 'tame' users before launching it to a wider audience.

You lose the immediacy, portability of paper, so need to make up for this with the interactivity and malleability of on-line. Also, you need to establish a 'brand' through the style, look and feel of your information product.

7.1.7 Make navigation and orientation easy

One of the merits of a conventional library is that you have a rich source of contextual clues when looking for a particular item. For instance, you may well recall that the book you seek is green, is situated on a high shelf, is near to the fire exit, is crammed between two big dictionaries.

These contextual clues need to be recreated if users are to find their way around. You have to be able to establish some sort of map to make best use of a complex information set. If there are no physical features, then there have to be memorable icons and consistent signposts.

Well-thought-out structure and navigation will allow the user to get information quickly, by minimising the number of user actions and using simple navigation.

Make the structure obvious – embed the map, don't ask the users to create their own. Consistent navigation and location icons let users know where they are and where they can get to. In terms of complexity, getting around an information product is much like exploring a large, unfamiliar building. It helps a lot if each floor or area is colour coded, if rooms are numbered and if signs are visible. So it should be for a complex piece of on-line real estate. Each page should carry its own identifiers, signposts and escape routes.

7.1.8 Build it for the users environment

It is very easy to get carried away with the sheer variety of icons, colours, textured backgrounds, etc. that are there and ready for use. What looks like a masterpiece on your screen may not cut the mustard, though. For a start, others may not see it as you do (different browsers will reproduce colours and layouts differently; sometimes not at all how they were intended). Furthermore, some people may take so long to gain access (usually traceable to too many pictures) that they give up. Do bear in mind that a considerable proportion of users are colourblind. Also that some may not have the applications to interpret the file formats you have used.

Always design for use as well as for the eye – 'form follows function!'

7.1.9   Record the design and configuration

There is little doubt that you will want to update it, check that it is consistent etc., even if you didn't plan to. The reason that configuration management has been stressed throughout is that it always came back to bite in software engineering and is likely to do the same to the media engineer. Forewarned is forearmed.

7.1.10   Automate

You cannot keep the details of a product of any complexity in your head. When hundreds or thousands of links need to be maintained, acres of source files kept in step, and reams of build information kept, you need some level of automation.

Much of DIVA was motivated by a need to get a firm grip on these issues. In a sense, the above are the requirements for our method. And the guidelines contained in Chapter 5 are the supplementary notes for applying the method.

The authors are convinced that DIVA goes a long way in supporting the systematic development of information products. We are equally convinced that there is more ahead of us in media engineering than there is behind us. We close the book with a glimpse of what might lie ahead.

7.2   WHITHER INFORMATION

The evolution of information over the last twenty years is well illustrated by what has happened on the Internet.

In the early days, there was the 'Steam Internet'. This allowed one computer user to connect to a variety of remote computers and use their facilities. We could characterize this era as one where specialists used Telnet to log on to a networked system.

As the Internet became more sophisticated, people started to use software utilities such as Gopher to access the file index of a remote computer. We could say that we have moved into a second era, where the user connects to files.

The third era of information networking is familiar to many people –

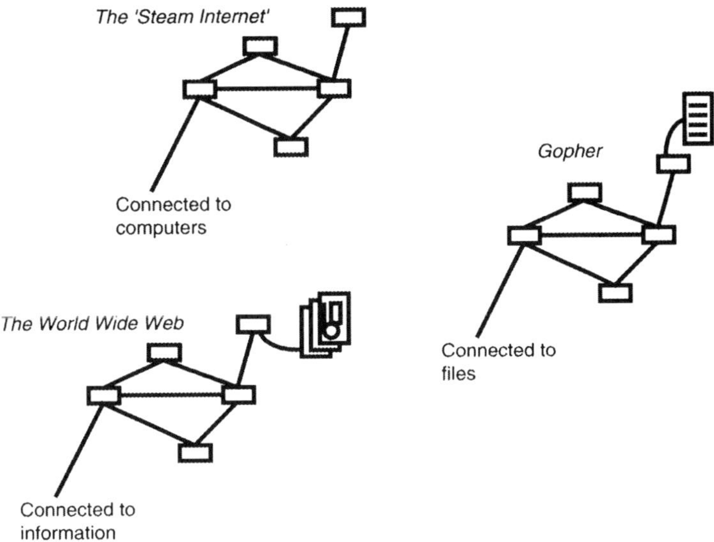

Figure 7.1
Three eras of information networks

direct connection to remote information, most notably to pages on the World Wide Web. By now, the specialism of the user has been diluted to the extent that no knowledge of the details of the underlying computer network are necessary – the user connects to information.

The three era are illustrated in Figure 7.1.

The transition between the three eras has been rapid – at least in terms of social evolution. So, connecting to information is very much a new phenomenon, one that has yet to fully develop. It seems likely, therefore, that media engineering will also have to develop as this era settles down (and as new technology emerges). It should be clear, though, that (networked) hypermedia is here to stay.

At the start of this book, we argued that media are defined more by their limitations than by their capabilities.

At different periods of man's history there have been a range of factors which limited the communication of information. Before the invention of the printing press, information was limited by the rate of output of the small number of skilled scribes: the cost of a single book was so great that very few could have access to them. Even in the case of printed media, a major limitation was until recently the sheer cost of the materials: indeed Penguin Books invented the paperback medium largely to bring books within the reach of working class people. Throughout history, of course, the other limitation has been the lack of universal literacy: the skills to read the information contained in books.

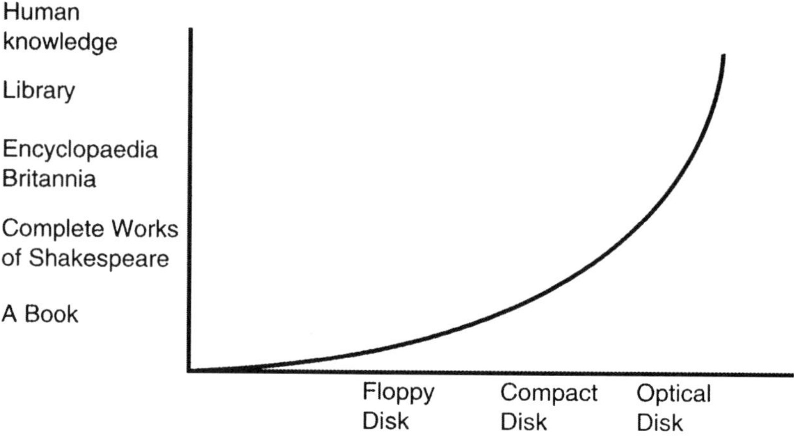

Figure 7.2
The ever-growing capacity of technolgy

With the advent of modern electronic media, the cost of the medium is no longer the limitation. A compact disk (CD), for example, costs about 30p to manufacture and holds some 650 million characters; likewise, access to the Internet is free or at very low cost from many parts of the world. Admittedly, the equipment needed to extract the information from either CDs or the Internet (i.e. a PC) is beyond the means of all but the wealthiest classes on Earth, but certainly the trends in computing costs have continued to fall exponentially and these electronic media are ever coming within reach of more and more people. It seems that it will not be long before all human knowledge can be consigned to a piece of plastic the size of a credit card. The progress in this direction is illustrated below.

So what is the current limitation on information access? Increasingly, it is the ability to search and 'navigate' the material and, ironically, all the other trends (those that make it easier to publish information as well as those that make it cheaper to store and distribute information) conspire to increase the complexity of the information and make it ever more difficult for the end user to navigate the 'information space'. CD technology allows us to put the contents of 1000 books in an object the size of a beermat: it does nothing to assist in finding the required 'needle' in this highly compressed 'haystack'. The next generation of CDs will allow us to put 15 000 books (more than the average person reads in a lifetime) on a similar beermat. The situation with the Internet is the same: the World Wide Web offers the end user at least 50 000 000 pages of information and almost no structure.

Webwatcher Gordon Bell's verdict is nicely summed up thus -

> I claim that we are all cats. Why? Well cats chase mice. And what is our life
> about? It's mousing up and around these trees and then going up the trees
> and then down the trees by clicking on the browser's Back button. That's
> how we're spending our time.

It seems that our exploitation of this medium will be limited by how well
the information it carries is engineered. With such quantities available, a
free format WWW would rapidly become a World Wide Waste of time.

7.3 WHEREVER NEXT?

Many of the messages in this book are fairly obvious. Most people who
have worked on a software project will be able to relate to the ideas and
techniques. Hopefully, they would testify to their effectiveness. Yet the
idea of media engineering has received scant attention to date. Before
closing, we speculate why this might be and what the future holds.

First, why so little attention to media engineering? The answer
probably lies in the diversity of its roots, from computer science, to
graphic design, to telecommunications. These hitherto disparate areas are
converging on a new market – the information market. Each is sure that
they have a role to play in the provision of reams of high-quality
information to the masses. But there is little agreement on exactly what
the respective roles are! Do the Disneys, Warner Brothers and News
Internationals of this world adopt new technologies and build their own
distribution networks? Or do the likes of AT&T, NTT, BT and France
Telecom start to provide information services over their existing infrastructure. In practice, both are happening and the convergence of the
computing, telecommunications, electronics and entertainment providers
is more of a collision.

It should come as no surprise, therefore, that the principles and
procedures for building information products are immature. By way of
illustration, the vast majority of content posted to the World Wide Web as
of early 1997 was hand crafted using basic editors to create the HTML.

The dazzling expansion of on-line and multimedia offerings seems
likely to push the pace of evolution. It took many years and several high
profile project disasters to advance the state of software engineering.
Consumer pressure (and the growing realisation that there is money to be
made in delivering quality information products) could see media
engineering well established in just a few years.

Prediction is futile, but it does give our descendants something to laugh
about, so here goes.

As presented in Chapter 2, a reasonable way to gauge advances in an
engineering discipline (which is what you need to cope with anything that

demands reproducible quality) is in terms of the tools and theory that help the practitioner to do their job.

Just now, we have virtually no theory – there are a few languages (HTML, SGML) along with some utilities to get the products onto a network (Perl, CGI). The design method and guidelines contained in these pages is about all that you get in terms of how to apply the base tools.

The picture on the tool front appears to be a little rosier (but close examination soon dampens any enthusiasm). There are a variety of tools for content development, analysis and site management (see Appendix 2 for a brief overview). These allow the designer, developer or manager to create multimedia pages, check that they appear as and when they should and keep a collection of pages in step with its surroundings.

In practice, there is little integration between the various tools. In any case, few of them allow an information product to be created, managed and maintained as described here. Doubtless, the various providers will get together to provide tool suites, just as software providers did in the 1980s. A caveat here would be that the all-singing, all-dancing Integrated Project Support Environments (IPSEs) that promised to regularize all software development failed to deliver.

Alternatively, the development of Media Engineering might take a different turn if some of the software engineering tools vendors adapt their products to the media problems. We may find that CASE tools provide an ideal design and development environment and that conventional relational databases displace HTML storage.

There are, doubtless, some barriers to the development of effective tools. The two major ones so far can be summed up as 'power to the people' and 'my browser is better than yours'. The former stems from the global cottage industry (discussed earlier) and the author = publisher equation. The down side of this democracy and devolution is that practitioners require a low cost of entry to the market and are disinclined to accept any sort of discipline that might exclude them. The second point is the product of the browser wars in which each vendor continues to try and leapfrog its rivals by adding new features and extending the hypertext language. The net result is a continuing growth of features but a very unstable base technology on which to base tools and techniques.

Perhaps more significant than tools, though, will be the development of a soundly based development method for information products. The pragmatic notation, method and guidelines explained here have certainly worked for the authors. Hopefully they will add value elsewhere, but a more general approach, based on rigorous theory, may be required. Again, there is precedence in software engineering, where the formal design notations (e.g. Z, LOTOS) developed during the 1980s did not make a major impact. Just as the IPSE was found to be too constraining a

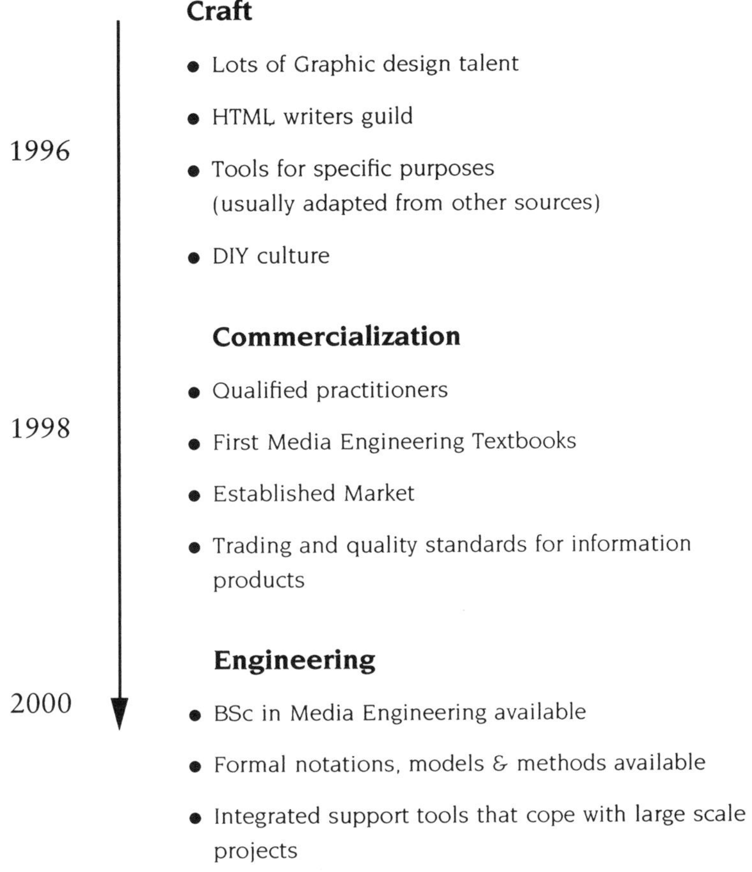

Figure 7.3
Progress towards an engineering discipline for information products

tool, so formal notations were generally taken as overly precise for the job in hand.

So, what of Media Engineering? There seems little doubt that it addresses an area where something needs to be done. And there is certainly something there at the moment. Perhaps an academic treatment will add weight to a sound set of principles. Hopefully, practitioners will extend the range of application of DIVA and widen the base of developers who share a common way of doing business. After all, information is easy – no problem. It is our ability to control it that needs to be enhanced.

Futile or not, our guess of the evolution of Media Engineering for the years ahead is shown in Figure 7.3.

We have already seen a bit of progress down this path – a Scandinavian degree course in media engineering that touches on some of the ideas we have covered. Hopefully, this is a portent of things to come.

7.4 SUMMARY

We would contend that the distinction between authors and publishers is blurring, indeed disappearing. In this book we have explored the consequences and implications of another major step along the path that began with the invention of the printing press.

In the very near future, information dissemination will be limited by the ability to navigate. So the information provider (and we believe that means just about everyone) will be limited by their ability to structure what they want to say: not by their access to technology nor by the value of their utterances.

The usability (and therefore attractiveness) of any publisher's offerings will be determined by the rigour with which they prepare their wares. A large part of our purpose in defining Media Engineering has been to outline how to go about building coherent information maps. With so much information on line and on disk, more and more understanding comes from tracing relationships between one idea and the next. Exploration is, and will increasingly be, the way that we assimilate the world around us.

Once upon a time the message was the message; then the medium was the message; now the map is the message!

Backword

> *This is not the end. It is not even the beginning of the end.*
> *But it is, perhaps the end of the beginning.*
>
> Winston Churchill

The authors hope that the above quote will come to be as relevant to Media Engineering as it was in its original context. In this book we have presented a systematic approach to the development of information products. This is based on established good practice and is supplemented with our own ideas and experience. At the outset, we did not seek to do any more than catalogue some hints, tips and guidelines. As it turned out, each part seemed to fit with each other and we 'discovered' media engineering. The question we are left with, having committed to print, is 'what next'?

One last lesson from software engineering that we might dwell on is that a few simple ideas can have far reaching effects. They have to be the right ideas, of course, and their development usually relies on the imagination and inspiration of many people. But once the first few steps are taken, some momentum is established and new insights begin to emerge.

So what are these insights likely to be? Since completing this text, we have tried to take our own medicine and observe how far it goes in curing all known ills. So far, the verdict is that we have something useful on the shelf and now have raised expectation. The prospect of information product interfaces (much like the software engineer's pet, the application programmer's interface) have been envisaged by some of our more imaginative colleagues. In effect, this takes our idea that information can be treated as a product on by one logical step.

Where do the other conceptual refinements and extensions lie? The most likely answer is *you*. Anyone who has read this far will have followed a simple idea through in some detail. They may dismiss it. On the other hand, they may see new possibilities. We hope it is the latter. And if it is, please let us know.

Steve West and Mark Norris can be contacted via the publishers.

Appendix 1
Checklists and Templates

What follows is a straightforward collection of the various aides-memoires and standard documents that we have used. They are not intended to be rigorous – simply to cover the key issues. Hopefully they will serve other media engineers as well as they have served us: it is surprising how often an oversight is picked up by using a standard checklist!

The organization of the appendix is in line with the sequence of activities for developing an information product. The few that we couldn't fit into this structure are included in the last two sections.

A1.1   REQUIREMENTS PHASE

A1.1.1 Checklist of items to be completed

At the end of this phase, you should have completed:

Mission statement	
Subject scope	
Target audience	
List of key requirements (desirable/mandatory)	
Table of delivery choices	
Estimate of size and complexity	
Project plan	
Tool section	

A1.1.2   Sample template for browser choices

Browser Support	Must/Should/Wont
HTML 2.0	
HTML 3.2	
Tables	
Internationalization	
Inserted objects	
Client-side image maps	
Forms-based file upload	
Style sheets	
Frames	
Floating frames	
Multi-column text	
Font sizes	
Background colour	
Background images	
Mail to URLs	
FTP URLs	
New URLs	
SSL security	
Java	
Java script	
In line JPEG images	
Animated GIFs	
PDF	

Shock wave	
Real audio	
Midi sound	
Quicktime	
VRML	
Server push	
Client pull	

A1.1.3 Planning checklist

Estimated number of pages	
Estimated number of pictures	
Estimated number of links	
Number of video items	
Number of sound items	
Number of image maps	
Is source material in 'raw' form?	

A1.1.4 Tools checklist

Authoring and editing	
Post-edit link insertion	
Post processing (include files)	
Testing	
Configuration management	
Graphics editing, conversion and resizing	
Server scripting	
File transfers to server	
Browser choice for testing	
Server logging and analysis tool	
Search engine	

A1.2   ANALYSIS PHASE

A1.2.1 Checklist of items to be completed

At the end of this phase, you should have completed:

Storyboard	
Use cases	
Prototype screens	
Top level design	

A1.2.2   Use case template

Use Case Number	
Use Case Title	
Preconditions	

User action	System response	Event response number

Alternative events

A1.3   DESIGN PHASE

A1.3.1 Checklist of items to be completed

At the end of this phase, you should have completed:

Complete logical design	
Name and document all structured links	
Name and document all pages	
Complete physical design	
Name and document all physical directories and files	
Document mapping logical to physical design	
Naming conventions for physical design	

A1.3.2   Template for logical/physical mapping

Logical page name	Directory path	File name	Version No.	Notes

A1.4   IMPLEMENTATION

A1.4.1 Checklist of items to be completed

At the end of this phase, you should have completed:

Obtained or written all source material	
Conversion to hypertext	
Build in links and anchors	
Document unstructured links	
Use post-processor	
Implement configuration management process	
Transfer to live environment	
Re-edit any absolute links that were specific to the development environment	
Page test (each page)	
System test	
CAT test	

A1.5   MAINTENANCE

Checklist of items to be completed

At the end of this phase, you should have completed:

Established responsibilities for live operation	
Established policy for monitoring remote links	
Established process for handling feedback	
Established logging and reporting process	

A1.6   GOOD PRACTICE CHECKLIST

Do you know what you want to say, and who do you want to say it to?	
Are you sure the audience find it of interest?	
Have you made your message tightly focused and captivating in its delivery?	
Do you know what effect you want your message to have and have you achieved it?	
Have you related your message to existing messages elsewhere in Cyberspace?	
Have you considered process and legal issues?	
Is the level of security or privacy clear?	

Is the source of information known?	
Is there a feedback address?	
Is it clear what the status of the information is?	
Is the information appropriate for your chosen medium?	
Is copyright covered?	
Are trademarks acknowledged?	
Are adequate warranties in place?	
Is page size appropriate?	
Are any pages too big?	
Is navigation intuitive?	
Is the structure explicit?	
Have you over-used gratuitous graphics?	
Does it make sense without the images?	
Are there text alternatives to image maps?	
Are images re-used?	
Is the first page inviting?	
Are all links valid?	
Will the user see what was intended?	
Is maintenance catered for?	
Are product delivery standards established?	
Is there a material check?	

A1.7 BAD PRACTICE CHECKLIST

It may seem a little trite to include this but we have found that you often find out what *will* do by discovering what *will not* do. The following is a list of things to avoid:

Page under construction	This is a sure sign that configuration management is out of control and offers no possible value to the reader.
Centred, blinking text	Although this is a matter of taste, people of good taste are unanimous about this one.
Using absolute sizes of table cells as a layout hack	Absolute sizes for table cells are dangerous because you don't know the size of the end user's screen. Using them to position items in particular places on the screen is doomed to failure.

Background images that are too narrow	Don't forget that some people have very wide screens. If you use background images that are too narrow, they are repeated horizontally as well as vertically. This looks particularly bad in cases such as those where the background image provides a stripe down the left of the screen. Instead, use extremely wide images.
ALT text with image height and width	If you specify height and width for your images, make sure that any 'ALT' text will fit the box size of the image. Particularly avoid the image being placed between tags that will affect the text size (e.g. including the image within <H1> tags.
Pictures that look terrible on 256 colour PCs	Choose your colours from the correct 216 colour default palette.
Pictures with the wrong 'Gamma'	Display devices of different machines have different 'gamma' values which measure the non-linearity of the display device. Generally, professional graphics workstations, including Apple Macs and Silicon Graphics workstations, have some form of gamma correction. Most PCs do not, and middle tones tend to look darker.
English spelling	In HTML <centre> does not work – the American spelling, <center> is required.
Frames that don't work properly	When designing systems that make extensive use of frames (and particularly when the frame behaviour is controlled by complex JavaScripts), it is very easy to produce a system that disappoints the user. Common problems arise from unexpected behaviour of different navigation options such as the 'Back' button and in-frame links. The solution is to test thoroughly and consider every possible user navigation action.

Appendix 2
Technology

If the map and the terrain disagree, believe the terrain.

Army Handbook

The focus of this book has been on how to design useful information products. Most of the effort in achieving this is goes in the systematic organization of the source materials, the user requirements and your own thoughts. But at some point, even the best laid plans have to meet the real world to be realized. So, some recognition needs to be made of the basic technologies that are available to host an information product.

There are currently two practical mechanisms for getting volumes of multimedia information into a computer: a high-capacity disk and a network connection to another computer. The former is to be found in the guise of the compact disk, the latter is exemplified by the Internet and its close relation, the World Wide Web. In this appendix, we explain a few of the basics for both technologies.

In addition to the delivery technology, we also need to explain a little about the production technology that is commonly used to build information products. The two aspects of this that we touch on here are the markup languages used to turn plain text into hypertext, and some the tools that help the developer to create, manage and maintain their product.

Space precludes anything like complete detail on any of these topics. In any case, they are all evolving at such a pace that you really have to be actively working with or using the technology to be *au fait* with all of the latest nuances. Fortunately, there are many excellent textbooks on some of the topics touched on here that provide more than enough solid grounding for the practitioner.

The last part of this appendix deals with some of the research ideas that look as though they might provide better, more powerful (or simply different) facilities for the media engineer to work with.

Given the association in many people's minds between on-line information and the Internet, we start by building up a description of the Internet that leads into some detail on the World Wide Web.

A2.1 THE INTERNET

The Internet is a communications network that spans the globe. It is essentially an interconnection of many local area and regional networks that works by passing data using a communications protocol know as Internet Protocol (IP). The IP protocol can be used on many types of computer and over almost any network infrastructure: local and wide area. The Internet has an associated naming and addressing scheme, Domain Name Service (DNS) whereby resources (information, services and people) on the Internet can be easily located. It is the universal acceptance and wide availability of IP, DNS and some other key standards that give the Internet its global reach, its broad availability and its vast user base.

One of the basic functions of the Internet is that it allows the transfer of information from one computer to another – and hence, from one person to another. This was initially effected thanks to a file transfer application (known as FTP) which was typically part of the TCP/IP package; many networked PCs have a pre-installed FTP client program. Simple FTP clients can connect FTP hosts, view directories of files (much like Mac Finder or Windows File Manager) and download them according to user choice.

Typically, FTP servers require a username and password before they will allow connection. There are some FTP servers that will allow anonymous login, these require the username anonymous and a password that is either your Internet Protocol (IP) address or your Internet email address.

In many ways, the World Wide Web (WWW or web) builds on the established file transfer capability of the Internet. Like FTP, web browsers (e.g. Netscape Navigator, Internet Explorer – software packages that give a user access to the system) use a simple file transfer protocol, known as HTTP, to connect to web hosts and can download information in any file format. The user is provided with a simple and intuitive interface for navigating information that is distributed throughout the Internet. Access to Web pages does not usually require you to enter a username or password (although some commercial sites do require registration and/or a fee).

What makes the Web so much better than its predecessors is that the information, its addressing and referencing all abide by a common encoding standard, HyperText Markup Language (HTML – see later for more on this).

What the Web browser does is to access and read files written in HTML. It is the HTML coding that defines the files' text layout and style when diplayed on the browser. The HTML standard is quite basic but has a feature that fits the problems of distributed information well – the Hypertext link (or anchor). The hypertext link is a simple definition within the language that can be used to highlight a word or phrase within the text of the file, this is known as the anchor. This definition associates an address (a logical location) and a file reference with that anchor so that when it is selected by the browser (a simple click of the mouse with the cursor or pointer over the anchor) an instruction is sent to the browser to fetch the file that is referenced. This is a bit of a long-winded explanation for a simple concept that works very intuitively in practice.

The power of hypertext used in this way has been demonstrated over the last few years by the phenomenal growth in the Web. The simple concept of linking one file to another through an explicit and contextual reference in the text means that many of the problems associated with redundant information and searching for a needle in a haystack can begin to be addressed. It also means that the Internet itself is no longer in the realm of the scientist or engineer. The Web has brought point-and-click usability to the Internet, just at a time when the growth in the home PC market has itself entered a period of vertical acceleration and the image of the PC in many a business is no longer the executive's toy but an indispensable tool for the job.

A2.2   THE WORLD WIDE WEB

To reiterate an important (but often misunderstood) point, the World Wide Web is a multi-media[1] hypertext information retrieval system that sits on top of the Internet. It draws on many of the Internet's concepts and combines them to provide the ultimate in point-and-click navigation systems – huge, ubiquitous, global and intuitive.

The Web is actually implemented as a client–server system. This means that software is distributed so that one end (the client) is usually the information consumer, the other end (the server) is the provider. A practical implication of client–server systems is that there are typically

---

[1] The information stored in web servers consists of text, images, sounds, and movies. A single web document may contain all of these.

many more client than servers. This imbalance is not a problem as the client to server interface is uniform, so there is a natural balance of performance and client to server ratios.

The realization of the client is the now ubiquitous Web browser. These are rich (and getting richer) in functionality and, as mentioned above, use a simple file transfer protocol (HyperText Transfer Protocol, HTTP) to connect to web servers to download and view files that have been written in a format known as HyperText Markup Language (HTML). So the web provides the user with a uniform and intuitive interface for navigating information that is distributed throughout the Internet.

The files (or pages) that web browsers view appear within the browser window on your PC screen as formatted text and graphics. Embedded within the text of each document there are usually a number of hyperlinks. Each of these is a reference to another file somewhere on the web. This reference is known as a Uniform Resource Locator (URL) and has a similar format to established Internet addresses (e.g. www.disney.com).

The real beauty of the web is that its addresses do not have to be exposed directly to the user – the thinking is that this gets in the way of the web's intuitive interface (but see below for a brief exposé on IP addressing. Many people memorize URLs – they are usually pretty obvious and are routinely flashed up during TV adverts. Even if they didn't they could still easily navigate the Web. By clicking on a hyperlink with the mouse, the web client will retrieve and display the referenced document. The user can then browse through the web of information by clicking on the links on each page.

The development of the PC is now at a stage where it is the vehicle for the delivery of multimedia information, whether it be text, graphics, video or audio. These media forms can now all be digitized and stored as data on computer disks at relatively low cost. The power behind the web is in exploiting these trends through the very simple language of HTML and the context of hypertext. HTML is used to define the layout of a computer screen combining text (in a range of typographical styles) and images whilst combining the ability to address other forms of information through hypertext links.

At the heart of hypertext is the anchor. This is a very simple construct within the HTML specification that identifies text, a single word or a string, as a hypertext link. An anchor is typically of the form:

```
Just an  <A HREF='http://www.expl.com/expl.html'>example</A>
of an anchor.
```

Where the link, 'example', would be shown by the browser in blue or some other colour rather than the default black. To click on the anchor would result in a request being sent from the client to the server (`http://www.expl.com/`) defined in the Hypertext reference (HREF). The request would be sent as an HTTP request, asking for the file 'expl.html'. The file would then be sent to the browser and displayed.

If a file is not an HTML document, it will usually have a suffix that denotes its type (e.g., .txt, .doc, .ppt etc.). When the server encounters this suffix it will prepare the file according to its local type definition within its configuration and send it to the browser. The browser, on encountering a file type that is not HTML, will also look up the file suffix in its helper application configuration and if it is defined as suffix type or associated with a particular application, it will either save the file to disk or boot-up the application so that it (and not the browser) can handle the file. For example, a file with suffix '.pdf'[2] will result in the browser booting Adobe Acrobat for it to be read.

HTML is easy to read and write since it consists of plain text delimited by tags (the special characters in chevrons) and for this reason, it is easy to see just how extensible this language is. For example, an anchor always starts with <A ...> and ends in </A>.

To give some idea of its pace of development, HTML has seen at least two revisions per annum since it went under change control and now includdes a whole raft of features, from tables to text fields, buttons, check boxes and context-sensitive image definitions.

The combination of features and concepts has pushed the web far beyond the capabilities of the basic Internet utilities of mail, file transfer and bulletin boards. Much of this functionality has been subsumed in many implementations of the web browser. This is just as well since the web performs the functions that basic file transfer could not – the display of information within the files that were downloaded.

The more sophisticated browsers now bundle in mail and news client software within the same interface, offering a single software entry to all the resources on the Internet. This trend continues but in a more cooperative way, where web browsers are now the platform for integration of plug-in functionality for specific purposes.

Because the basic concept of the web – hypertext – is not dependent on file type, the linking action can be used by the requested web server to interface to an application prior to sending any results back to the requesting client. What this means is that an anchor reference may be an application process that can accept input and return a result. For example, a typcial web page can be used to display a field and a button; the user can fill-in the field and by clicking on the button, invoke a hypertext link that

---

[2] The suffix '.pdf' stands for portable document format. It is a standard for document presentation that helps to ensure that a page of information, when viewed, is in the format that the originator intended.

sends the filled-in field back to the server for the attention of an application script.

The script can be accessed by the server through a Common Gateway Interface (CGI) and so these scripts are generally referred to as 'CGIs'. The CGI performs some operation on the text submitted through the filled-in field and returns a result back to the server/end-user. This result would be in the form of a page of HTML. What has just been described here is, in effect, the front-end of a search engine for the web.

Another benefit from hypertext is the ability to pull-in and collect a much greater body of information than hitherto. Special programs can be written to behave as web browsers that can download a web page, cache its links and then traverse all the links, pulling in each page, caching its links and so on. By crawling across the Web like this, the cache of links soon grows and forms a substantial database of information. Coupled with some software to perform searching on this database and the web form (discussed above) it is relatively easy to build a powerful web search engine.

Because of the ease in which this can be done and the flexibility of HTML and of CGIs, it hasn't taken long for multiplicity of different search engines to appear on the web. Whilst it is sometimes difficult to choose which one to use, the web search engines are still many times more powerful than previous Internet offerings such as WAIS. Some of the better known of the web search engines are YAHOO, Lycos and Alta Vista.

A2.3   THE INTERNET PROTOCOL

To complete our whistle stop tour of the Internet, we return to addressing on the network and explain how information gets from A to B to Z and beyond.

Firstly, everyone is familiar with communications protocols, we use them everyday; from when we grunt when we get out of bed in the morning, wave to our friends on the way to work, write to our colleagues using email and memos and talk to fellow humans on the phone.

A protocol defines the expected behaviour between entities, a set of rules to which the communicating parties comply. The only difference with the Internet (and we are including the Web here) is that the protocols it uses can only be understood by machines, which means that they have to be precise and unambiguous. The protocol needs to define the information to be conveyed, how it is sent and received, who it is addressed to and who it is sent from, and its meaning within its relative context.

More commonly the Internet Protocol is referred to as TCP/IP since this is the collective term used for its many implementations (and many component protocols) on PCs and UNIX computer systems. It gets its name from two of its components Transmission Control Protocol (TCP) and Internet Protocol (IP). In practice Internet applications use either TCP or User Datagram Protocol (UDP); the differences between these two are that UDP is for unreliable connectionless packet delivery, and TCP is for reliable connection-oriented byte-stream delivery. So UDP tends to be used for simpler services that can benefit from its speed, TCP for more demanding ones where it is worth trading a little efficiency for greater reliability. The difference between the two is explained further below.

Communications protocols can be (and in practice, always are) viewed as layered structures – a stack. This model has been used extensively to describe the communications systems and TCP/IP has not been exempt from the treatment. The stacking or layering within the protocol is a convenient way to separate function in the protocol as follows:

4. The *application layer* defines the application software, its processes and the protocol it uses to convey its data to the communications protocol stack. In the case of email, the protocol it uses is Simple Mail Transfer Protocol (SMTP). Email applications wrap-up email messages with start and end markers and attach header information about who the mail is from and who the mail is to be sent to. This is passed to the layer below to be sent on its way; much like putting a letter in an envelope, writing the address on the front and dropping it into a postbox.

3. The *transport layer* wraps-up the application layer message in its own data that defines the application that is sending and the application to receive; these are known as the source and destination ports. It will also add data to specify the overall length of the message and number, the checksum, to use to check if any of the data it is carrying has been corrupted. This is the layer in which both TCP and UDP reside. UDP is generally used to convey small messages of a request–response nature within single packets and TCP is used to convey larger messages within a byte stream.

    The reasoning behind this difference is that, for small messages, the overhead of creating connections and ensuring reliable delivery is greater than the work of re-transmitting the entire message. To this end, TCP will attach further information to the message passed from the application to ensure that the reliable connection is maintained during the transmission and that the segments of the byte stream all arrive at their destination.

2. The *Internet layer* provides the most important function of the TCP/IP

stack by structuring the data into packets, known as datagrams, moving the datagrams between the network access layer and the transport layer, routing the datagrams from source to destination addresses and performing any necessary fragmentation and re-assembly of datagrams. The Internet layer wraps up the transport layer data in its own data, which includes the length of each datagram, and the source and destination addresses (the IP addresses), which specify the network and host of the source and destination.

1. The *network access layer* is perhaps the least discussed of all the layers since the protocols within it are generally specific to a particular hardware technology for the delivery of data. Therefore, there are many protocols, one or more for each physical network implementation. The role of the network access layer is to ensure the correct transmission of IP datagrams across the physical medium and mapping of IP addresses to the physical addresses used by the network.

The examples above explain how an application may send data across the Internet using the TCP/IP suite of protocols, from application layer to network access layer. The reverse is also true when data is received by the network access layer. The roles of each layer are the same, the difference being that the data is 'peeled' as it ascends the stack, each layer removing the layer-specific data put there by the source TCP/IP. The concept of wrapping up data layer by layer in this way is referred to as encapsulation.

A.2.3.1 Addressing

From an engineer's point of view, one of the real beauties of Internet lies in the way in which the IP datagrams are addressed to named hosts on the network.

Each host on the Internet has a unique number, known as an IP address (this concept and the fact that there are a limited number of these were discussed earlier in this chapter). The IP address is a 32 bit number that can be used to address a specific network and host attached to the Internet. This does not mean that every Internet user has a permanent IP address. For instance, dial-in users using the point to point protocol (PPP) to connect an ISP are 'loaned' one for the duration of their connection. Enduring IP addresses relate to specific host on a specific network.

The 32 bit IP address needs therefore to be split to define both a network part and host part. This split occurs in different positions within the number according to the class of the address, and there are four classes, A through D.

- Class A addresses are within the range 001 to 126.XXX.YYY.ZZZ. The first byte is used to define the network (bit 1 = class A, bits 2–8 the network). The remaining 24 bits are used to address the hosts on the network, therefore millions of hosts can be addressed.

- Class B addresses are within the range 128 to 191.XXX.YYY.ZZZ. The first two bytes are used to define the network (bits 1 and 2 = class B, bits 3–16 the network). The remaining 16 bits are used to address the hosts on the network, therefore thousands of hosts can be addressed from thousands of class B networks.

- Class C addresses are within the range 192 to 223.XXX.YYY.ZZZ. The first three bytes are used to define the network (bits 1, 2 and 3 = class C, bits 4–24 the network). The remaining 8 bits are used to address the hosts on the network, therefore 254 hosts can be addressed from millions of class B networks.

- Class D addresses are within the range 223 to 255.XXX.YYY.ZZZ and are special reserved addresses for multicast protocol address (they can be safely ignored).

There are two class A addresses missing from the list above, these are 000 and 127. These are special addresses that are used for default and loopback routing – used when configuring a host. Also, host numbers 000 and 255 are reserved; 000 defines the network itself and 255 is often used to broadcast to every host on the network.

Occasionally it is necessary to define additional networks from an address range. This can be done by using host address bits in the range as additional network address bits. By doing this the total number of addressable hosts is reduced but the number of networks increased. These networks are known as subnets. The need to define subnets is usually not technical but managerial or organizational. Subnetting caters for the delegation of address assignments to other organizations; however, subnets are only locally defined and the actual IP address of a host is still interpreted as a standard IP address.

Subnets are defined by applying a bit-mask (the subnet mask) to the IP address. If a bit is 1 in the mask it defines a network bit, if a bit is 0 in the mask it defines a host bit. It is best to define subnet masks on byte boundaries (it makes them easier to read); a standard class A address would therefore have a subnet mask of 255.0.0.0 (all the bits in the first byte are 1, defining the network; all the bits in bytes 2, 3 and 4 are 0, defining the millions of hosts that are addressable on a class A network).

So how does this all relate to the various addresses that you may have encountered on a good day's surfing. To complete this section, we take a uniform resource locator (URL) and break it down into its constituent parts – each of which has been explained at some point already.

Let's take the full version of the URL used in the previous section to explain the concept of an anchor. It was:

```
http://www.expl.com/expl.html
```

and it can be broken down into a number of parts.

http://

This part tells the client which protocol that it needs to use on this occasion. In this example, it is a standard access to a Web page, so HTTP is chosen. If the URL was targetted on a filestore, the first would most likely be ftp://.

www.expl.com

This is the readable version of the IP address as explained above. It resolves into the right address of the machine that you want to get your information from. So, assuming that the target machine is part of class B network, the Domain Name Service would resolve the mnemonic for the intended server into something like 146.139.16.17 – the server's IP address. Sometimes, there are qualifications to this address field (e.g. www.expl.com:8080). The part after the colon is not part of the address as such – it is there to route an incoming request to a particular port on the host machine. This may be included for security or operational reasons.

expl.html

And finally, we get to the file that you are looking for. The extension .html should give you a warm feeling that all is well and that you are going to get an HTML coded document, as you would hope, using HTTP. Many addresses are a lot longer than the one in our example, e.g. `http://www.expl.com/net/faq/basics/expl.html`. The intermediate references between the machine address and the final document reference are simply there to get to the right part of the directory structure on the host.

There is a lot more that could be said about the Internet and World Wide Web, but the above skim should be enough for the media engineer to get by with. Later on in this appendix, we return some of the production technologies that have been driven, to a large extent, by the development of the Web. Before that, though, we say a few words about the other delivery medium for information products – the compact disk.

A2.4   THE COMPACT DISK

The compact disk, usually referred to as the CD, is a type of computer medium that resulted from audio technology first developed by Philips in the early 1980s. They are now used to carry much of the software (and music) that is sold to the general public. The reason for the rise in popularity of the CD is its very capacity. It has proved itself to be a very popular medium for delivering high-quality information products – a major industry in CD-based encyclopaedias, games and guides has sprung up in a few short years.

A standard commercial CD can hold around 650 million bytes of data; the equivalent of more than 400 conventional floppy disks. This means that a single disk can carry over an hour of high quality music, the text and diagrams from several hundred books like this one or an entire feature film. To illustrate, the UK telephone directory – 17 million entries – fits onto one CD.

Some of the potential capacity of the CD is not used for data storage. About 15% of the available storage is used to check the integrity of the rest of the data. This error detection and correction overhead is important for error intolerant information, such as software, raw and processed data.

The most common type of CD is the CD-ROM (compact disk – read only memory). They cannot be reused, as you can on a floppy disk, because each disk is made by burning a sequence of tiny holes into the reflective base material. The pattern of holes etched on the disk is interpreted as digital information when the laser contained in a disc reader scans it. As the disk spins, light from the laser is either reflected or not. And this provides a stream of zeros and ones that can be turned into music, software, picutres or anything else that can be digitally encoded. The way that it works make it very robust; no physical contact is required to read the information.

The CD-ROM is one of a larger family of CDs. There are a number of related compact disks, all based on the same technology and coding but with different index structures to suit specific applications. Perhaps the best known is the interactive CD-i. The family is growing rapidly and CDs that can be written to are now emerging, albeit at a price. Instead of burning holes in the reflective material, these are made by heating up a magnetic material which then changes its optical properties.

Despite having huge storage capacity, the compact disk did have some initial drawbacks. Perhaps the main one was the speed at which information could be retrieved. Early disk drives could get data at a rate of 150 Kbits/s – giving an average access time of several hundred milliseconds, compared to about 20 ms for a hard disk. Modern drives have speeds much closer to that of the hard disk thus giving considerable improvements in performance.

As would be expected, the access times to retrieve information from a

CD are considerably less than those to retrieve it from most networks – notably, the Internet Likewise, the incidence of errors between source and application is reduced to a much lower rate.

Affordable CD writers, which allow information to be put onto a CD direct from a computer (just as it would save files to a floppy disk) started to become available from the mid 1990s. If they follow the general trends in the computer industry, it is likely that they will be a run of the mill part of a computer system. And given that the availability of modems was one of the popular triggers to the growth of the Internet, we may well see a significant rise in the variety of information products delivered on compact disk.

A2.5 MARKUP LANGUAGES

We are all familiar with 'what you see is what you get' (WYSIWYG) word processors that allow the user to produce documents that employ complex formatting that was once the province of the professional publishing industry. The most humble word processor probably allows the use of different fonts, bold and underlined text, distinctive titles, indented text and a whole range of other features for customizing the appearance of documents. It follows that when a word-processed document is saved onto a computer disk, not only is all the text, or 'content' stored, but also a mass of information relating to the layout and appearance of the document must be saved too. Each word-processor manufacturer has its own proprietary method for encoding all this structuring information which must accompany the basic text. It is the difference between these methods that leads to the incompatibilities that often prevent a document created using one word-processing package to be viewed using a different manufacturer's product. In fact these word-processor file formats are so intimately bound up with the particular formatting features offered by a particular product that there is often an incompatibility between document formats generated by different variants of the same vendor's product.

Word processors use a variety of ways of encoding formatting information. Some embed cryptic sequences of codes interspersed in the text to indicate such features as bold text or changes of font. Others embed pointers within the text which refer out to a table of 'styles' which are defined (again in an encoded format) at either the beginning or the end of the document file. All these share a number of features:

- They are not 'human readable'. They can be interpreted by the word-processing application but not by the person who tries to decode the file.

- They are not 'standards' (either amongst vendors or even product versions of the same vendor). Neither are they generally published or open.

- They are designed to optimize the editing process from the end-user viewpoint. This means that they are optimized for efficient handling by the computer.

Whilst word processors have been developing with ever more powerful features and proprietary file formats have evolved with corresponding complexity, a separate strand of activity has been underway in the industry, to develop 'markup languages'. Like a word-processor file, a markup language is intended to encode information about a document's structure and content. However, the concept of markup has its origins in the publishing industry, with the marks that authors or editors employ to indicate how parts of the text should be formatted in the typesetting and printing stage of a document. Hence, computer markup languages are human-readable (if a little cryptic) and made up of characters accessible from the normal computer keyboard. So that they can be distinguished from the textual part of the document, they have to have some distinguishing character sequence that instantly identifies them as markup sequences. For example, the most commonly used markup languages which we shall be discussing enclose their markup 'tags' within a pair of angle brackets: <>. For example, the symbol for the start of a new paragraph could be <P>; the symbol for a title, <TITLE>, and so on. Some of the characteristics of markup languages are:

They are (as noted already) human readable and writable (with some effort). There have been considerable attempts to standardize them internationally.

To further clarify the difference between a markup language and a word-processor file, we can think of a document as containing three things:

- *The content.* The words, pictures and other items that it contains. In a multimedia document this can include sounds, video or any other media.
- *The structure of the document.* How it is divided into paragraphs, headings, chapters, and similar items.
- *The rendition.* The way that the structure is portrayed on the screen or printed page. What size and weight of font is to be used for titles; how

the break between chapters is to indicated; and so on.

In the case of a word processor, the top feature is generally usability and that means that the 'what you see is what you get' feature is paramount. This in turn leads to the three things being mixed up together. On the other hand, markup languages seek to separate these out and are aimed primarily at structure.

In particular, markup languages do not generally make any statements about rendition. This may seem at first sight to be a weakness: what is the use of a language that tells you the structure of a document but doesn't tell you how it should appear on the page? In point of fact, this becomes an advantage when one is dealing with multimedia documents delivered over a medium such as the Internet. One of the problems with such a delivery is that the author and publisher have no knowledge of the particular computer that will be used by their reader. Hence, there is an advantage in delivering a document in the form of content + structure and leaving it to the client computer to decide how to render it on the screen.

We now discuss the main developments in markup languages and their contribution to Media Engineering.

A2.5.1 SGML

Standardized Generic Markup Language (SGML) is the most important markup language that has been standardized internationally. It is sometimes described as a 'meta language', meaning that rather than being a complete markup language in itself, it is actually a language framework that can be used to define any number of markup languages for specific purposes. As we shall see, one such use of SGML has been to define the hypertext markup language HTML which has been central to the development of the World Wide Web and hypertext publishing.

SGML, in keeping with the philosophy of markup languages that we have discussed, sets out to encode (using markup tags) the structure of a document and not its rendition. For example, we might decide that there is a particular type of document called a novel, whose structure consists of a book title followed by a series of chapters. Each chapter begins with a chapter title followed by a series of paragraphs. To describe the structure of such a document, we might define the following markup tags:

- start of novel: <NOVEL>

- end of novel: </NOVEL>

- start of book title: <BTITLE>

- end of book title: `</BTITLE>`
- start of chapter: `<CHAPTER>`
- end of chapter: `</CHAPTER>`
- start of chapter title: `<CTITLE>`
- end of chapter title: `</CTITLE>`
- start of paragraph: `<P>`
- end of paragraph: `</P>`

There are several things to note about the markup tags: the first is that they are always enclosed in angle brackets to distinguish them from the content of the document; the second is that the end tag for a particular element of structure is indicated by the solidus '/' sign.

If a simple novel was structured using the above markup, it might look like:

```
<NOVEL>
    <BTITLE>
    The Gumbleton Saga
    </BTITLE>

    <CHAPTER>
        <CTITLE>
        In the Beginning
        </CTITLE>

        <P>
    Josiah Gumbleton never forgot the first day he arrived in
London. He had taken the coach from Deal and had arrived at the Turk's
Head in Newgate Street. From there he had hired a cart to take himself
and his wife to the their new premises in East Lane, Walworth . . .</P>
</CHAPTER>
<CHAPTER>
        <CTITLE>
        The next instalment
        </CTITLE>
        The next year . . .
</CHAPTER>
</NOVEL>
```

Various features are apparent:
In general, elements of the document are enclosed in matching sets of tags such as

<CHAPTER> ... </CHAPTER>.

Some tags are not necessary. Their effect can be inferred from the context. For example, the end of a paragraph is always followed by the start of a new paragraph (a <P> tag) or the end of a chapter (a </CHAPTER> tag). Hence, the </P> tag is not strictly needed to mark the end of a paragraph.

Some tags might appear anywhere (<P> paragraph tags could appear almost anywhere) whilst others can only appear in certain places (<CTITLE> for instance can only occur within a chapter). SGML provides a language for defining tags and includes such characteristics as we have just encountered:

- whether it must have an obligatory matching end tag;

- whether it can appear anywhere or only nested within some other pair of tags.

A set of tags defined using SGML for a particular purpose is known as a document type definition (DTD). The markup languages widely used for Internet-based multimedia are defined as SGML document type definitions.

A2.5.2   HTML

Hyptertext Markup Language (HTML) is the most widely used DTD for on-line multimedia systems. Although HTML is formally defined in terms of an SGML DTD, most practitioners make full use of HTML without delving into the complexities of SGML.

This book does not aim to give a complete guide to writing HTML. What is relevant to this book is the way that markup languages are evolving and the impact of this on Media Engineering.

In practice, WWW practitioners have not sat down and worked out the perfect markup language: instead, a set of tags was devised that was adequate for the original WWW development and this has evolved largely through browser vendors adding features that they think people will use. The standards process has trailed some way behind, picking up the features that are generally agreed as a common set and then tidying them up and formalizing them as an SGML DTD. The bulk of the 'basic' tags have been capture in the HTML 2.0 standard which has been issued as an Internet RFI and is now being adopted by ISO. This includes:

- the character set (including codes for various symbols and the accented characters needed for a range of languages);

- stylistic tags for emphasis;

- lists: bullet lists and numbered lists (known as unordered lists and ordered lists);

- forms;

- embedded images;

- hypertext links.

HTML standards

HTML 2.0

The nearest thing to an international standard for hypertext markup is HTML 2.0. This is being standardized as an Internet standard, as RFC 1866. It is very much a subset of what is supported by existing browsers and omits such 'essential' items as tables and text-flow around images.

HTML 3.2

The World Wide Web Consortium (W3C) includes the principal vendors such as IBM, Microsoft, Netscape Communications Corporation, Novell, Softquad, Spyglass and Sun Microsystems. They have jointly agreed a standard which is intended to provide a common HTML specification. Nevertheless, this is not preventing individual vendors from adding their own extensions. Because this is the common specification for most of the current generation of browsers, we summarize the complete set of tags defined in HTML 3.2.

HTML 3.2 Document structure

An HTML 3.2 document is structured as follows:

```
<!DOCTYPE HTML PUBLIC ''-//W3C//DTD HTML 3.2 Draft//EN''>
<HTML>
<HEAD>
    Head elements go here . . .
</HEAD>
<BODY>
```

```
    Body elements go here . . .

</BODY>
</HTML>
```

The `<!DOCTYPE>` declaration is needed to distinguish documents employing HTML 3.2 from those using other HTML versions.

HTML 3.2 Head elements

The head must include a document title, using `<TITLE>` and `</TITLE>` tags. Other optional elements of the head are:

- BASE. This gives the base URL for any relative URLs used elsewhere in the document, e.g.
  ```
  <BASE href=``http://www.norwest.com/''>
  ```

- ISINDEX. This tells the browser that the page is to present an input field for the user to fill in. The contents of this field will then be sent back to the server: actually it will be sent to the URL defined by BASE. e.g.
  ```
  <ISINDEX PROMPT=``Enter a line of text and hit Return''>
  ```

- LINK. This provides a way of defining relationships with other documents. However, its use seems to be completely ignored by everyone, including browser vendors.

- META. This allows user-defined meta data to be recorded as name/content pairs, e.g.
  ```
  <META NAME=``Author''CONTENT=``Mark Norris''>
  <META NAME=``Version''CONTENT=``2.1''>
  <META NAME=``Last edited''CONTENT=``21 Nov 1996''>
  ```

- SCRIPT and STYLE. At the time of writing, these exist in the draft standard but their usage is undefined.

Body elements

The BODY tag itself can include information about colours or can include a link to a background image, e.g.

```
<BODY BGCOLOR=``#800080'' TEXT=``#000000'' VLINK=``#FFFF00''
ALINK=``#0000FF''>
```

specifies the background colour as Purple (800080 hexadecimal), with Black text (000000), visited links being Yellow (FFFF00) and unvisited links being Blue (0000FF). Colours are specified as hex numbers in the form rrggbb.

```
<BODY BACKGROUND=``http://www.abc.def.gh/graphics/gb.gif''>
```

This example specifies a background image.
The other tags that can be used are:

A. The hypertext anchor tag. The two main attributes are 'NAME' and 'HREF'. The 'NAME' attribute associates a name with the anchor, e.g.:

```
<A NAME=``ninths''></A>Ninth chords consist of the root, major
third, perfect fifth, minor seventh and ninth.
```

The 'HREF' attribute denotes the anchor as a hypertext link, e.g.

```
<A HREF=``guitar/chords#ninths''>Click here to find out about ninth
chords</A>
```

The <A> tag can also include the following attributes, not much seen in practice:

    REL A forward relationship to another linked document
    REV A reverse relationship to another linked document
    TITLE A title for a linked resource

ADDRESS. Information enclosed within ADDRESS tags will be displayed by browsers in an appropriate form for a name and address. Usage would be something like:

```
<ADDRESS>Steve West, <BR>19, Railway Cuttings, <BR>East Cheam
</ADDRESS>
```

APPLET. This denotes an embedded Java Applet.

BASEFONT. This tag set the default font size for the page. Font sizes can be from 1 to 7, so <BASEFONT SIZE=``2''> selects a small font as the default for the page.

BIG. Text attribute to put text in a large font. Quite often used to make initial letters bigger than the rest of the text, e.g.

```
<BIG>T</BIG>he <BIG>H</BIG>oliday <BIG>H</BIG>ome
<BIG>F</BIG>or <BIG>P</BIG>ets <BIG>P</BIG>ie <BIG>C
</BIG>ompany
```

BLOCKQUOTE. This tag is used to enclose quotations:

```
``Work is the curse of the drinking class''
</BLOCKQUOTE>
```

B. Bold text, e.g.

```
<B>Text to be emboldened</B>
```

BR. Tag for a line break. Has a special use with images aligned against the left or right margins with text flowing round them: the CLEAR attribute ends the flowing of text round the image and returns to normally placed text. <BR CLEAR=LEFT> starts the next text below any left-aligned image and <BR CLEAR=RIGHT> does the same for right-aligned images. <BR CLEAR=ALL> does the same for either left or right aligned images.

CENTER. This is a Netscape extension for centering text. The construction:

```
<DIV ALIGN=CENTER>
```

is the preferred way of signifying centring of text.

CITE. Text attribute that denotes a citation or reference, e.g.

```
Please refer to <CITE>Media Engineering by Steve West and Mark Norris </CITE>
```

CODE. Text attribute denoting that the text is to be rendered like a computer program:

```
<CODE>
main{
    writeln(''Hello world/n'');
    }
</CODE>
```

DFN. Text attribute denoting the definition of a term, e.g.

```
<DFN>PAF</DFN> Patent Applied For
```

DIR. Directory list. List items are denoted by <LI>. Browsers will ideally display it as a multi-colum list. For example,

```
<DIR>
<LI>First item
<LI>Second item
</DIR>
```

DIV. This tag starts a new division of a document (i.e. some new logical section). It is used to apply formatting features to the section – notably left, centre or right alignment of text, e.g.

```
<DIV ALIGN=CENTER>
```

DL. Definition List. This consists of a list of items each of which includes a 'term' and a definition for the term. It is useful for creating things like glossaries. The terms are denoted by `<DT>` tags and the definitions by `<DD>` tags, e.g.

```
<DL>
<DT>BLOB<DD>Binary large object
<DT>FRED<DD>Federated Relational Enterprise Database
</DL>
```

EM. Text attribute that tells the browser to emphasize the text (e.g. by rendering it in italics):

```
The <EM>love of</EM> money is the root of all evil.
```

FONT. This tag is used to change the size and/or colour of the font, e.g.

```
Normal text, <FONT SIZE=``7'' COLOR= ``ff0000''>Huge red text</
```
FONT> and normal text.

The size can be an absolute integer from 1 to 7 (in increasing size) or can be relative to the last font used, such as `<FONT SIZE='-2''>` which yields a font that is two sizes smaller than the current one.

Headings H1 to H6. For example:

```
<H1>Top level heading</H1>
<H6>Sixth level heading</H6>
```

HR. Horizontal rule. It can include attributes: **align** (left, right or center), **noshade** (to make it a solid colour rather than '3D'), **size** (height in pixels) and **width** (as a number of pixels or a percentage), e.g.

```
<HR ALIGN=``LEFT'' SIZE=``10'' WIDTH=``50%''>
```

I. Italic text, e.g.
```
<I>Text to appear italicized</I>
```

IMG. Tag for an embedded image, e.g.

```
<IMG    SRC=``/images/cat.gif''    ALT=``Tabby    cat    image''
ALIGN=``top''
WIDTH=80 HEIGHT=60 BORDER=0 HSPACE=10 VSPACE=10>
```

The ALT attribute provides a text alternative for non-graphical browsers. The ALIGN attribute can position the image vertically in relation to the current text line (ALIGN=top, middle or bottom). Alternatively, the ALIGN attribute can be used to position the image against a left or right margin, with subsequent text fitted in beside it, e.g.

```
<IMG SRC=``images/cat.gif'' ALIGN='left''>This picture shows my
cat Molly asleep in our conservatory<BR CLEAR=ALL>Our next picture
shows a historic steam engine.
```

The `<BR>` tag with the `CLEAR=ALL` attribute is used to indicate the end of the text that is supposed to be beside the image. The sentence about the steam engine will come after the picture.

The WIDTH and HEIGHT attributes are optional but allow the browser to size the space for the picture before it has been loaded. The HSPACE and VSPACE attributes indicate the number of pixels of white space to be left beside the picture, in the horizontal and vertical directions, respectively.

The BORDER attribute is mainly used to turn off the border that appears by default around a clickable image.

The other possible attributes are USEMAP (which denotes the image as a client-side image map – see the **MAP** tag) and ISMAP (which denotes the image as a server-side image map).

KBD. Text attribute used to denote example text typed by user, e.g.

To list your files type `<KBD>ls -</KBD>` in response to the prompt.

MAP. This tag is used to define a client-side image map. For example:

```
<IMG SRC=``/images/violin.gif'' BORDER=0 USEMAP=``#violinMap">
<MAP NAME=``violinMap''>
<AREA HREF=``strings.html'' ALT= ``Violin strings'' SHAPE=rect
COORDS=``20,65,170,35''>
<AREA HREF=``pegs.html'' ALT=``Violin pegs'' SHAPE=circle
COORDS=``180,50,10''
<AREA HREF=``body.html'' ALT=``Violin body'' SHAPE=poly
COORDS=``10,25,25,5,40,20,80,10,120,40,120,60,80,90,40,80,25,85,10,75''>
<AREA HREF=``help.html'' SHAPE=default>
</MAP>
```

The map consists of a number of 'hot' areas which may be circles, rectangles or polygons. The coordinates are specified as numbers of pixels, with the top left corner of the image being 0,0. For circles they denote *x-coord of centre, y-coord of centre, radius*; for rectangles they denote *top left x, top left y, bottom left x, bottom left y*; and for polygons they denote *x1,y1,x2, . . .*

SHAPE=`default` is used to specify the default HREF for the whole image area (and should be placed last in the list).

The ALT attribute provides text alternatives for browsers that cannot display the image.

A particular area can use a NOHREF attribute (in place of the usual HREF) to define a non-clickable area in the middle of a clickable one. The list of areas is parsed from top to bottom so the NOHREF item needs to precede the area which it is supposed to mask.

MENU. Menu list. List items are denoted by `<LI>`. For example

```
<MENU>
<LI>My first point
<LI>My second point
<LI>My third point
</MENU>
```

The result is probably much like a `<UL>` list.

OL. Ordered list (i.e. a numbered list). List items are denoted by `<LI>`. For example

```
<OL>
<LI>My first point
<LI>My second point
<LI>My third point
</OL>
```

P. The tag for the start of a new paragraph. Optionally this can include an alignment attribute, e.g.

```
<P ALIGN=LEFT>
```

PRE. Preformatted text. The browser should display this using a fixed-pitch (typewriter) font such as Courier and should preserve line breaks and spaces, e.g.

```
<PRE>
        Month      Sales
        Jan        12
        Feb        15
</PRE>
```

SAMP. Text attribute to denote sample output (e.g. from computer programs), e.g.

```
The computer prompts you: <SAMP>Please enter user name and password</SAMP>
```

SMALL. Text attribute to put text in small font, e.g.

```
<SMALL>This text will be smaller than the rest</SMALL>
```

STRIKE. The text attribute to generate strike-through text, e.g.

```
<STRIKE>This text will have a line struck through it</STRIKE>
```

STRONG. Text attribute for strong emphasis. Browsers may, for example, render this as bold text.

SUB. Subscript text, e.g.

The formula for water is H₂O

will be rendered as: The formula for water is H_2O

SUP. Superscript text, e.g.

E = mc²

will be rendered as $E = mc^2$

TABLE. Rather than describe all the intricacies (which can be found in the standard, we simply give an example:

```
<TABLE BORDER ALIGN=CENTER CELLSPACING=10 CELLPADDING=4>
<CAPTION ALIGN=BOTTOM>Example of an HTML table</CAPTION>
<TR ALIGN=CENTER VALIGN=CENTER> <TH ROWSPAN=2>Month
<TH CHOLSPAN=2>Sales
<TR ALIGN=CENTER VALIGN=TOP> <TH>Area A<TH>Area B
<TR ALIGN=LEFT> <TD>Jan<TD>12<TD>15
<TR ALIGN=LEFT> <TD>Feb<TD>20<TD>17
<TR ALIGN=LEFT> <TD>Jan<TD> <TD> 
</TABLE>
```

The <TABLE> tag specifies that the table has a border, that it is centred on the page (ALIGN=CENTER), that the cells have a 10 pixel spacing between them (CELLSPACING=10) and that the cell contents are spaced 4 pixels from the edges of the cell (CELLPADDING=4). The <CAPTION> tag gives the table a caption. This table makes use of ROWSPAN, to specify that a particular cell occupies two rows, and COLSPAN to make one of the cells span two columns. We have chosen to fill the 'empty' cells with 'non-breaking space characters' ( ) because some browsers render completely empty cells as though they were part of the cell borders.

TT. Teletype text (i.e. a monotype font such as Courier) e.g.

<TT>Text that should look like it's been typed on a typewriter</TT>

U. Underlined text, e.g.

<U>Text to be underlined</U>

UL. Unordered list (i.e. a bullet list). List items are denoted by <LI>. For example:

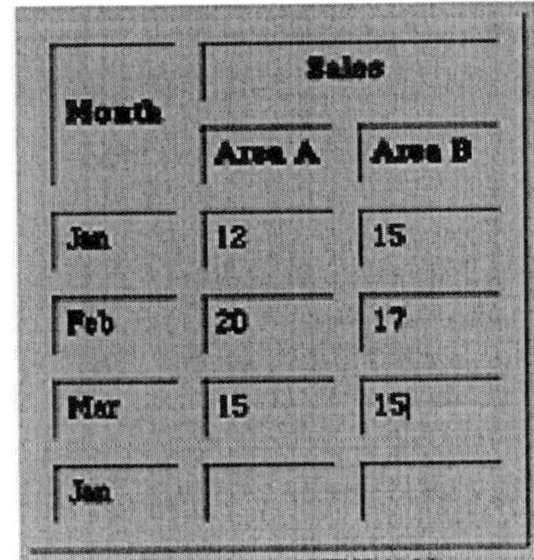

Figure A2.1

```
<UL>
<LI>My first point
<LI>My second point
<LI>My third point
</UL>
```

VAR. Text attribute that denotes variables in example computer programs or scripts, e.g.

```
This function takes two inout parameters: <VAR>string1</VAR> and
<VAR>string2</VAR>
```

Forms

HTML 3.2 forms are defined by `<FORM>` and `</FORM>` tags. Form tags have the following attributes:

- **ACTION.** This attribute specifies a URL to which the data from the form is to be submitted. This will often be a CGI script or can be a 'mailto' URL, in which case the form data is sent as an e-mail.

- **METHOD.** There are two methods for sending data to servers: Get and Post.

- **ENCTYPE.** This determines the mechanism for encoding the form data.

A form consists of a number of fields. In general, a field will have a name and the result of submitting a form will be to generate a set of name–value pairs corrsponding to the set of fields in the form. The values will then be processed by an application or script.

The form fields are defined by three tags: INPUT, SELECT and TEXT AREA. The types of form field are:

Text fields. These are the usual form fields in which the user can type a line of text. They are created using an INPUT tag with TYPE=text. For example:

```
< INPUT TYPE=TEXT SIZE=50 MAXLENGTH=100 NAME=username VALUE=''Type
your name here''>
```

This produces a text field 50 characters wide into which the user can type a string of up to 100 characters. The default text, before the user types anything, is 'Type your name here'. The field is named *username*.

Password fields. These are like text fields except that the user's input is echoed as asterisks to obscure the text from casual observers, e.g.

```
INPUT TYPE=password SIZE=50 MAXLENGTH=20>
```

Checkboxes. Checkboxes allow the user to select items independently. For example:

```
Vehicle particulars:
Automatic transmission < INPUT TYPE=checkbox NAME=automatic >
Leather seats < INPUT TYPE=checkbox NAME=leather >
CD Player < INPUT TYPE=checkbox name=cd CHECKED >
```

The CHECKED attribute denotes that the box is initially selected as a default.

Radio buttons. These let the user select one out of a list of items. Again they use the INPUT tag but with TYPE=radio. For example:

```
< INPUT TYPE=radio NAME=instrument VALUE=''Oboe''>
< INPUT TYPE=radio NAME=instrument VALUE=''Violin''>
< INPUT TYPE=radio NAME=instrument VALUE=''Viola''>
< INPUT TYPE=radio NAME=instrument VALUE=''Guitar'' CHECKED>
< INPUT TYPE=radio NAME=instrument VALUE=''Cello''>
```

The NAME attribute must be the same for all radio buttons within a group. The CHECKED attribute is used to select the default item that is checked at startup.

Select menus. These are lists of options, usually in the form of drop-down menus. They have their own SELECT and OPTION tags rather than being types of INPUT tags. For example:

```
< SELECT NAME=''instrument''>
< OPTION VALUE=''Oboe''>Oboe
< OPTION VALUE=''Violin''>Violin
< OPTION VALUE=''Viola''>Viola
< OPTION VALUE=''Guitar'' SELECTED>Spanish Guitar
< OPTION VALUE=''Cello''>Violincello
```

```
</SELECT>
```

The SELECTED attribute identifies the default option.

Text areas. These are multiline text fields. They have their own TEX-TAREA tag. For example:

```
<TEXTAREA NAME=haiku ROWS=9 COLS=70>
Type in your haiku here. . .
</TEXTAREA>
```

The text between the tags is the default that will appear before the user types anything.

Attached files. The INPUT tag supports a TYPE=FILE attribute. The browser will probably handle this by providing a text field into which the user can type a file name, or it will provide a button which, when pressed, brings up a file requester through which the user can select a file. Either way, the contents of the selected file is sent with the form when it is submitted, e.g.

```
<INPUT TYPE=file name=attachedFile SIZE=25 MAXLENGTH=32>
```

Note that SIZE is the size of the text box into which the user can type the filename and that MAXLENGTH is the maximum length of the *filename* not the file.

Hidden. Hidden fields are not displayed by the browser. They provide a means for an application to send information with the form that will be returned when the form is submitted, e.g.

```
<INPUT TYPE=hidden NAME=formId VALUE=``1234''>
```

Submit button. This is the button that the user clicks to submit the form to the server. For example:

```
<INPUT TYPE=submit VALUE=``Enter''>
```

The VALUE will appear as the name of the button on the user's screen.

Image. An image can be used in place of a submit button. For example:

```
<INPUT TYPE=image SRC=``button.gif''>
```

Reset button. The reset button resets the contents of a form to its default settings, e.g.

```
<INPUT TYPE=reset VALUE=``Restore defaults''>
```

Ongoing standardization work

It will be seen that even HTML 3.2 does not include such familiar hypertext features as frames and scripting. At the time of writing, a number of major areas of standards work are under way within the W3C consortium. Some of the main ones are discussed below.

Cascading style sheets

HTML began as a neat way of displaying text with some simple formatting and embedded images. However, people want it to develop into something much more complex: either an environment for developing complex applications or a complete publishing environment. It is this latter requirement that is leading to ever richer facilities for defining the layout and style of pages. HTML itself defines the elements of structure and content of a page but says nothing (or very little) about how it is rendered by a browser. The idea of a style sheet is to provide a means of specifying how particular pages are to be rendered on the screen.

A style sheet contains a set of rules for rendering particular HTML elements. For instance, it might include rules that an H1 heading was to be rendered in 14 point Helvetica font and coloured green. Any HTML page could contain a reference to a style sheet that specified how all the elements of the page should appear (or, as now, it could accept the default style offered by the browser). For example this would be specified by the following:

```
<STYLE TYPE=''text/css''>
H1 {
    font-weight: bold;
    font-size: 14pt;
    font-family: helvetica;
    color: green
    }
</STYLE>
```

Having dealt with the concept of a style sheet let us now move on to the cascading part. As an example, a browser will probably have a default style sheet. The author of a particular page will then create a style sheet for the page: this will override some of the defaults, but in areas where this style sheet makes no declarations, the defaults remain in force. The user may also define a style sheet which specifies his or her personal preferences. Again, this does not completely replace the other style sheets: it only changes them in the areas where the user has explicitly overridden the styles specified by the author. It can be seen that a whole hierarchy of style sheets can apply to a single document – in this case, one provided by the browser vendor; a second supplied by the document author; and a third constructed by the end user. Each of these does not completely supplant the others: it merely adds its own modifications. This approach, in which the final observed style is built up from a hierarchy of style sheets, is known as 'cascading style sheets'.

Frames

Most browser vendors support some variant of frames. Frames either divide a browser window into a number of 'tiled' areas, each of which can hold its own hypertext contents, or else they appear as multiple overlapping browser windows on the computer desktop. They serve a number of purposes:

- Supporting complex page layouts in which a number of textual and graphical elements have to be placed in particular positions on the page. Borderless frames can provide more powerful ways of defining page layouts than can be achieved with simple left- and right-aligned images and flowing text.

- Combining scrolling material and fixed material. For example, a navigation bar can remain in a fixed frame at the top of the window whilst the main content of the page is displayed in a scrolling frame below it. As the user scrolls through the document, the navigation bar remains accessible.

- Separating content and structure. In Chapter 5 we described how frames can be used to maintain some separation of content from structure.

Current approaches to frames are mostly based around the use of a <FRAMESET> tag which signals the start of some frame definitions, together with <FRAME> tags that specify the details of the frame. However, these tags are not yet part of a recognized standard and they are not without their problems:

- In all but the simplest cases, the syntax for defining them becomes quite complex.

- They open up many opportunities for poor usability. For instance, most designers do not consider every possible user action, including clicking on links in any one of the frames or usig the back and forward buttons of the browser toolbar. Some combination of these actions often leads to unexpected consequences (from the user's point of view).

- Not all browsers support frames and although there is a <NOFRAMES> tag to define the alternative behaviour for these browsers, the programming is quite cumbersome in all but the simplest cases.

- The visual effect is quite dependent on the end user's screen size. In the case of a small screen, dividing it into a lot of frames can result in unusably small frames.

Current standardization work recognizes that for anything but the simplest cases, a comprehensive model of frames is required – a couple of extra HTML tags are really not sufficient for the job. The proposed approach is to make use of style sheets to define the properties of frames. The syntax for defining styles has been extended to define a nested set of frames and to determine which parts of the document go into which frame.

Object insertion

Early implementations of HTML allowed the embedding of images, using the image tag. As the multimedia potential of web browsers has developed, additional ways have been developed for embedding other kinds of multimedia resources in a web page – for example, Microsoft's DYNSRC tag, Netscape's EMBED and Sun's APPLET tag.

The standards community is working on a consistent model and notation for embedding multimedia objects into HTML pages. The idea is to define a new <OBJECT> tag that can be used to embed any kind of object:

- graphic
- sound
- Applet
- Active/X control
- Shockwave file
- etc.

Meta data elements

We have described the use of the META tag in HTML headers. This allows the definition of named data elements to which values can be associated. There is, however, the need to define a core set of 'standard' names so that HTML meta data can be machine-readable. For example:

- title
- subject
- author
- publisher
- date
- language.

PICS labels

PICS stands for 'Platform for Internet Content Selection'. It is a labelling system for Internet pages that allows pages to be labelled in such a way that they can be filtered on the basis of their content. For example, pages with pornographic content can be filtered out for certain users.

HTML has been extended to allow the following to be encoded into the page:

- a reference to a third party rating service: the people who define the rating system;

- identification of the rating system in use;

- a set of attribute/value pairs that describe the document in terms of the particular rating system;

- other options such as the date when the document was rated.

A2.6   TOOLS

The whole tools market is extremely volatile. In the text we have noted that there are currently some very good point tools for some jobs but in other areas the tool support is poor. It seems likely that it will be some time before the market stabilizes sufficiently to offer comprehensive toolsets. Even then, if we compare this with our experience from software engineering, the results may not deliver all that was promised.

The following list is by no means comprehensive but includes some of the main contenders in each category.

For each tool we indicate whether it is available for the PC platforms (usually understood to be Windows 95) and/or the Mac platform (i.e. Apple computers, or compatibles, which most people still think of as Macs even if Apple call them something else).

Because of the rapid change cycle for tools, it is likely that some of the details of this section will need revising even before this book is published. Hence it is recommended that the following list be used as a starting point: at least one or two tools are pointed out for each of the main areas: it is up to the reader to try to improve on this selection!

Graphics tools

Adobe Photoshop

(PC and Mac). This is the industry standard application for processing bit-mapped images. A comprehensive professional package with a price tag to match.

Paint Shop Pro

(PC). A shareware image processing program. Good for converting between graphics formats.

Graphics Converter

(Mac). Shareware program for converting between a wide repertoire of graphics formats and will also perform straightforward image editing.

GIFBuilder

(Mac). Software Tool that creates animated GIFs.

Equilibrium DeBabelizer

(PC, Mac). A tool for conversion between large numbers of file formats. It includes scripting and batch features as well as palette conversions.

Media Research LView

(PC). Image editor conversion utility.

HTML editing

SoftQuad HotMeTaL Pro

(PC, Mac). Comprehensive HTML editor. Includes WYSIWYG viewer and graphics editor.

Adobe Pagemill

(Mac). WYSIWYG editor allowing HTML ages to be generated with no knowledge or visibility of HTML syntax. However, it lags a bit behind latest HTML developments.

Netscape Gold

(PC, Mac). The Gold versions of the Netscape browser allow WYSIWYG editing of pages. A good option for occasional editing where you can edit what you browse.

BBEdit

(Mac). Very widely used. Basically a simple text editor with some HTML extensions.

MS Notepad.

As basic and simple as you can get but more widely used for generating HTML than any of the WYSIWYG tools.

There are a huge number of tools available in the public domain or via shareware libraries, each offering slightly different features. The reader is advised to check via the Internet.

Tools to convert from proprietary formats

RTFtoHTML

(Unix, PC, Mac). Converts word-processor documents from RTF format into HTML. Most mainstream WPs have a 'Save as RTF' option. The conversion is table-based and so can be customized.

Microsoft Internet Assistant

(PC, Mac). Free add-on to Microsoft Office products which allows documents to be saved as HTML. At the time of writing it has some limitations but is likely to ve very good in the future.

A comprehensive list of conversion utilities is currently maintained by Rich Brandwein and Mike Sendall at `http://www.w3.org/hypertext/WWW/Tools/Filters.html.`

Newer versions of leading packages are increasingly offering direct conversion to WWW-compatible formats (e.g. using a 'Save as HTML' option on the 'File menu'). These include Adobe Pagemaker and Claris-Works, for example. It seems likely that this is the way that the market will develop: for example, the next generation of Microsoft Office products will probably integrate the functionality of Internet Assistant into the applications.

HTML syntax checking

weblint

(Unix, PC, Mac). This is a Perl script for checking HTML syntax.

Spyglass HTML Validator.

This is downloadable from

http://www.spyglass.com/products/validator/.

Some integrated tools such as Adobe Sitemill and Microsoft FrontPage will also perform this function.

Link checking

see entry Adobe Sitemill (below)

Integrated Web suites

Adobe Sitemill

(Mac). Includes WYSIWYG page creation, linking and error checking. The newbie can set up a small to medium website with very little knowledge. For the industrial-strength webmaster, the facilities for syntax checking and link integrity checking are most useful.

Microsoft FrontPage

(PC). This includes a browser, editor, personal HTTP server and extensions for existing servers. The personal server is useful for testing pages before uploading to the operational server. Good link checking and analysis facilities.

Claris Home Page.

Supports frames and includes a library function for reusing page components (e.g. page templates).

Specialized multimedia tools

Macromedia Director

(Mac, PC). A tool for integration of media objects such as 2D and 3D graphics, video, sound and text. It can produce stand-alone multimedia systems for CD-Rom publication. Alternatively, multimedia objects can be created for inclusion in Web pages in 'Shockwave' format. This latter option requires users to install a (free) Shockwave plug-in for use by their Web browser.

Macromedia Authorware

(Mac, PC). Top of the range Multimedia authoring tool from Macromedia. Powerful and easy to use. Aimed at producing stand-alone CD works.

Apple Media Tool.

Consists of two parts: the simpler allows media systems to be constructed using point-and-click approach; the more advanced allows complex programming.

mTropolis.

Sophisticated object-oriented multimedia tool suite aimed at the top-end professional market.

Audio tools

Progressive Networks RealAudio

(PC, Mac). The client end of RealAudio is bundled with some browsers but must be installed as a plug-in with others. This works in conjunction with a RealAudio server (working with the HTTP server) to play 'streamed' audio. This means that the sounds play as they are downloading – much preferable to earlier systems where an entire sound file had to be downloaded before it could be played.

Logging and analysis

Net.Genesis net.Analysis.

Comprehensive site analysis and reporting tool based on the use of a relational database. Aimed at both systems administration and marketing requirements.

Software WebTrends.

Another comprehensive analysis and reporting tool.

Content management

BT Ubiquity.

Uses an object relational database to store and manage multimedia objects. Aim at serious, large scale multimedia applications.

NetCarta Corporation Webmapper.

Sophisticated Web site management and analysis capabilities. Uses a spider to follow all links and build a graphical map of the site. Finds broken links, analyses site structure and object properties, and performs a variety of other Web site management tasks.

Programming tools

Sun Java Development Kit.

A royalty-free version of the Java development kit can be downloaded over the Internet from Sun's Web site. A more fully featured product is also available as a commercial product from Sun.

Symantec Cafe

(PC, Mac). Cross-platform visual Java development toolset.

Perl

(PC, Mac). Shareware versions of this scripting language are available for many platforms including PC and Mac. It is widely used for creating simple CGI applications for use with an HTTP server.

Image map creation

Mapedit

(PC). A shareware WYSIWYG map editing tool that includes both server-side and client-side map capabilities.

Webmap

(Mac). A shareware WYSIWYG map editing tool for the Mac.
Also a number of the WYSIWYG page generation tools (Adobe Sitemill, for example) include map creation, though not all support client-side maps.

Appendix **3**

Polycontiguity – A Case Study Using JavaScript

In Chapter 5 we gave some illustrations of how *polycontiguity* would be applied in practice. In this appendix, we take the example from that chapter and provide some detail of how it would be implemented using Javascript. The example of Chapter 5 described a hypothetical set of process documentation relating to the authorization and initiation of projects. Five distinct cases were covered:

- projects above £10M;

- projects between £1M and £10M with capital budgets greater than £250K;

- projects between £1M and £10M with capital budgets below £250K;

- projects below £1M with capital budgets above £250K;

- projects below £1M with capital budgets below £250K.

Each of these cases requires a set of documentation, some of which is common to other cases and some which is not.

The documents are titled 'Document A', 'Document B' . . . 'Document K'.

Our task is to implement five 'tours' through the documentation, corresponding to the five cases identified above.

The documents are implemented as eleven HTML files named 'DocA.html', 'DocB.html', . . . 'DocK.html'. In addition, we want a home page that points the user to the five tours: this will be 'index.html'.

Our design approach is as follows:

We construct an array which holds the URLs for the pages. For simplicity, we assume that everything exists in a single directory and that all URLs are relative. Hence, the array contains the items shown in Table A3.1.

Index	Entry
1	DocA.html
2	DocB.html
3	DocC.html
4	DocD.html
5	DocE.html
6	DocF.html
7	DocG.html
8	DocH.html
9	DocI.html
10	DocJ.html
11	DocK.html
12	index.html

This table is implemented as a JavaScript array and is referred to as 'A-table'. This array is a key variable in the scripting of pages.

A tour is defined by some sequence of index numbers relating to this table. The way that we have implemented this in practice is to define a string which consists of the required sequence of numbers, separated by '/' characters, and to store this string in the browser's cookie file as a cookie named 'tour'. So, for example, the JavaScript statement:

```
document.cookie = ''Tour=/1/3/7/''
```

would construct the data for a tour that visited DocA.html, DocC.html and DocG.html.

The complete home page (index.html), including all the necessary JavaScript is as shown on page opposite:
This page displays a list of tours each of which appears as a hypertext link. However, when the user clicks on the link, the JavaScript 'onClick' event is activated. This executes one of five functions which we have defined in the page header: doA(), doB(), doC(), doD() or doE(). Each of these functions will write an appropriate set of data to the document cookie.

When the user clicks on one of the hyertext links, as well as activating one of these functions, the normal hypertext behaviour will also be executed using the 'HREF'. In all cases this takes us to DocA.html – simply because this is the first document in all the tours.

The main document pages (DocA.html . . . DocK.html) carry the 'intelligent' buttons that are the main feature of this case study. These

```
<HTML>
<HEAD>
<TITLE>Main Menu</TITLE>
<SCRIPT>
function doA() {document.cookie=''Tour=/12/1/2/11/5/10/7/12/''}
function doB() {document.cookie=''Tour=/12/1/3/9/5/10/7/12/''}
function doC() {document.cookie=''Tour=/12/1/3/9/5/8/7/12/''}
function doD() {document.cookie=''Tour=/12/1/3/4/05/10/7/12/''}
function doE() {document.cookie=''Tour=/12/1/3/4/5/6/7/12/''}
</SCRIPT>
</HEAD>
<BODY>
<H1>Project authorization documentation</H1>
Select your type of project from the following list:
<UL>
<LI><A HREF=''DocA.html'' onClick = ''doA() ''>Projects &gt; £10</A>
<LI><A HREF=''DocA.html'' onClick = ''doB() ''>Projects £1 to £10M
including capital &gt; £250K</A>
<LI><A HREF=''DocA.html'' onClick = ''doC() ''>Projects £1 to £10M
including capital &lt; £250K</A>
<LI><A HREF=''DocA.html'' onClick = ''doD() ''>Projects &lt; £1
including capital &gt; £250K</A>
<LI><A HREF=''DocA.html'' onClick = ''doE() ''>Projects &lt; £1
including capital &lt; £250K</A>
</UL>
</BODY>
</HTML>
```

buttons perform 'forward' and 'back' functions, but do so in the context of the tour.

One of the aims, here, was to use a completely general script that could be used on every page within the tours and was specific neither to the page nor to the tour.

When the user clicks on, for example, the 'forward' button, a JavaScript, named DoNext(), is executed. This does the following:

- It uses the JavaScript document document.URL object to find out which page the user is currently accessing.

- It searches through the A-table array to find a matching URL and notes the index number of that entry.

- It accesses the 'Tour' cookie and finds the index number in it.

- It takes the next index number, in sequence, from the cookie and uses this as an index number into A__table.
- It loads the page pointed to at this index position in A__table, using JavaScript 'location='.

This sequence of is illustrated in Figure A3.1.

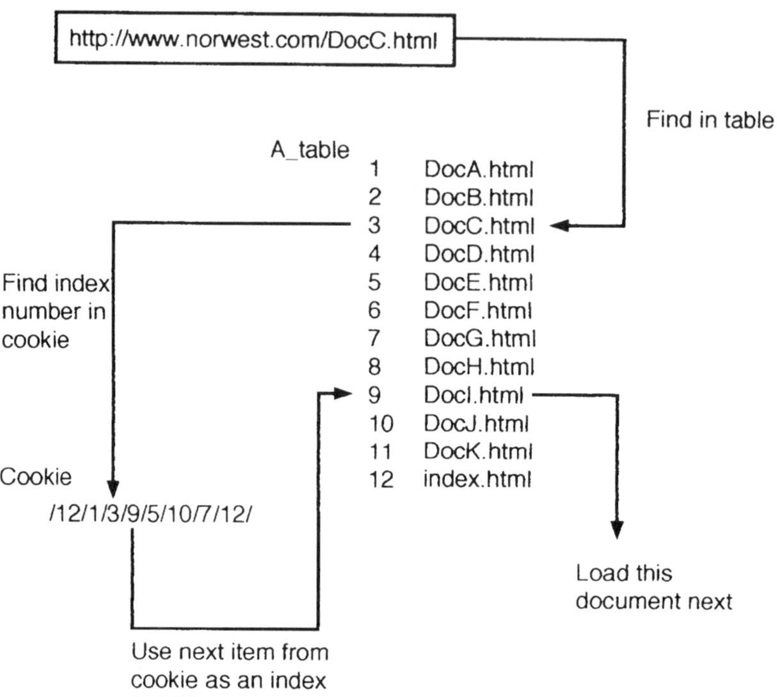

Figure A3.1
Sequence for Tour

The 'back' button is scripted in a similar way, though, of course, this time the destination is found from the index which *precedes* the current one in the cookie.

The two buttons are implemented as JavaScript functions: doNext() and doPrev(). Some of the common elements of these scripts are factored out as three additional JavaScript functions:

- `inString(string1, string2)` which finds the first occurrence of string1 in string2;

- `nthCookieItem(n)` which returns the *n*th item from the cookie;

- `findInTable(string1)` which returns the index number of the array element that matches string1.

The following extract is the complete script to implement the intelligent buttons, including the initialization of the array A__table. Note that to retain some clarity of structure, we have not included all the checking for exception conditions that would be present in a full implementation. In reality, it would be necessary to consider cases such as those where the cookie file is missing or damaged. Also, in practice, it would be necessary to test the code against a wide range of different browsers – in our case we have tested only against Netscape 3.0.

```
//Script contained in file buttons.js


function inString(string1, string2)}
//This function checks to see if string2 contains string1.
//If successful, the function returns the offset of the character
//immediately AFTER the first match for string 1 in string 2.
//If unsuccessful, it returns -1
    var i=0
    for (i=0; i<1+string2.length-string1.length; i++)}
        if (string1 == string2substring(i, i+string1.length))}
            return i+string1.length
            }
        }
    }
    return -1
    }


function nthCookieItem(n)
    }
    }
//This function parses a cookie named ``Tour'' of the
//form ``/first item/second item . . ./''.
//it returns the nth slash-separated item
    var i=0
    var j=0
    var p=0
    I = inString(``Tour='',document.cookie)
    for (j=0; j<n; j++)
        }
        }
        i+=
inString(``/'',document.cookie.substring(i,document.cookie.length))
        }
    j=inString(``/
'',document.cookie.substring(i,document.cookie.length))
    return parseInt(document.cookie.substring(i,i+j-1))
    }
function findInTable(string1)}
//This function searches the array string array A_table and returns
//the index of the first array element that 'matches' string1.
//We count it as a match if the array element is a substring of
string1.
    for (var i=1; i<13;i++)
        }
        j = inString(A_table[i],string1)
        if (j>0) return i
```

```
        }
    return -1
    }

function DoNext(){
    var i=0
    var j=0
    var current_index=0
    current_index = findInTable(document.URL)
    if (current_index<0) location=A_table[12]
    while (current_index !=nthCookieItem(i)){i++}
    location = A_table[nthCookieItem(i+1)]
    }
}

function DoPrev(){
    var i=0
    var j=0
    var current_index=0
    current_index = findInTable(document.URL)
    if (current_index<0) location=A_table[12]
    while (current_index !=nthCookieItem(i)){i++}
    location = A_table[nthCookieItem(i-1)]
    }
}
A_table = new Array(15)
A_table[1]  = ''DocA.html''
A_table[2]  = ''DocB.html''
A_table[3]  = ''DocC.html''
A_table[4]  = ''DocD.html''
A_table[5]  = ''DocE.html''
A_table[6]  = ''DocF.html''
A_table[7]  = ''DocG.html''
A_table[8]  = ''DocH.html''
A_table[9]  = ''DocI.html''
A_table[10] = ''DocJ.html''
A_table[11] = ''DocK.html''
A_table[12] = ''index.html''
```

In our implementation, the whole of this script was stored in a single file
'buttons.js'.

This same file was made available to all pages which participate in the
guided tours, using the <SCRIPT SRC=....> tag.

So, for example, the skeleton for Document A is as follows:

```
<HTML>
<HEAD>
<TITLE>Document A</TITLE>
<SCRIPT SRC=''buttons.js''>
</SCRIPT>
</HEAD>
<BODY>
<H1>Document A</H1>
```

```
This document describes how to prepare a project proposal and obtain
customer sign-off. . . .<P>
<HR>
<CENTER>
<A HREF=``javascript:DoPrev()''><IMG SRC=``bak.gif'' BORDER=0
<A HREF=``javascript:DoNext()''><IMG SRC=``for.gif'' BORDER=0
ALT=``Next''></A>

</CENTER>
</BODY>
</HTML>
```

In this document, the clicking on either of the two buttons (bak.gif and
for.gif) causes the execution of one of the JavaScript functions DoPrev()
or DoNext(). This is achieved using JavaScript 'pseudo HREFs' such as:

```
<A HREF=``javascript:DoPrev()''
```

Precisely the same script can be used for all the other documents.
This approach is very flexible:

- A tour can be edited simply by editing the string that is written to the
  cookie on the index.html page.

- A new tour can be constructed simply by inserting a new line on the
  index.html page, with a new string to be written to the cookie.

In a real HTML application, we were required to provide an 'à la carte'
tour, in which the user could put together a customized tour from a menu
of pages. The approach that we have described in this appendix allows
such a system to be implemented quite simply. For reference, the
following HTML page implements an à la carte tour using the documents
DocA.html . . . DocK.html that we have used in our worked example. The
idea of constructing such a customized tour may not be appropriate to our
example of a process for project initiation, but the principle works well.

```
<HEAD>
<TITLE>Main Menu</TITLE>
<SCRIPT>
function compute()
    {
    var ckie=``/12/''
    var j=0
    for (var i=0;i<11;i++)
        {
            if (j==0)}j=i+1}
            ckie+=i+1+``/''
            }
        }
    if (ckie!=``/12/'')
```

```
                }
                ckie+''12/''
                document.cookie=''Tour=''+ckie
                location = A_table[j]
                }
        else alert(''Check some boxes please!'')
            }
A_table = new Array(15)
A_table[1]  = ''DocA.html''
A_table[2]  = ''DocB.html''
A_table[3]  = ''DocC.html''
A_table[4]  = ''DocD.html''
A_table[5]  = ''DocE.html''
A_table[6]  = ''DocF.html''
A_table[7]  = ''DocG.html''
A_table[8]  = ''DocH.html''
A_table[9]  = ''DocI.html''
A_table[10] = ''DocJ.html''
A_table[11] = ''DocK.html''
A_table[12] = ''index.html''
</SCRIPT>
</HEAD>
<BODY>
<H1>A la carte guided tour of the documents</H1>
Select your chosen sequence of documents and hit ''Start Tour'':
<FORM NAME=''form1''>

<BR><INPUT TYPE=''checkbox'' NAME=''C1''>Document A
<BR><INPUT TYPE=''checkbox'' NAME=''C2''>Document B
<BR><INPUT TYPE=''checkbox'' NAME=''C3''>Document C
<BR><INPUT TYPE=''checkbox'' NAME=''C4''>Document D
<BR><INPUT TYPE=''checkbox'' NAME=''C5''>Document E
<BR><INPUT TYPE=''checkbox'' NAME=''C6''>Document F
<BR><INPUT TYPE=''checkbox'' NAME=''C7''>Document G
<BR><INPUT TYPE=''checkbox'' NAME=''C8''>Document H
<BR><INPUT TYPE=''checkbox'' NAME=''C9''>Document I
<BR><INPUT TYPE=''checkbox'' NAME=''C10''>Document J
<BR><INPUT TYPE=''checkbox'' NAME=''C11''>Document K
<BR><INPUT TYPE=''checkbox'' NAME=''C12''>Main menu

<P>
<INPUT TYPE=''button'' VALUE=''Start Tour'' onClick=''compute()''>
</FORM>

</BODY>
```

This page includes a form with a set of checkboxes: one for each
document. The user can select the chosen set of documents for the tour by
clicking in the boxes. When the "start tour" button is clicked, the
JavaScript function compute() is executed.

This function tests each of the checkboxes (which are sequenced the same as the elements of our old friend A__table) and constructs an appropriate tour cookie. It then selects the appropriate page from A__table to load at the start of the tour. As a default, the home page is included at the end (and before the start) of the tour.

Appendix 4
Glossary

> *Today we have naming of parts. Yesterday,*
> *We had daily cleaning. And tomorrow morning,*
> *We shall have what to do after firing. But today,*
> *Today we have naming of parts*

Henry Reed

If there were no computers, software or networks, then there would be no media engineering. But there are computers, software and networks, and media engineering builds on all of them. Given this, there are, inevitably, many terms and concepts from all of these well established areas scattered throughout this book. In an attempt to assuage the worst aspects of multi-disciplinary confusion, we proffer this extended glossary.

Active-X
: Microsoft's technology for embedding information objects and application components within one another. For example, an Active-X button can be embedded in an HTML page displayed in a browser window.

Address
: A location identifier for any Internet connected device. Addresses can be logical (131.146.6.11, an IP address for a workstation) or personal (name@organisation.domain, to reach an individual).

Agent
: A piece of software that carries out a particular set of pre-defined tasks. For instance, a mail agent might be installed on a PC to monitor and filter incoming messages.

Anchor
: A named location in a hypertext page or document that is the destination for a hypertext link. When the user "clicks" on a piece of link text, the media system loads a new hypertext page and displays the section named by the anchor. In HTML, an anchor is denoted by the tags: `<A NAME=`` ''></A>`.

Applet
: This is a mobile application program that can be accessed over a

network (typically the Internet). It is self-contained, in that it carries its own presentation and processing logic, and can run on whatever type of machine imports it. Although fairly new, applets are being used as plug in units that form part of a larger application.

The concept of the applet is tied to that of Java (a compact and portable interpreted language).

Application program	More usually referred to simply as 'application', this is a complete, self-contained program that performs a specific function directly for the user. Editors, spreadsheets, and text formatters are common examples of applications. Network applications include clients such as those for FTP, electronic mail and telnet.
Asynchronous	An arrangement where there is no correlation between system time and the data that is exchanged, carried or transmitted over the system. For instance, an asynchronous protocol sends and receives data whenever it wants – there is no link to a master clock. The penalty for this freedom is that extra information has to be added to announce the start and stop of a communication.
Bandwidth	The amount of information that can be exchanged over a link – a measure of network capacity. Usually measured in bits per second
Binding	The connecting together of components. In software engineering this refers to the joining together of modules of code to create a complete application. Such modularity is desirable so that, for example, different modules an be implemented by different teams, the modules can be tested separately, and modules may be re-used in future applications. In Media Engineering an analogous process in the linking together of hypertext pages using, for example, HTML links and anchors.
Bitmap	A data file or structure which corresponds bit for bit with an image displayed on a screen, probably in the same format as it would be stored in the display's video memory. A bitmap is characterized by the width and height of the image.
Bits per second	The basic measurement for serial data transmission capacity, abbreviated to bps. Usually has some form of modifier – kbps is thousands of bits per second, Mbps is millions of bits per second. Typically, a domestic user will have an Internet line running at a few tens of kbps. Backbone links are usually 2Mbps and more.
Bookmark	A reference to the location (usually a network address) of a document which may or may not be on the same server to which a user is connected. Most Worldwide Web and Gopher clients can save a file of bookmarks to allow you to quickly locate documents to which you want to refer frequently.

Browser	A program which allows a person to read hypertext information. The browser gives some means of viewing the contents of nodes and of navigating from one node to another. Mosaic, Lynx and Netscape are browsers for the Worldwide Web. They act as clients to the array of remote servers on which web pages are hosted.
Bundle	General term used when a variety of products or services are combined and presented as a single offering. Bundling is increasingly prevalent on the Worldwide Web, with the content coming from one source, the computers it is presented on from another and the networks it is delivered over from another.
Cache	A small fast memory holding recently accessed data, designed to speed up subsequent access to the same data. Used for keeping a local copy of data that has been accessed over a network and is likely to be required again (e.g. several pages of Worldwide web information may be cached).
CGI	Common Gateway Interface. An interface protocol associated with web servers. CGI is used by the web server to invoke and pass data to applications that process information captured from web clients.
Circuit	A communications path with a specified bandwidth (i.e. capacity in bits per second, bps). Can be either dial-up or permanent.
Client	A requester of a service – typically a PC accessing information over the net. More precisely a client is an entity – for example a program, process or personthat is participating in an interaction with another entity and is taking the role of requesting (and receiving) the required service.
Client–Server	The division of an application into two parts, where one acts as the 'client' (by requesting a service) and the other acts as the 'server' (by providing the service). The rationale behind the client–server split is to exploit the local desk top processing power leaving the server to govern the centrally held information.
Compiler	A program that converts source code into machine code. The input to a compiler is high-level language text and the output is a binary sequence that executes a series of commands on a computer.
Connection-oriented	This is the familiar form of communication on the telephone network. A call is initiated by setting up an end-to-end connection between participants and this connection is kept for the duration of the call. It may not be efficient in terms of network usage, but there are some assurances of delivery.
Connectionless	This refers to a communication where two or more participants do

	not have a fixed path between them. Each of the packets that constitute the communication looks after its own routing. This arrangement is subject to the vagaries of network availability but can be a very efficient overall way of using a network.
Cookie	A token of agreement between cooperating programs that is used to keep track of a transaction. At a more concrete level, a cookie is a fragment of code that holds some information about your local state – your phone number or home page reference, for instance. You probably have cookies that you don't know about. The Netscape and Explorer browsers both support them, with the cookie being presented to the server to control your dialogue.
CU-SeeMe	An application that enables suitably equipped users to see and speak to each other. It is interesting in that it allows visual communications (traditionally expensive and bandwidth hungry) over standard Internet links.
Cyberspace	A term used to describe the world of computers and the society that gathers around them. First coined by William Gibson in his novel *Neuromancer*.
DBMS	Database Management System. A set of software tools used to manage large data stores. Often complex entities in their own right.
Discrimination	In the DIVA method, this term is used to denote the separation of the concerns of the *structure* from those of the *content* of a multimedia system.
Dithering	Images are often made up of more colours than the user's computer can display: many PCs, for example, can only display 256 colours on the screen. Graphic display programs (including Web browsers) simulate colours that they cannot actually display by a process called dithering. This is achieved by creating patterns of closely spaced dots of different colours: at a distance, these approximate to the required colour although, on close inspection, the image appears speckled. Dithering is usually more visually acceptable on photographic-style images (where the speckling is harder to see) rather than on block-colour images.
DIVA	Documented Information Visualisation Approach. An engineering methodology for managing the complexity of designing, building and maintaining information products.
DNS	Domain Name Service. A general-purpose distributed, replicated, data query service used on Internet for translating hostnames into Internet addresses, e.g taking a dot address such as jungle.pdq.com and returning the corresponding numerical addresses.
EFF	Electronic Frontier Foundation. A group established to address

social and legal issues arising from the impact of the Internet and related computer-based communications networks on society. A non-profit public interest organisation with an aim of protecting freedom of expression, privacy, and access to on-line resources and information.

Electronic mail — Messages automatically passed from one computer user to another, often through computer networks and/or via modems over telephone lines.

Electronic mail address — The coding required to ensure that an electronic mail message reaches its specified destination. There are many formats of mail address, perhaps the best known being the dot address used for Internet mail e.g. 'name@organisation.domain'.

Emoticon — Symbols such as :-) (for happy) and :-((for sad), used to convey, when viewed sideways, an emotional state in electronic mail or news. Originally intended as a joke (and known as smileys), now virtually mandatory under certain circumstances.

Encapsulation — The implementation of components as "Black Boxes" whose function is defined by the interface they offer to the outside world rather than by their internal workings.

FAQ — Frequently Asked Questions. As its name suggests a list of questions and their answers that provide a compendium of accumulated knowledge in a particular subject. FAQs tend to be maintained by volunteers made widely available over the Internet. The collection of all of the FAQs is quite impressive and contains a huge wealth of up-to-date expert knowledge on many subjects of common interest, some technical, some social.

Firewall — In general, this refers to the part of a system designed to isolate it from the threat of external interference (both malicious and unintentional).

Firewall machine — This is a dedicated machine that usually sits between a public network and a private one (e.g. between an organization's private network and the Internet). The machine has special security precautions loaded onto it and used to filter access to and from outside network connections and dial-in lines. The general idea is to protect the more loosely administered machines hidden behind the firewall from abuse.

Freeware — Software that is provided at no charge. Freeware is similar to shareware, except that the former is given away to whoever wants it with no strings at all.

FTP — File Transfer Protocol. The high-level Internet protocol for transferring files from one computer to another (it is defined in RFC 959).

Anonymous FTP is a common way of allowing limited access to publicly available files via an anonymous log-in.

Gamma

When dealing with a graphics display system, it is usually understood that when the input levels are zero (e.g. rrggbb values are zero), the output is also zero (i.e. black. Also, when the input is at its maximum (eg rrggbb = ffffff) the output is white. However, in between these extreme cases, there is generally some non-linear relationship between the levels that are put into the system and those that are seen on the screen. The 'gamma' of a device is a way of characterizing that non-linearity between input and output. The formula is:

$$output = input^{gamma}$$

i.e. the output is equal to the input raised to the power gamma. Here, the range of values for both input and output are chosen to be in the range 0 (black) to 1 (white). If the display system was perfectly linear, the value of gamma would be 1.0 – however, display systems are not perfectly linear. A 'raw' monitor has a gamma of about 2.5. Apple Macintoshes use a gamma correction in the computer which corrects it to about 1.25; most PCs, on the other hand, do not employ gamma correction and the effective gamma of the display system is thus around 2.5. Variations in gamma explain why images drawn on one computer may look quite different on another. For example, images that look good on a Mac may appear dark and dingy on a PC.

Gateway

An interface between two incompatible networks, a gateway acts as a translator that enables applications to work between the two.

GIF

Graphics Interchange Format. An image file format widely used on the Internet. More compact than the alternative JPEG (.jpg) standard but lower quality pictures. GIF files are easily spotted by their .gif extension. GIF images are compressed with an algorithm developed and owned by one of the leading On-line Service Provider, CompuServe.

GIFs support a maximum of 256 colours (i.e. 8 bits per pixel) and uses the LZW compression algorithm. There are two main variants to the format: GIF87a, the form developed in 1987 and GIF89a, an extension of the standard to include transparency and animation.

GNN

Global Network Navigator. A collection of free services provided by O'Reilly & Associates. These include The Whole Internet Catalog (which describes the most useful Internet resources and services), the GNN Business Pages (which lists companies on the Internet) and the Internet Help Desk that provides help in starting Internet exploration.

Gopher

One of a number of the early Internet-based services that provided information search and retrieval facilities. Gopher, which could be cast as a manual precursor to the Web, is defined in RFC 1432. To gain access you need a gopher client and you also need to know the name of a gopher server.

Groupware
A general term to denote software-based tools that can be used to support a distributed set of workers. This covers applications as disparate as Windows for Workgroups through to PC video-phones. More formally called Computer Supported Co-operative Working (CSCW).

Header
A header is the part of an electronic mail message or news article that precedes the body of a message and contains the sender's name and e-mail address, the date and time the message was sent and details of the route taken.

Home page
On the World Wide Web, the introductory document relating to a particular site. This often has a URL that is just a hostname (for instance, http://www.isoc.com/, the home page for the Internet Society) and it serves to explain the structure of, and provide links to, underlying information.

Host
Usually refers either to the large mainframe computer that a dumb terminal connects to. Also used for a networked computer that you can establish a session with and can get some services from (i.e. a server).

Hotlink
A mechanism for sharing a piece of data between two applications. Changes made within one application (e.g. updating a spread-sheet) are reflected in the other's copy (e.g. that same spreadsheet, shown as a table in a text document).

Hotlist
A feature of most World Wide Web browsers that allows a configuration file containing hypertext links to be stored. A means of quickly reaching specific or pages on the Web.

HTML
Hypertext Markup Language. HTML is the language used to describe the formatting in World Wide Web documents. As well as text layout, HTML is used to place pictures, insert buttons, and specify links to other documents. See Appendix 2 for a lot more detail.

HTTP
Hypertext Transfer Protocol. The basic protocol underlying the World Wide Web system. It is a simple, stateless request–response protocol.

Hypermedia
Term used to describe media systems in which the user can follow arbitrarily complex navigation threads through the material using, for example, hypertext links.

Hypertext
A means of presenting documentation so that links to related text

is readily apparent. Hypertext systems allows a user to select certain words, pictures or icons and immediately display related information for the selected item. Hypertext requires some form of language (like HTML) to specify branch labels with a hypertext document

Image map	A "clickable picture" in a multimedia system (or more strictly, the behind-the-scenes template that instructs the system what to do when a part of the picture is clicked on). Clicking the mouse pointer on different parts of the picture results in the activation of predetermined hypertext links. In WWW systems, image maps are classified as client-side or server-side. In a client-side image map, the translation from the position of the pointer in the picture to the hypertext destination is resolved by the browser: with a server-side map, this resolution is undertaken by an application running on the WWW server machine.
Information object	An identifiable multimedia item. eg a disk file containing hypertext or a single graphical image, video clip or sound. It is the smallest item that is managed in the engineering process of Media Engineering.
Information superhighway	A much used (and abused) term that refers to a combination of high-speed networks and sophisticated applications for information handling. The term was first coined in the US Clinton/Gore administration whose plans to deregulate communication services began with their 1994 legislation to promote the integration of concepts from Internet, telephone providers, business networks, entertainment services, information providers, education, etc.
Internet	The Internet is the largest network of computers in the world. It actually comprises many smaller networks that use the TCP/IP protocols to communicate and share a common addressing scheme and naming convention. The Internet is recognized as the largest and most important data network in the world. It is growing at a phenomenal rate and has sparked a wealth of technical and social innovation over the years. See Appendix 2 for a bit more on some of the key technical features of the Internet.
internet	With a lower case 'i', this term denotes any set of networks interconnected with routers and using applications such as browsers.
Internet address	The 32–bit host address defined by the Internet Protocol (IP) in RFC 791. The Internet address is usually expressed in dot notation, e.g. 128.121.4.5. The address can be split into a network number (or network address) and a host number unique to each host on the network and sometimes also a subnet address.

The dramatic growth in the number of Internet users over the last few years has led to a shortage of new addresses. This is one of the issues being addressed by the introduction of a new version of IP, IPv6.

InterNIC

Internet Network Information Center. The InterNIC provides a huge range of information about the Internet. It was started by the National Science Foundation who, in cooperation with the Internet community, prompted Network Information Service (NIS) managers to provide and/or coodinate services for the NSFNet community.

Interpreter

This is a piece of software that carries out the same task as a compiler (turning source code into machine code) except that it does so a line at a time rather than working on the whole program.

Intranet

A private network implemented with the same technologies as the public Internet.

IT

Information Technology. A very general term, coined in the 1970s to describe the application of computer science and electronics and engineering to the specification, design and construction of information-rich systems.

Java

A compact and portable language that looks as if it will have significant application in the building of highly portable applications (or applets). Java is designed to run on a wide range of computers and to look after its own security and operation. With Java users can download anything they like the look of over the Internet without having to have all of the software to use it on their local machine.

JPEG

Joint Photographic Experts Group. The original name of the committee that designed the standard image compression algorithm. JPEG is designed for compressing either full-colour or grey-scale digital images.

In general, JPEG coding yields better picture quality than the comparable GIF coding, albeit at the cost of larger file sizes. An image file using this technique can be recognized as it uses a .jpg extension.

Most people refer to JPEG files. Strictly speaking, JPEG is just the standard for the compression algorithm – the file format is called JFIF – JPEG File Interchange Format.

Kiss

Keep it simple, stupid. A software engineering motto that is also very relevant to Media Engineering.

Link

Used in several contexts to mean the joining together of components or the entity that implements that joining. In Media Engineering it generally describes the hypertext connection that

can exist between two information objects – a hypertext link. Within the DIVA method we consider a several categories of links:
– constructional links whose purpose is to create the rendition of a single page from several information objects;
– local links whose scope is limited to anchors within the current page of hypertext;
– unstructured links which take the user to a destination which has no structural relationship with the starting point;
– structured links which link information objects within clearly defined structure – often the links associated with a "button bar".

Lycos	One of many World Wide Web search facilities, Lycos is served by Carnegie Mellon University. It allows you to search on document title and content for a list of keywords. Lycos is probably the biggest such index on the web. Similar search facilities are available on the World Wide Web using Alta Vista, Yahoo and WebHound.
LZW	Lempel-Ziv Welch compression algorithm used for GIF images. It is 'lossless' in the sense that it does not discard any image detail when compressin the image. It has been patented by Unisys.
Media Engineering	The engineering discipline that relates to the designing building and maintenance of multimedia system such as those based around the World Wide Web. Like any engineering discipline it is concerned with understanding the materials that you work with; developing an end-to-end process and lifecycle; developing appropriate tools and techniques; and the recording of the specifics of particular projects, using a range of notations.
Mosaic	NCSA's browser (client) for the World Wide Web. Mosaic was described as 'the killer application of the 1990s' because it was the first program to provide an intuitive, multimedia and graphical user interface to the Internet's ever-expanding wealth of distributed information services.
MPEG	Moving Pictures Expert Group. A committee that generates standards for digital video compression. Also the name of their algorithm.
Multicast	Describes the transmission of a message to a number of recipients (usually, a distribution list). A more discerning one-to-many distribution than a broadcast.
Multimedia	Human–computer interaction involving text, graphics, voice and video. Usually includes concepts from hypertext.
Netiquette	Describes network etiquette. It covers the conventions of politeness recognized on Usenet and in mailing list. The most important rule of netiquette is 'Think before you post'. There are whole

books dedicated to Netiquette!

Netscape Navigator

A World Wide Web browser from Netscape Communications Corporation. Despite the first versions being released (free to the Internet) only in late 1994, it is now the most popular of the net browsers.

Netscape evolved from NCSA Mosaic (with which it shares at least one author) and runs on the X Window System under various versions of Unix, on Microsoft Windows and on the Apple Macintosh. It features integrated support for sending electronic mail and reading Usenet news, as well as encryption (based on the RSA standard) to allow secure communications for commercial applications such as exchanging credit card numbers with net retailers.

Network

In general, a system of interrelated elements that are interconnected with dedicated or switched links to provide local and remote communication (of voice, video, data, etc.) for the exchange of information between end users with common interests.

Also, the set of switches, routers, circuits, trunks and software that make up a communications facility. Examples of well-known networks that provide a particular service are the Public Switched Telephone Network and the Packet Switched Data Network.

Network interface

The circuitry that connects a node (e.g. a PC) to the network, usually in the form of a card fitted into one of the expansion slots in the back of the machine. It works with the network software and operating system to transmit and receive messages on the network (usually using a modem, or over an ISDN link).

Object Orientation

An increasingly popular approach to the design of network systems in which it is composed of a set of objects. Each object is an independent element with defined interfaces and actions. There is a significant formal basis behind this simple idea.

Open System

A general term for systems that are built with standard interfaces which allow components from different manufacturers to be connected together.

Parse

The breaking of a language into its constituent elements. There are many computing applications that require a set of instructions to be understood by a program and this is often accomplished by parsing the sequence of instructions so as to make sense of them.

PC

Personal Computer. Any computing system for use primarily by one person.

Perl

A widely used language for manipulating text, files and processes. Perl is a scripting utility that comes free with many Unix systems. It was invented by Larry Wells and is documented in the O'Reilly & Associates Perl book.

Polycontiguity — The principle that in multimedia systems there can be multiple navigation paths through the same body of information.

PNG — Portable Network Graphic (pronounced ping). It is intended to be a replacement for the GIF format: it is technically superior and uses a public-domain compression algorithm. It uses a compression method similar to that used in pkzip and related file compression utilities. PNG uses a 7–pass interlacing scheme which sends the gross outline of the image first and then sends increasingly fine levels of detail. It supports up to 48 bits per pixel and can stroe gamma information. Gamma determines how a compter display responds to image intensity levels. Hence it is possible to ensure that the image looks the same on all platforms. This can get over the problem that, for example, graphics produced on a Macintosh can look dark and dull on a PC.

Protocol — A formal set of rules used during the transmission of data across a network. There are lots of different sorts of protocols: for sequencing messages, error recovery, presentation of information etc.

PSTN — Public Switched Telephone Network. The collection of interconnected systems operated by the various telephone companies and administrations around the world. Also known as the Plain Old Telephone System in contrast to Integrated Services Digital Network which extends data as well as voice service to the end user.

Quality of service — Measure of the perceived quality of service. Usually based on tangible metrics such as time to fix a fault, average delay, loss percentages, system reliability etc.

Quicktime — Apple Computer's standard for integrating full-motion video and digitized sound into application programs.

RFC — Request For Comments. One of a series of numbered Internet informational documents and standards widely followed by commercial software and freeware providers in the Internet community. Early RFCs were discussion documents and ideas but more recently they have come to be practical standards.

RTF — Rich Text Format. A file format standard invented by Microsoft and widely used for transferring documents between dissimilar word processors.

Secure sockets — Applications such as WWW browsers communicate with the underlying TCP/IP communications software via entities called "sockets". The secure sockets layer (SSL) is a standard for

	encrypting data that is sent (via a socket) over a TCP/IP connection.
Server	An object which is participating in an interaction with another object (usually a client), and is taking the role of providing the required service. One half of client–server system.
SGML	Standard Graphical Markup Language. An international standard encoding scheme for linked textual information. HTML is a subset.
Shareware	Software that can be loaded from an open source such as the Internet is usually referred to as Shareware. It is usual for some licence to be payable on such software (often no more than a few dollars or a crate of beer), which distinguishes it from Freeware.
Site certification	One of the concerns when using WWW technology is to ensure that the site you are accessing is truly what it purports to be. This is especially important if you are about to authorize the site owners to charge a large sum of money to your credit card! Site certification is a technique by which a "trusted third party" uses cryptographic keys to issue "certificates" to both the server site and the client, in such a way that the client can be assured of the server's authenticity.
SLIP	Serial Line Internet Protocol. Software allowing the Internet Protocol (IP), normally used on Ethernet, to be used over a serial line, e.g. an RS-232 serial port connected to a modem.
Smileys	A popular way of conveying emotion in an on-line session. A typical smiley is:-) (tilt head left to view). There are scores of these, from the quizzical to the miserable. See Emoticon.
Staple	In the DIVA method this is the term used to describe attributes applied to particular kinds of information object so that they are distinguishable by the media system.
Syntax	The rules for composing legal statements in a language. You can follow the rules of syntax and still write rubbish, though. The meaning of the statements is the domain of semantics.
Teleworking	Using computing and communications technology to work away from an office.
Topology	The physical layout of a network. To illustrate, the topology of a local area network is usually divided into star, ring or bus.
Trading	The process of matching a request for service in a distributed system (like the Internet) to an appropriate supplier.
UDP	User Datagram Protocol. UDP is a connectionless protocol which,

like TCP, is layered on top of IP. It provides a simple and efficient, if unreliable, datagram service. It is defined in RFC 768. UDP is required to carry many of the more basic Internet services.

Unix
One of the most important of modern operating systems. It was created by AT&T but enhanced by universities and other vendors and gained popularity with practitioners because of its efficiency.

URL
Uniform Resource Locator. A standard for locating an object on the Internet and most widely known as the form of address for pages on the World Wide Web. Typical URLs take the form http://www.identity.com/, ftp://archive.ic.ac/fred or telnet://jungle.com. The part before the first colon specifies the access scheme or protocol. The part after the colon is interpreted according to the access scheme. In general, two slashes after the colon indicate a host name.

Use case
A technique invented by Ivar Jacobson for expressing requirements in terms of the proposed behaviour of a system as it responds to particular user actions. The technique has the merits that it can express requirements in a form that is readily understandable to customers and users (eg when the user presses button "x", the system responds by displaying "y" on the screen) yet it is sufficiently rigorous to direct detailed design work.

Veronica
Very Easy Rodent Oriented Net-wide Index to Computerized Archives. An Internet facility that is accessed through gopher. It allows a user to carry out a keyword search on gopher titles.

Virtual Team
A group of people, working together on the same project, who are physically separate, their only link being via a network and computer screen.

VRML
Virtual Reality Markup Language. An extension of the HTML concept into virtual reality. VRML provides a language for coding virtual reality images that can be accessed over a network by anyone with a compatible browser.

WAIS
Wide Area Information Server. One of a number of Internet utilities, used for public database text searching. The search returns a list of documents, ranked according to the frequency of occurrence of the keyword(s) used in the search.

Webmaster
A nominated keeper of a set of World Wide Web pages. Often the system administrator for the server providing the pages.

White pages   Rather like the telephone directory, this is a computer network directory service for locating individuals on the Internet by name.

World Wide Web   Also referred to as the Web, WWW and W3. It is the Internet based distributed information retrieval system that uses hypertext to link multimedia documents. This makes the relationship of information that is common between documents easily accessible and completely independent of physical location.

WWW is a client–server system. The client software takes the form of a 'browser' that allows the user to easily navigate the information on-line. Well known browsers are Netscape and Mosaic. A huge amount of information can be found on World Wide Web servers.

X/Open   A standards consortium, probably best known for the fact that it owns the Unix trademark.

Yahoo   Yet Another Hierarchically Organized Oracle. One of the many search utilities that can be used to trawl and crawl through information held on World Wide Web. Others include Lycos and Alta Vista.

Yahoo is rumoured to stand for any of Yet Another Hierarchical Officious, Obstreperous or Organised Oracle. Yahoo is probably the biggest hierarchical index of the Worldwide Web.

Zip   A commonly used application that is used to compress files so that they can be more easily transmitted over a network.

Bibliography

We proffer no direct references to support what this book is all about: there aren't any! In just the same way that programming books preceded those on software design, so we have seen a plethora of books on the mechanics of World Wide Web page production, hypermedia authoring and information networks but we believe this to be the first on media engineering. For all that, there are some excellent texts that relate to media engineering.

Atkins J. & Norris M. *Total Area Networking*, John Wiley & Sons (1995)

Barfield L. *The User Interface*, Addison Wesley (1993)

Barnatt C. *Cyber Business: Mindsets for a Wired Age*, John Wiley & Sons (1995)

Belkin N. J. Information concepts for Information Science, *Journal of Documentation* 43(1) (1978)

Berk E. *Hypertext Hypermedia Handbook*, McGraw-Hill (1991)

Berners-Lee T. World Wide Web: an illustrated seminar http://www.w3.org.pub/WWW/Talks/General.html (1991)

Berners-Lee T. Universal Resource Identifiers in WWW http://www.w3.org.pub/WWW/Addressing/URL/uri-spec.txt

Booch G. *Object Solutions*, Addison Wesley (1996)

Budgen D. *Software Design*, Addison Wesley (1994)

Cohill A & Kavanaugh A. *Exit One on the Information Superhighway: Design of the Blacksburg Community Network*, Artech House (1996)

Desfray P. *Object Engineering*, Addison Wesley (1994)

Dodsworth C. *Digital Illusion*, Addison-Wesley (1996)

Drucker P. *Post Capitalist Society*, Butterworth Heinemann (1993)

Egan B. L. *Information Superhighways II: the Economics of Multi Media*, Artech House (1996)

Fisher S. *Multimedia Authoring*, AP Professional, Cambridge MA (1994)

Foley J. D., Van Dam A., Feiner S. & Hughes J. F. *Computer Graphics: Principles and Practice*, Addison Wesley (1996)

Frost A. & Norris M. *Exploiting the Internet*, John Wiley & Sons (1997)

Gibbs S. & Tsichritzis D. *Multimedia Programming: Object, Environments and Frameworks*, Addison Wesley (1995)

Gore A. Infrastructure for the Global Village, *Scientific American* (1991)

Graham I. *The HTML Sourcebook*, John Wiley & Sons (1996)

Gray M., Hodson N. & Gordon G. *Teleworking Explained*, John Wiley & Sons (1993)

Handy C. *The Age of Unreason*, Arrow (1990)

Handy C. *The Empty Raincoat*, Hutchinson (1994)

Hoft N. *International Technical Communication*, John Wiley & Sons (1995)

Howell G Building *Hypermedia Applications: A Software Development Guide*, McGraw-Hill 1992

Illich I. *Deschooling Society*, Harper & Row (1971)

Jacobson I., Christerson M., Jonsson P. & Overgaard G. *Object-oriented Software Engineering: a Use Case Driven Approach*, Addison Wesley (1993)

Kelly K. *Out of Control*, Fourth Estate (1995)

Minoli D. *Distance Learning Technology and Applications*, Artech House (1996)

Naisbitt J. *Global Paradox*, Nicholas Brealey Publishing (1994)

Negreponte N. *Being Digital*, Hodder & Stoughton (1995)

Norris M. & Rigby P. *Software Engineering Explained*, John Wiley & Sons (1992)

Norris M. & Winton N. *Energise the Network*, Addison Wesley (1996)

Ohmae K. *The Borderless World*, Harper Collins (1990)

Reich R. *The Work of Nations*, Simon & Schuster (1991)

Smedinghoff *The Software Publishers Association Guide to Online Law*, Addison-Wesley (1996)

Stein L. *How to Set Up and Maintain a World Wide Web Site*, Addison Wesley (1997)

Steinhauer L. *Web Multimedia Publishing*, John Wiley & Sons (1996)

Stoll C. *Silicon Snake Oil*, Pan Books (1996)

Tilton E., Steadman C. & Jones T. *Web Weaving*, Addison Wesley (1995)

Woodhead N. *Hypertext and Hypermedia*, Addison Wesley (1991)

Index